TAKING THE WORD TO HEART

Taking the Word to Heart

*Self and Other
in an Age of Therapies*

Robert C. Roberts

WILLIAM B. EERDMANS PUBLISHING COMPANY
GRAND RAPIDS, MICHIGAN

Printed in the United States of America

Library of Congress Cataloging-in-Publication Data

Roberts, Robert Campbell, 1942-
    Taking the word to heart: self and other in an age of therapies /
Robert C. Roberts.
        p.   cm.
    ISBN 0-8028-0659-7 (paper)
    1. Psychotherapy — Religious aspects — Christianity.
    2. Christianity — Psychology. 3. Pastoral psychology. I. Title.
BV4012.R594   1992   92-34333
261.5'15 — dc20   CIP

Unless otherwise noted, all Scripture quotations are taken from the Revised
Standard Version of the Bible, copyrighted 1946, 1952 © 1971, 1973 by
the Division of Christian Education of the National Council of the
Churches of Christ in the U.S.A., and used by permission.

This book is dedicated to

My sister Lissy (1947–1986) and

Her daughter Catherine,

Who also did not survive her birth

CONTENTS

ACKNOWLEDGMENTS

I've had lots of help along the way in writing this book, which has been my education in psychology (a one-sided education, no doubt, weighted heavily in the direction of psychotherapy and personality theory). I thank Wheaton College for giving me some teaching-load reductions when I started teaching there in 1984, which allowed me to take courses in psychotherapy from David Benner, Stan Jones, and Fran White, and to do some initial thinking about the "integration of psychology and Christianity." A number of people have read parts of the book at various stages and offered comments: Ivan Boszormenyi-Nagy, Deb and Rich Butman, Rodney Clapp, Judy DeBoer, Steve Evans, Kirk Farnsworth, Janice Harrison, Dan Horn, Al Howsepian, Melissa Jacobsen, Alan Johnson, Eric Johnson, Brenna and Stan Jones, Barbara Kay, Mike Mangis, Mickey Maudlin, Karen Mehlbrech, Richard Olmsted, Neal Plantinga, Elizabeth Vanderkooy Roberts, Julius Scott, Paul Warning, Janice and Jay Wood, and several anonymous reviewers for the *Journal of Psychology and Theology*. I am indebted to the students who have taken my courses Psychology 611 and 494 since 1984, for their patience as I gropingly worked out some of the ideas that appear in these pages, and for instruction in psychology. I'm also grateful to various church groups to whom I presented some of this material, for their interesting reactions. I thank my pastor, Father Ray Cole, for cautions and hints received via his preaching and for conversations. Thank you to Frederick Buechner for permission to use the passages from *Telling Secrets* that appear on pp. 225-26. Some of the chapters were written in 1989-90, when my family and I enjoyed the hospitality of Juniata College, where I was the J. Omar Good visiting professor. I especially thank Dale Wright for helpful chats, and Andy Murray for help with Chapter Fifteen.

A few paragraphs in this book are taken from published articles (always, I think, in revised form): "Children: Who Needs Them?" (*Christianity Today*, 17 April 1985); "Therapy for the Saints" (*Christianity Today*, 8 November 1985), especially the material from the interview with pastors, which the *CT* staff arranged; "Competition and Compassion" (*Christianity Today*, 4 April 1986); "Forgiveness as Therapy" (*The Reformed Journal* 36 [August 1986]); "Psychotherapeutic Virtues and the Grammar of Faith" (*Journal of Psychology and Theology* 15 [1987]); "Reconcilable Differences," coauthored with Elizabeth Vanderkooy Roberts (*Christianity Today*, 12 June 1987); "I Win, You Lose" (*Christianity Today*, 23 April 1990); and "Mental Health and the Virtues of Community: Reflections on Contextual Therapy" (*Journal of Psychology and Theology* 19 [Winter 1991]).

PREFACE

It is often hard to tell when a book begins, but I think this one started with a sermon I preached at Christ the Victor Lutheran Church in Fairfax, California, in February of 1986. I went at the invitation of my sister Elisabeth Roberts (Wulzen), who two and a half months later died in childbirth. I have given the book the title that the sermon bore (except for the subtitle) partly to remember that occasion, which in light of the subsequent event has acquired such a tone of sadness, but partly too because Christians are people of God's Word, called daily to take it to heart and thus to be formed, as persons, by the sound of his voice. This book is all about becoming persons who dwell, in a variety of ways, among other persons. Our relations to those others (and thus our selves) are shaped by some "word" or other, some account of what it is to be a person. Several non-Christian "words" — and thus non-Christian forms of personhood — are discussed in the book, but the centerpiece is the Word of Christ, in whom is all comfort and joy and fulfillment. This Word, as the book contends, is the background of all deepest and truest healing of persons, because it is the one by which persons are truly formed. This word is the "logy" of the true psychology; it is the Word of the soul, which must be brought to the fore and asserted once again, and thought through and placed in perspicuous comparison with the other psycho-logies that sound daily in our ears and bid to form us in their image. At the time of her death, Lissy was straining, like so many of us, to hear again the voice of God amid the din of voices that ring in our ears, making confusing claims about what it is to be a person. I pray, and am confident, that she hears God more clearly now, and in virtue of that hearing is more gloriously and precisely a person than ever she was on earth.

CHAPTER ONE

Introduction: Psychology and the Life of the Spirit

Foreign Spirits in the Church

The church has often been haunted — hindered and helped — by alien spirits. Time was when the ghosts skulking behind pulpits and visiting in the choir stalls were mostly philosophers: Plato, Aristotle, Kant, and more recently Hegel, Marx, Whitehead, and Heidegger. In the best cases their conversation stimulated Christian thinking and threw light on aspects of our life and calling that we would otherwise have missed. But sometimes these philosophers affected the pulpit more than the gospel of Jesus did; it was their spirit, rather than the Holy Spirit, that became the spirit of the community; it was their word, and not the Word of Life, that was taken to heart by the congregation.

Recently psychologists have taken over much of the role formerly played by philosophers. *I'm OK — You're OK* has wormed its way into the Sunday school curriculum. Seminars in "rational Christian living" teach believers how to avoid depression, anxiety, unproductive anger, and overeating through rational self-management. In Episcopal congregations the air is often thick with the mysterious breath of Carl Jung.

1

Small-group Bible studies have a distinctly encounter-group air about them, what with all the sharing of feelings and "needs" that goes on there. We hear about sensitivity and openness and being in touch with our feelings; about being vulnerable and going with the flow and having a healthy self-concept and experiencing growth. We seek spontaneity and personal presence and unconditional acceptance and being real and in touch and human; after all, life is a process. We learn to accept ourselves and avoid anxiety and depression by avoiding global self-evaluation, irrational self-talk, and thinking we can't be happy if life isn't perfect. We seek to get in touch with our unconscious, or the child within. We class ourselves as introverted or extraverted, as feelers or thinkers, as sensers or intuitives. Smother-mothers have learned to describe themselves as codependent. We welcome accountability, try to invest ourselves in our decisions, and feel pressure to become more self-disclosing and assertive; we worry about our self-esteem, our identity crisis, our mid-life crisis, and communications breakdowns with our significant others. Do you hear what I'm saying?

One reason that therapists have been so unquestioningly welcomed is their low profile. Like their philosophical predecessors, they often come in the back door and remain largely incognito. William Kirk Kilpatrick has aptly named Carl Rogers "the *quiet* revolutionary." Many church people who fluently speak his language and have drunk deeply of his spirit have no idea who the man is, or even that there is a man behind their vocabulary. In what is probably the most developed book on RET-based Christian counseling, Ellis's name is mentioned only once or twice, and then in a way that doesn't begin to indicate the depth of his influence. (See Chapter Three for a discussion of that book.)

In the chapters of Part One of this book, I want to raise the profiles of these secular contributors to church life, and also to look at a psychologist — Heinz Kohut — whose ideas seem to be on the rise among Christians, as well as a representative of the family therapy movement, which is also very much on the rise these days. I think we will see more promise, or perhaps a different kind of promise, in these newcomers than in the psychologies that have dominated the church in recent decades. But the psychologists are, one and all, a mixed blessing. Or rather, a real blessing, but a dangerous one because their psychologies are so likely to be taken over uncritically and whole hog. They offer insights and practices that can be helpfully adapted for Christian use, but each has a very real potential to lead us astray. Part One is devoted to sorting out the help from the misguidance.

What Sort of Thing Is Psychotherapy?

Let's begin with a stupid question: Why is the church so interested in psychology? Why does psychology tend to weave itself into sermons, prayers, Bible studies, pastoral care, retreats, spiritual self-reflection, and vestry meetings? Why does the church's language not get equally infused with the latest developments in fiber optics or subatomic particle physics or genetic engineering? The question is stupid because the answer is obvious: The church is not in the business of physics or genetics, but it *is* in the business of transforming persons from being damaged, poorly functioning, unfulfilled, hostile, and anxious, to being whole, well functioning, fulfilled, loving, and at peace. From the earliest days a central task of the church has been to form and restore persons. In other words, the church has always dealt in practical psychology.

A term by which the church has sometimes designated its concepts and disciplines for dealing with the development of persons is *spirituality*. Christian spirituality (or psychology, if you will) says that persons are creatures who are in some sense mirrors of God, something like his children, and designed quite specifically to be "in love" — above all to love God and find their peace and satisfaction in him, and also, very importantly, to care for and to be cared for by the human beings they find around them. The Christian disciplines of worship, prayer, meditation on God's Word, meditation on special exemplars of human excellence (saints), service to others, gift-giving (especially to the poor), and fellowship with other Christians are ways of pursuing this proper personal life and shaping our character as mirrors of God and sisters and brothers of one another.

To draw the connection in the other direction, we could say that the psychologies of Rogers, Ellis, Jung, Kohut, and others are really alternative spiritualities: like Christianity, they are ways of conceptualizing what it is to be a person, along with sets of disciplines by which to arrive at better "health" — that is, to grow toward true personhood or away from various forms of failure to be proper persons. These psychologies are of course in various ways unlike Christianity in what they take persons to be, so I call them *alternative* spiritualities, and that is why Christians, who insist that persons be formed as children of God, must understand these psychologists' spiritualities and know just where the continuities and discontinuities with Christianity lie. The danger is that these psychologies may to one degree or another *replace* Christianity without most people even noticing that any substitution has taken place. In some instances the influence of the therapies — even from within the church — may be so strong that our character and relationships are no longer Christian but are now Rogerian, or family-systemic, or Jungian, or rational-emotive. Our love may be Rogerian empathy, our courage the updated Stoicism of RET, our forgiveness motivated by our "right to be free from hate" (see Chapter Ten). In short, under the influence of these psychologies, our souls may turn out Therapeutic rather than Christian.

But to interpret psychologies as alternative spiritualities goes against the popular understanding of them. Isn't psychology a science? Isn't psychotherapy a branch of scientific medicine? Many psychologists desire to see themselves as scientific, and they often write in a language suggestive of science.

Even as subjective and loose a thinker as Carl Rogers tried to support his "findings" by statistical research; and Freud and Jung, who were offering philosophies of life if ever anyone did, made strong claims to be scientifically rigorous. Among lay people, the prestige of psychotherapy derives in part from its association with scientific medicine. Therapists vary in the degree to which they think of themselves as "scientist practitioners"; some see psychotherapy as much more like an art than a science. But many lay people would trust their therapist less if they thought he or she were offering them just another philosophy of life that has many rivals.

I won't deny that psychology is scientific (or can be, in the hands of some practitioners; "science" is, after all, a term of praise, and some psychologists practice their craft better than others). The concept of science has been considerably humanized in the past twenty years, following the work of Thomas Kuhn[1] and others. Thus the boundaries have been blurred between science on the one hand and ethics/philosophy of life/religion on the other. The most creative work of physical scientists depends on a global "vision" of their subject matter that is not strictly entailed by their data, and this vision is analogous to the "visions" of human nature with which psychologists work when (as is so often the case) their inquiries depend on, or bear on, general questions about what persons are and what proper human functioning is. In Part One of this book, which is a tour of a few of the options in therapeutic psychology today, we will see quite an array of visions of human nature.

The variety of rival views on basic issues in psychology is one of the main things that lead people to say that psychology is not a science and that psychotherapy is not a branch of scientific medicine. There is simply nothing like the same variety of disagreeing views on, say, the question of how a

---

1. His famous book is *The Structure of Scientific Revolutions* (Chicago: University of Chicago Press, 1962).

kidney functions and what it is for it to be functioning well. So psychology in its present state is unlike the most securely established parts of the physical sciences. But even in the physical sciences at times a variety of basic views conflict, as happens today in cosmological theory (the theory of the origin of the universe), and as happens at crisis points throughout the history of science, as Kuhn has shown. The mere fact of basic disagreement does not disqualify an area of inquiry for the title of science.

But if we do allow the rather conflictual variety of views and methods of inquiry in established psychology today to count as science, then perhaps we should not withhold this title from analogous bodies of thought about the nature of persons and their well-being that have not traditionally been thought of as scientific views. In particular, those expressed in Aristotle's *Nicomachean Ethics*, Epictetus's *Enchiridion* and *Dialogues*, Augustine's *Confessions*, Thomas Aquinas's *Summa Theologiae*, René Descartes's *Passions of the Soul*, David Hume's *Treatise*, and Søren Kierkegaard's *Sickness unto Death* may then also count as scientific psychology. Conflictual though these views may be, among themselves and with various twentieth-century views, they are no more in conflict than the twentieth-century views are among *them*selves. All the views I have just mentioned are based on careful observation — just as careful, though in a different way, as the highly methodical observations, worked up statistically, that fill the pages of our contemporary psychology journals. The striking differences that separate these views from much of contemporary psychology are of course the less formal methods of observation, the lack of mathematics in the work of the earlier psychologists, and the fact that they made no pretense of divorcing psychology from ethics and spirituality.

We must admit that there is a narrower use of the word *science* than the one I have just employed, and it is important to distinguish the kind of psychology that this book deals with from the kind that has the best claim to be scientific in this narrower sense. The most scientific psychology, as it has developed in the twentieth century, is characterized by highly controlled observation, rigorous use of statistics, and an avoidance of grand and philosophical/religious questions about the meaning of life, how people should live, and how personalities should be shaped. This ideal is very difficult to maintain in psychology, where questions about meaning and value so naturally arise and may operate where even the scientific practitioner himself is not aware that they are controlling his work. B. F. Skinner is a psychologist who sought to be a scientist in this stricter sense but who, almost everyone would now agree, was offering a broad philosophical construct about human nature and its conditions of flourishing that made claims far beyond anything that could be established by the methods of strict science. Also, one could question whether psychology, when it does succeed in restricting itself to being scientific in this narrower sense, is very interesting or can be adequate to its subject matter, those valuing, self-interpreting animals that we call persons.

The kind of psychology dealt with in this book makes general claims about human nature, the meaning of life, and what constitutes living well, and can be regarded as scientific only in the broader sense that allows the views of Aristotle, Kierkegaard, and Aquinas to count as scientific psychology. The "method" of the older psychologists, if one can generalize, was (1) to listen acutely to what others have said about the nature of persons, (2) to observe persons of their own acquaintance, not least themselves, (3) to have vigorous discussions with others who have observed and thought about persons and their well-being, and (4) to articulate, in writing and conversation, the views that arise from these discussions and observations. The combination of this disciplined method and a native acuteness makes these older psychologists worthy to be listened to hundreds and thousands of years after their deaths.

It seems clear to me that the originators of the six psychotherapies that I will discuss in Part One use basically the same methods as the supposedly nonscientific psychologists of earlier ages: they know some of the things their predecessors have said about persons, they closely observe their clients as they attempt to help them and are alert to their own reactions as they do therapy, they discuss their clients with colleagues, and they articulate, in writing and conversation, the views that arise from the aforementioned activities. It seems to me that "clinical" psychologists are especially likely to have interesting and important things to say precisely because their knowledge of persons is based primarily on this more informal humanistic method of inquiry, which tends to keep them focused on the essential issues of human existence. It is also for this reason that their psychologies conform so nicely to the model of a "philosophy of life" and resemble the church's millennia-old framework for spiritual formation of its members.

Another way that psychotherapies are unlike medical technologies is the extent to which they aim to help people with ordinary life. A few decades ago a stigma attached to getting help from a therapist: therapy was thought to be for people with severe mental illness such as paranoid schizophrenia, suicidal depression, multiple personality disorder, and anorexia nervosa. This view of the therapist is pretty well gone, and people now see her as a helper in more ordinary problems of life, such as fear of flying, marital discord, poor self-esteem, less-than-clinical anxiety and depression, grief, juvenile delinquency, loss of meaning in life, poor motivation in school or workplace, and many other things that a reflective Christianity will also have strategies for addressing. You don't have to be a public scoundrel to profit from being a member of the church; you just need to be an ordinary sinner. Neither do you have to be mentally ill to profit from the services of a therapist. Many wealthier people regard their therapist as able to help them develop a more mature personality and a richer life. Psychotherapy does, of course, also address itself to horrendous pathologies, but the six therapies we will look at in Part One are typical in approaching the more commonplace problems of life. All these therapies assume that they can help just about anybody to live a fuller, richer, more relaxed and productive life. Thus they are not, in the last analysis, primarily medical technologies but instead practical ideologies of the good life. Each of them invites us, as a more or less explicit part of the therapy, to adopt a certain philosophy of life, to see ourselves and our world (especially our social world) through some particular set of conceptual lenses.

Like Christianity, psychotherapies are powerful shapers of selves, spirits, souls, persons. In the chapters that follow, we will treat them as spiritualities *formally* like Christianity, while in some instances strikingly different from Christianity in the particular shapes of spirit that they promote.

Soul and Word

Charles Taylor notes that having a self is quite different from having a liver. You can have a liver without having any ideas about livers, but to have a self necessarily involves having some ideas about what it is to be a person, about what is important in life, about what the goal of life is, and about what persons can do. Human beings are, as Taylor says, "self-interpreting animals." As selves, they live not by bread alone but also by the "words" in terms of which they interpret themselves. So we can expect that people will differ from one another according to *how* they interpret themselves. Those who seriously interpret themselves in Christian terms will tend to have Christian selves; likewise, those who seriously interpret themselves in Rogerian or Jungian terms will tend to have Rogerian or Jungian selves. One of my central tasks in Part One of this book is to display for the reader what a number of alternative forms of selfhood are like, and to compare each of these with Christian character. I do this by looking at the central "virtues" of each of the therapies under discussion: the traits that a person would have if his therapist succeeded in making him into a fully functioning person — that is, according to that therapist's idea of what a fully functioning person is.

The various originators of the therapies that I shall look at will probably want to raise objections to my procedure. All of them will object that I make them look like ideologists rather than the careful thinkers that they are. Each of them will think that his view of human nature is not just *a* possible way of construing human persons but *the* way human beings actually are. I don't think that any of these therapists is completely wrong about what persons are, but every one of them deviates from one or more of his colleagues in such a way that they cannot all be right in all respects. And further, they all contradict Christianity in one central way or another, or at a minimum leave out something essential. So if Christianity's view of human nature is correct, we must adopt a certain critical distance from all the therapists in answering the question of what it is to be a fully functioning person. "Ideology" may be too harsh a term for what these thinkers offer, and I think that "philosophy of life" is actually a fairer and more accurate expression; they are all serious thinkers about personhood, and are, to varying degrees, open to criticism and correction in a way that true ideologists are not. But they offer, I will maintain, rival "words" about human nature. And these are not just theories; the therapists are all practical people, intent on changing our lives for the better. ·They mean their "words" to be taken to heart, to shape our souls, and their therapies are potent methods for planting their ideas in us so that we may grow in the shapes that they ordain.

A second objection would come in particular from Carl Rogers, and to a lesser extent from Jung. I have been saying that the kind of persons we become (the kind of character we develop) is a function of how we think about ourselves, and that therapists form us by "indoctrinating" us, by getting us to think about ourselves in the terms of their particular philosophies of life. They shape us by giving us a creed about ourselves (you will find, in most of the following six chapters, my formulation of the creed that I think each therapist would have us live by). But Rogerian therapy fastidiously shuns giving the client any ideology, any direction, any advice on how to live her life or how to think about herself. The Rogerian view is that each client must be turned back, away from all social teaching, to consult the wisdom of her own "organism," that she must be allowed to grow freely in her *own* way. But of course the claim that each individual has a completely trustworthy sense of his own needs, which, if only liberated from social conventions, would always guide his or her life correctly, is itself a highly controversial philosophy of life. And it is an idea that comes across to the client in the therapy, even if the therapist never lays it out in an explicit credo such as I present in Chapter Two.

If Rogers thinks that it is no philosophy of life, but rather the organism which forms the self in Rogerian therapy, Jung thinks it is the unconscious which dictates the shape of maturity in Jungian therapy. Jungian therapy merely aims to put us in touch with the unconscious, which will then, of itself, give us the deepest instructions about living. Jung is less insistent against ideology than Rogers because, as an heir of psychoanalysis, he recognizes the therapeutic importance of *interpreting* what the unconscious is saying. Still, he sometimes speaks as though one cannot go wrong if only one listens carefully enough to the unconscious. The unconscious, he says, does not lie. In Chapter Six I will try to show that a Christian interpretation of what the unconscious says is also possible and leads to a quite different formation of character than the Jungian reading. I think that Rogers's and Jung's hope of finding a voice somewhere in human nature that speaks unambiguously and without the need of venturesome and deeply controversial interpretation is vain.

Self and Other

A striking feature of the Christian Word about selves is that healthy selves are never entirely on their own. "To be the self that one truly is" (to use the title of one of Carl Rogers's essays) is always, in the Christian view, to be *in communion with others*. To be a self is to be a lover, an obeyer, and a glad receiver of gifts from God; and to be a helper, a fellow worker, a partner, a parent or child, a friend, a host, a spouse, a fellow member of the body of Christ, to some other human beings. On the Christian interpretation of persons, this is not something optional or coincidental to mental health; it is not as though one first becomes a self, and then relates to God and neighbor in healthy ways. Rather, to love God with all one's heart and one's neighbor as oneself is what it *is* to be a fully functioning, fully formed, healthy person. This is what the Christian Word about persons tells us, and it is by this Word that Christians interpret themselves and so become formed as selves.

An important difference between Christianity and most of the therapies discussed in Part One of this book is that they construe our relationship to particular other persons as more or less incidental to our selfhood. Two are exceptions. Heinz Kohut, with his stress on the importance of "self objects" (particular other persons — usually parents — who are essential in the formation of one's self), makes an important point that can help us draw out insights as we try to formulate a Christian psychology. And Ivan Nagy makes a suggestive contribution with his notion of "ontological relatedness" and the importance of justice, trust, gratitude, and other social virtues in satisfying the human needs that arise from our ontological relatedness to our family members.

But critical evaluation of what secular psychologists believe about personhood is no substitute for plain Christian thinking about the issues. If we are to meet the hunger for psychology that we see inside and outside the church today, and to avoid the captivity to secular thought that I described in the opening section of this chapter, we Christians must have our own psychology, a psychology not derivative of the secular ones but nevertheless formulated explicitly in conversation with them. That is why a project such as I undertake in this book must have two parts — a critical part, in which the psychologies are sympathetically understood and carefully evaluated, and a constructive part, in which distinctively Christian thought (in this case, thought about the various kinds of relationships that impinge on or constitute our selfhood) is pursued. This makes possible a genuine dialogue in which Christians speak in their own voice from the strength of their own psychology, the psychology inherent in the Bible and Christian tradition, and thus as full participants converse with the reigning psychologies of our day. I think the dialogue of Christians with psychology has been less than full because we have been held captive by the alien spirits, have not drawn with full decisiveness on the rich resources available within our tradition for understanding persons, their problems, and their well-being. And as a result we have not had much of our own to contribute to the conversation with non-Christian psychologies. I hope that by the end of this book the reader will have the impression not only that the Christian tradition has a psychology, at least implicitly, but also that its psychology is deeper and more adequate to our humanity than any of the modern non-Christian alternatives.

Part Two of this book is a series of Christian reflections about various relationships in which most Christians sooner or later find themselves. Chapters Eight and Nine are about the place of competition in our lives and our attitudes: What is healthy competition, and what can be done to promote mental and relational health in this arena? These chapters will be an occasion to think about the concept of sin, which is very basic in Christian psychology. Chapter Ten is about our relation to those who have offended us. What is the Christian psychology of forgiveness, and how does one achieve mental health in this area? Chapters Eleven and Twelve are about marriage and children respectively, and the next three chapters deal with our relations with strangers, friends, God, and fellow members of the church. These topics are all rich in psychological relevance, and they are ones to which the Christian tradition has much to contribute. I cannot treat these topics in depth; each might be worth a book on its own. But I hope that perusing this range of topics within the compass of a single book and addressing them in the setting of a dialogue with the therapists of Part One will clarify some general lines of a Christian psychology and distinguish it from the reigning psychologies of our day in such a way as to mitigate the Christian captivity to psychology and promote both critical and basic psychological thought on the part of Christians.

. A Christian psychology would not *have* to be pursued in dialogue with secular psychology — at least not if the psychologist in question were Augustine, or Kierkegaard, or Saint John of the Cross. But I can think of two reasons why we more ordinary Christian thinkers are well advised to do our psychology in dialogue with important secular psychologists. First, the influence of psychology is unavoidable in our culture, so we might as well address it head-on — frankly, self-consciously, and critically. Absorbing these other psychologies systematically, rather than haphazardly and by cultural osmosis, will allow us to hold more clearly and faithfully to the psychology that is implicit and explicit in the Bible and the Christian tradition. Second, Christians can learn some things from these psychologies: we can adapt certain positive insights and strategies for changing people. The therapies can remind us of features of our own psychology that we have forgotten, thus aiding us in the retrieval of our own psychological tradition. After all, Christianity has been extremely influential in shaping the thought of Western culture, so it should not be surprising if we occasionally see a distorted version of a Christian theme arise in the theory and practice of a psychologist who may have no clue where the idea came from. We should be humble and willing (as long as we are careful to make the right distinctions) to gain insights wherever they may be found. And sometimes, by the sheer starkness of their contrast with Christianity, these other psychologies can highlight features of our own psychology that we might otherwise have missed.

PART ONE
THERAPY AS
HEART-FORMING WORD

CHAPTER TWO

Unconditional Acceptance

Rogerian Therapy

If you go to a Rogerian for "counseling," you won't get much counseling, not in the sense of advice on how to solve your problems. But you probably will come away feeling more self-confident, liking yourself better. You'll be more aware of your feelings about what's bothering you, and more relaxed about them, and some of the negative feelings will go away.

Why will this happen? Because the therapist will bathe you in a warm atmosphere of "empathy." You sense, no doubt, that others have a limited tolerance for hearing your problems, and if you just hauled off and told people some of the shocking things you've done and thought and felt, you would be in for a gagging dose of condemnation. So you mostly keep your mouth shut. And with that stopped mouth your feelings get clogged up too, so that you're not even sure what they are. What a pleasant surprise, then, when the therapist speaks to you with that tender voice and looks at you with those empathic eyes that say, "I'd really like to hear about *you*. Please tell me your story, and don't hold anything back, because we have lots of time, and no matter what you tell me, there is now no condemnation. In my presence you can let it all hang out; you are *totally free* to be yourself."

17

The result of this active listening (and ideally, this is just about all that a Rogerian therapist wants to do) is a kind of emotional liberation. Because somebody actively and unconditionally accepts you just as you are, you are set free to accept yourself, to be the self that you truly are. You don't need to put up artificial, defensive fronts, either for yourself or for others, because there is no longer anything to defend yourself against. And being undefensive, you become accepting of others, regardless of *their* faults. The therapist's acceptance of you translates into your acceptance of others (so goes the theory, anyway), and your acceptance of them translates into healthier, happier relationships.

According to Rogers, all psychological problems can be traced to a person's failure to listen to, experience, and obey the dictates of her or his natural self. As we grow up, most of us fail to some degree to follow the leading of our own inner light, because other people impose their values on us in a very effective way. We need to think highly of ourselves, and this takes the form of wanting to be well regarded by others. We wish to be patted on the back, smiled upon by approving faces, hugged when we accomplish something. Our concern to win the approval of others makes us vulnerable to psychological enslavement by them. If Joey resonates to music and wants to spend his time listening and practicing, but his parents think he should find a career in which he can make lots of money, they may "manipulate" him by withholding approval from him when he spends his time at music and letting him know (perhaps very subtly) that the way to get their approval is to show enthusiasm for business-oriented activities. Since he wants their approval so badly, he may be willing to deny his true, musical self and construct a false, entrepreneurial self in its place. He learns to think of himself as an entrepreneur, to want the things that entrepreneurs want, and to feel the feelings that entrepreneurs feel.

Rogers will say that Joey has "introjected" his parents' "conditions of worth." That is, his parents have implicitly laid down conditions for ascribing personal worth to him (for giving him approval), in particular the condition that he function like an entrepreneur. And since their approval is so important to him, he has actually, in a sense, become — in terms of his behavior and feelings and self-concept — an entrepreneur. He has absorbed his parents' conditions of worth, made them components in the makeup of his self. But such a person is also likely to experience psychological problems, such as depression and anxiety, because the self that he projects to himself and the world is not the true Joey, but a Joey created according to the unnatural specifications of his parents. There is a rift between his true self (the artist) and his self-concept (that of entrepreneur). The anxiety and depression are just symptoms of the true problem, which is the lack of congruence between what Joey is and what Joey takes himself to be, between what he deeply wants to be (his true, musical self) and what he superficially wants to be (his false, entrepreneurial self).

According to Rogers, each of us is an "organismic valuing process" that gets more or less covered up and obscured by the conditions of worth which we have introjected from our social environment. All of us carry within ourselves a completely reliable source of judgments about what is right for us, and that source is our own "organism." To the extent that we consult outside sources for our judgments of value — say, rules imposed by the church or some other moral authority, the standards of our culture, the opinions of family and friends, or even the theories of our psychotherapist — we will not be "congruent" and thus fully functioning. The prescription for all of our failures to realize our human potential is to get in touch with this organismic valuing process, to tune in to our true selves.

How do we do this? Since we cannot avoid the need to receive positive regard from others, and since the *conditional* positive regard of others is the source of all our dysfunction, the solution would seem to lie in finding someone who will give us not advice about how to live, but unconditional positive regard. We need someone who will "love" us into becoming ourselves, who will facilitate our getting in touch with our organismic valuing process. This is what the Rogerian therapist does. She listens carefully to what the client says, trying not to direct him in any one direction rather than another, but letting him express his feelings. She not only refrains from any "judgment" about what he expresses but also communicates to him a sense of her positive regard by entering empathically into his "internal frame of reference," trying to feel his feelings after him as though they were her own. As Joey begins to see through his false, entrepreneurial self and to feel some of the feelings and valuations of his true, musical self, he will no doubt feel threatened and anxious. But his sense of being regarded positively and accepted unconditionally provides the safest possible setting for him to get in touch with himself, and gradually the conditions of worth he has absorbed (his sense that he is worthwhile only if he is an entrepreneur) dissolve, and his organismic valuing process begins to operate clearly and self-consciously. He is getting in touch with himself and is on the road to becoming a fully functioning person.

In the introduction I noted that just as Christianity's word — the Word of God — is preached and taught and assimilated in such a way as to form people's character, so each of the psychotherapies has its own "word" that operates in the therapist's mind and gets communicated to the client, a word that is assimilated by the client and thus shapes his soul. If we put the Rogerian "word" in the form of a confession, it goes something like this:

> I am basically good. If I listen to my organism and not to the voices of those who would impose upon me conditions of my worth, I will be at harmony with myself, and I will love myself and be in touch with myself and feel good about myself and be free to grow in my own unique way. I will not let anyone make me feel worthless because I do not measure

up to her standards. My deepest need is to be in touch with myself, and that need is met through my therapist, who accepts me unconditionally.

Rogerian theory resists the idea that Rogers is imposing a theory on his clients and shaping their self-understanding in terms of this theory. After all, Rogers's theory is that the therapist should impose nothing upon the client but should simply enable the client to blossom according to the urges of his own organismic valuing process. The therapist is not supposed to be "judgmental," to tell the client what is good and what is bad. But the Rogerian cannot in fact escape doing this. Even if it is not said in so many words, it comes across quickly to the client that it is *bad* to let his behavior and feelings be guided by his culture or by the church, and *good* to let them be guided by his organismic valuing process. The client does assimilate the Rogerian "word," and as the following chapters will demonstrate, the Rogerian word is just one word among many therapeutic words that are available and influential in our culture today, soul-shaping words on offer as alternatives to the Christian Word. We must ask what sort of character is shaped by the Rogerian word and how that character measures up to Christian character. Since "congruence" is the main Rogerian virtue, that is what we must take a look at.

But before I do that, I want to present a schema which is derived from one of Rogers's writings but which I think is schematic enough to be separable from Rogers's particular conception of congruence. By using it to sketch a Christian concept of congruence, we will come to understand both Rogerian and Christian character — both Rogerian and Christian psychology — more clearly, both in their similarities and in their differences from one another.

Our Four Selves

Rogers is by temperament not a careful or systematic thinker. He prefers to write in a chatty style laced with references to his personal experiences, his "learnings" and his "growth." But he accepted an invitation to write a systematic statement of his thinking that he entitled "A Theory of Therapy, Personality, and Interpersonal Relationships, as Developed in the Client-Centered Framework." In this essay, the most rigorous of his writings, he distinguishes the self from the self-concept and the ideal self;[1] elsewhere he uses the idea of the true self.[2] If we combine these ideas, we get a schema for thinking psychologically about the self, one that can be useful in Christian psychology. I want to begin by expounding the schema, not as Rogers would, but in a more general way. In the next section we will look at the particular Rogerian application of the schema, comparing it with a Christian application.

The ACTUAL SELF is constituted of whatever features would actually identify a person at a particular time. These features might be personal traits such as courage or kindness; abilities such as skill at public speaking or playing the piano or plumbing; relationships such as being mother of so-and-so, supervisor at such-and-such a workplace, friend of so-and-so; age; sex; past history, such as being one of the persons who painted the Golden Gate Bridge in 1980; and so on. In other words, they are the features that a sensitive and accurate describer of the person, perhaps a biographer, would mention in answering the request, "Tell me about so-and-so. Who is she? What is she like?" Obviously, some of a person's traits,

---

1. In *Psychology: A Study of a Science*, vol. 2: *Formulations of the Person and the Social Context*, ed. Sigmund Koch (New York: McGraw-Hill, 1959). Even here Rogers's vocabulary is fluid: he often uses "self" or "self-structure" where he intends "self-concept," and "experience" where he intends "self" or "self-structure."

2. See *On Becoming a Person* (Boston: Houghton Mifflin, 1961), especially pp. 107-24, 163-82.

accomplishments, relationships, and so on are more important than others and thus more central to his actual self, so what counts as a person's actual self will depend on this evaluative concept of "importance." A biographer, attempting to delineate a particular individual's actual self, is constantly deciding what is central and what is peripheral to his subject's character. There is no such thing as a value-neutral account of any person's actual self.

The SELF-CONCEPT, by contrast, is what the person *takes* himself to be, or *construes* himself to be, or *feels* himself to be. The self-concept can easily lack congruence with the actual self. A pianist who is really very good may think herself woefully inadequate, or even if she knows "objectively" that she is one of the very best, she may still *feel* herself to be quite poor. A sagging, middle-aged man may take himself to be dashing, and drive around in sports cars with women twenty-five years his junior to reinforce this concept of himself. A person who is in fact quite anxious in social situations may behave aggressively and think of himself as bold and self-confident. A woman who is manipulative in her relationships may sincerely regard herself as respectful of others' autonomy. In many of the psychotherapies, and also in Christianity, one of the aims in the development of the person is that his self-concept should come to represent more accurately his actual self. This is called self-knowledge, and it is considered a virtue. In Rogerian terms it is the "congruence" of self and self-concept.

To distinguish self from self-concept and to note that the two can lack congruence is not to say that the two do not influence one another. Most of us do not *completely* lack congruence, and this means that what we actually are has an influence on our self-concept. If I am very self-confident about my competence, it is probably because I am in some ways competent. But just as importantly, one's self-concept influences one's actual self: to think of myself as competent helps make me actually competent. Christian preaching and teaching aims to change people's self-concept, to get them to think of themselves as beloved of God, as forgiven, as accepted into the new community of God's kingdom. The expectation and hope is that this new self-concept will lead to changes in the actual self.

We can distinguish as different from both the actual self and the self-concept the TRUE SELF. The true self is not the actual self, because it may *remain to be actualized*. Your actual self may fall far short of realizing your true potential, or what the Greeks called your telos (end or goal). Your true self is what you *would* be if you actualized your potential. It is sometimes clear that a person's actual self is a distortion of his or her true self; we think that he or she was "destined" to be a great mathematician or musician or politician but was forced because of circumstances to actualize something else: the musician in him was stifled when he became a businessman; the mathematician in her was neglected for the sake of her identity as wife-of-Everett. Thus we sometimes think of a personal or an individual true self.

But more importantly, different spiritual traditions have different conceptions of what it is to be a true human being. Christianity takes the true self to be a child of God, made in the image of God and related to God through loving obedience; our true selves will be fully manifested only in God's kingdom, as we fully recognize God's goodness and authority and live lives of harmonious interaction with our brothers and sisters. This is quite different from the Marxist concept of the true self as a communal producer of material things who makes and owns the means of producing those things. Our Marxian true selves will be manifested only after the Revolution, in the communist society. Both of these ideas of the true self differ radically from Albert Ellis's idea that the human being is most fundamentally a rational calculator of his own pleasant, trouble-free, and long-as-possible individual life. Our true self is actualized when we are calculating and behaving "rationally," thus achieving such a life (see Chapter Three). All three of these conceptions differ from Rogers's conception of the true self, which we will look at in the next section.

Obviously, a kind of congruence is also called for by the true self. The notion of a true self is the notion of a self *to be actualized*. When the Christian is actually living in obedience to God and love to neighbor, she is congruent with her true self, as is the communist when he is living in a community along with whose members he works and owns the means of his material sustenance, as is the Ellis adherent when he is rationally calculating a long and happy life for himself. It is clear enough that what we take to be the true self is a function of our philosophy of life. People who have different philosophies of life will not agree on what the true self is and so will have quite different ideas of what congruence is.

They may also have different ideas about what a person's actual self is like. A Christian biographer, being as objective as he can, is likely to see quite a lot of sinfulness in an individual's actual self — that is, disobedience to God and failure to love the neighbor. A Marxist, looking at the same individual, is likely to see alienation from the material means of production — whether the one he contemplates is the proletarian victim or the capitalist oppressor. Ellis, looking at the same individual, is likely to see irrational attempts to achieve the goals of a long and pleasant life. Each of these evaluators, in giving his "objective" account of the individual's actual self, will tend to miss what the others see: the Marxist and Ellis will miss the sin, the Christian and Ellis will miss the alienation, and the Christian and the Marxist will miss that particular brand of "irrationality" which seems so obvious to Ellis.

Some prominent thinkers today would respond to the preceding paragraph by saying, "This disagreement among people whose philosophies of life differ in fundamental ways — not only on what a person's true self is but even on the *actual* self that is, as it were, right before their eyes — shows that there is no truth in psychology. There is the 'vision' of this school and the 'vision' of that — the behaviorists, the Freudians, the Christians, the cognitivists, the humanists, the family systems theorists, the Buddhists, the New Agers. But there are no facts of the matter; there is no objective reality that psychology deals with. The Freudians can't convert the behaviorists, nor the behaviorists the Freudians. It is, as you say, just a matter of philosophies of life, ways of speaking, interpretations that *we* supply, games that we play: pay your nickel and take your pick."

This is not what I am saying. Christian psychology will be, in broad outline at least, the *correct* reading of human nature. First, the fact that we are not likely to be able to prove to everybody's satisfaction that Christianity represents human beings more accurately than behaviorism or Freudianism doesn't show that Christianity isn't a truer representation. Most Christian thinkers have admitted that a certain amount of faith is involved in the affirmation of the Christian truths; they are to some extent inaccessible to nonbelievers and unprovable to them. Second, if it were true, as the quoted view claims, that a science (that is, genuine knowledge) of psychology is not even a *possibility*, it would be surprising that psychologists from different schools interpret each other's data in their own terms and are forced to deal with data that their theories do not comfortably accommodate. Psychologists seem to be dealing with a common reality and disagreeing about *it*, not just making up a reality; even a behaviorist, for example, acknowledges that dreams are something to be dealt with in psychology. In addition, some views do seem to fall away because they are inadequate to the "data." Again, behaviorism is an example. Its theory was that our mental life (thoughts, intentions, emotions, mental images, etc.) is nothing but dispositions to move our bodies in complex ways in response to stimuli in our environment. This view is all but dead in scientific psychology today, and it is plausible to think that it died, in large part, of exposure to the facts of human nature — in this case, the virtually undeniable fact that humans have a mental life which is not reducible to patterns of physical behavior. In this book I take the position that psychology, in making claims about people's actual selves or true selves, is making truth claims and not just "playing games." And as a Christian I will assume that a psychology worked out in Christian terms is more likely to capture the way people really are (or really ought to be) than competing views.

The fourth aspect of the self that Rogers identifies is the IDEAL SELF. The ideal self is like the self-concept in being "subjective"; it is a matter of how a person *thinks* of himself and not of how he *is* (either actually or potentially). But it is not the same as the self-concept; the self-concept is the person's interpretation of who he *actually* is, and the ideal self is his interpretation of who he would be if he were *fulfilled*. Just as the self-concept is the subjective version of the actual self, so the ideal self is the subjective version of the true self — it is not what a person's true self *is*, but what a person *takes* his true self to be. For example, Christians know that the true self is a child and image of God, but a person may *take* his true self to be a rich and powerful lord of other persons. This is how he "idealizes"; it is the potential that he considers most fitting to realize. His actual self may be rather poverty-stricken and socially unpowerful, and he may know this (that is, his self-concept is pretty realistic), so his ideal self lacks congruence with his actual self and his self-concept, as well as with his true self as a child of God. A person whose ideal self lacks congruence with his true self is obviously headed down the wrong track in life, and this lack of congruence is very likely to show up in symptoms of dysfunction.

According to the schema of the four selves, a person is fully functioning (healthy, virtuous, mature) if his actual self is congruent with his true self (that is, he has actualized his human potential), if his ideal self reflects his true self (that is, the self he wishes to be is the self that he truly is), and if his self-concept and ideal self accurately represent his actual self. This schema suggests a number of claims about the person. First, to be a person is necessarily to have *thoughts* about oneself, to have some categories or concepts in terms of which one construes oneself. To be formed as a person is to have some "philosophy of life," as I put it in the introduction. We do not live, as I suppose the animals do, in an utterly unreflective state about what our life is and what it means. We are by nature thinkers, speakers, listeners; we live not by bread alone but by words as well, even if, as individuals, we are not very able to articulate in words what we think of ourselves. This is suggested by the ideas of the self-concept and the ideal self. Second, the schema suggests that it is not a foregone conclusion that we will achieve our true nature as human beings. Our physical development is more or less automatic, but we do not become integrated selves automatically. We need to live rightly, making correct choices and efforts at self-integration. The possibility of failure, not at this or that task but at *being a person*, is real. This point is suggested by the very idea of a lack of congruence between the various "selves." Third, the idea of the true self suggests that psychology is not simply value-neutral description of the way human beings are but is in the business of prescribing norms that are, broadly speaking, "ethical" and "spiritual" — that is, they prescribe what kind of person one should be and what kind of life one should live. As we go along, we will see that this is true of each of the psychologies discussed in this book.

A few paragraphs ago I commented that how the true self is conceived varies from one philosophy of life to another. A Marxist conceives it in one way, Rogers in another, Ellis in yet another, Jung in a still different way; and of course the Christian conceives the true self in a way that is different from all the others. But if our conception of the true self is central to how we are to be formed as persons and what influences we are going to have on the formation of other persons in our families and other communities, it is important to be clear about what we think the true self is. In recent decades Christians have been sloppy in their thinking about the true self and have sometimes polluted their church and family life with concepts of the true self that are alien to Christianity. A principal aim of this book is to alert us to how different the various concepts of the true self are, and how much these differences can affect our formation as persons.

Rogerian Congruence

What is the true self, according to Rogers? What kind of self does the Rogerian philosophy of life, at its most effective, produce? In becoming "congruent" in the distinctively Rogerian way, what do we become?

Rogers's technical term for the true self is the "organismic valuing process." Each of us, if only he can "get in touch with his organism," has within him a completely reliable set of rules or impulses or values by which to live. For Rogers, the very young infant is a paradigm of proper human functioning because she has not yet absorbed the alien and artificial rules of her social environment. She does nothing because she "ought" to, or because it is "expected" of her, or because Mommy and Daddy will think poorly of her if she doesn't. (Clearly, we are talking about a very young infant here.) If she feels like screaming, she screams; if she feels like sucking, she sucks; if she feels like pooping, she poops. Rogers points out that by acting purely in consultation with her organism, the baby is following rules and impulses that foster growth and constitute proper functioning for a baby.

Of course, an adult's organismic valuing process is more complex than that of a newborn infant. Like the infant, the adult needs to take in and eliminate food and to be hugged and talked to and smiled at and generally "loved." But in addition the adult will typically "need" to have challenging and meaningful work, a sex partner, affirmation by friends and colleagues, leisure time, freedom of movement, a certain amount of privacy, and many other things. If a person denies himself any of these things "on principle" or for the sake of others, chances are that he is out of touch with his organismic valuing process; in any case he is certainly creating incongruence between his true self (his organismic valuings) and his actual self (the patterns of denial of these natural urges and valuings).

The process of Rogerian therapy, then, aims to break the hold of such principles of self-denial by dissolving the client's introjected conditions of worth, thus liberating him to hear and heed the call of his "organism." Through the therapist's unconditional positive regard, the individual's actual experience (actual self) is brought into congruence with the organismic valuing process. His self-concept shifts from that of being, for example, a relatively unsuccessful pleaser of others to that of being a self with certain personal needs which it is perfectly all right for him to try to fulfill. And his ideal self (that is, the self that he wants to be) becomes identical with this self-concept.

Whereas the Rogerian true self is identified with the individual "organism" and its needs, in Christianity the true self is a self in fellowship with God and neighbor, a self that is defined as interacting with other persons as a member of the community, and whose well-being is thus found in compassion, gratitude, trust, justice, and a certain kind of self-denial (not, of course, denial of the true self, but instead denial, or possible denial, of the "organismic self"). For his "reality" the Rogerian looks not to God and the community but to himself as an individual and indeed as an "organism." Rogers insists that the congruent person is open to others and able to enter empathically into their "internal frame of reference." And there is a certain truth in the idea that if your individual needs are met and you are thus unencumbered by frustrations, you may be free to attend to others. But the Rogerian "word" teaches people to look first to the satisfaction of their own needs. Others function either as one more source of satisfaction for the individual (we have "social needs," we "need one another") or as optional vessels into which the congruent person pours from his abundance. Since most of us, and certainly most people who go for therapy, don't have much abundance to pour from, Rogerian congruence amounts to a narcissistic concentration on oneself and one's own needs in which other people get out of focus, becoming a sort of peripheral reality.

Carl Rogers's Theology?

Rogerian psychology has charmed pastors and theologians largely because of its emphasis on empathy and the liberating power of unconditional, nonjudgmental, positive regard, which bears a remote similarity to the Christian proclamation of forgiveness and Jesus' prodigal ministry to harlots, tax collectors, and other outcasts. Some pastors and theologians have even tried to argue that Rogerian therapy is a rediscovery of the essential dynamic of Christian ministry and spiritual transformation. A particularly clear example of this line of thinking is a chapter in Thomas Oden's *Kerygma and Counseling*, bearing the striking title "The Theology of Carl Rogers."[3] Oden published this chapter in 1966 and then republished it in 1978, shortly before his understanding of theology and ministry underwent significant change. My point in writing this section is not to take issue with Oden as a particular Christian psychologist but to alert the reader to a pattern of thought that is often encountered when Christians take to psychologizing. The pattern is not limited to advocates of Rogers's psychology; it may be seen virtually anywhere that Christians become enamored of a psychology. The pattern is to mistake analogies between Christianity and a particular psychology for identities, and so begin to see the constructs and practices of the psychology in question as "essentially" Christian.

The main body of Oden's chapter is an attempt to find Christian theological concepts under the surface of Rogers's

---

3. Oden, "The Theology of Carl Rogers," in *Kerygma and Counseling* (New York: Harper & Row, 1978), pp. 83-113.

psychotherapy. According to Oden, Rogerian theory and practice actually contain a (Christian) "theology" of sin, redemption, and sanctification. Essentially, when Rogers speaks of incongruence, he means what the church has called sin. When he speaks of the organismic valuing process, he is referring to what the theological tradition has called the *imago dei* (the image of God in the human person). "Introjected conditions of worth" is his phrase for what theologians have called "the orientation toward justification by works," and the communication of unconditional positive regard by a congruent therapist is redemption.

At the outset of his chapter Oden warns us against two misinterpretations of what he is doing:

> Mark carefully that, far from merely applying theological *terms* as an overlay to Rogers' concepts, we are, rather, asserting that he is already a theologian of considerable strength, whether or not he would wish to admit it. Neither are we speaking merely of *analogies* to a theology of man, reconciliation and sanctification, but of a constructive Rogerian *credo*.[4]

He is not just proposing a new meaning for some theological terms (for example, that we henceforth mean by "sin" what Rogers means by "incongruence," or that we use "incongruence" in the way that St. Paul uses the word "sin"). This would be merely a substitution of vocabulary, and could be done even if the Rogerian vocabulary has a very different meaning from the Christian vocabulary (though it would certainly be a confusing and pointless thing to do if the meanings are quite different). Nothing would be accomplished or proven by such a substitution, and Oden insists on the very strong claim that "sin" and "incongruence" (for example) already have the same meaning. It is just that Rogers and the theologians have not yet noticed this, so it is the psychologist-theologian's task

4. Ibid., p. 84.

to point it out. The other misinterpretation we are warned against is thinking that he is just pointing out some similarities between sin and incongruence (such as, for example, that they can both be interpreted in terms of our abstract four-self schema). No, he is not pointing out mere similarities between Christian and Rogerian concepts, but identities. The words in the two "languages" have the same meaning.

This project turns on a misunderstanding of how terms like "sin" and "incongruence" have their meaning. Sin is not just a failure to be congruent with one's true self but a failure to be congruent with one's true self conceived in a very particular way — namely, *as before God.* The concept of sin is the concept of disobedience to God, or disharmony with his purposes, or rebelliousness of attitude against him. The concept of God is essential to the concept of sin. Christian psychology conceives the true self as related to God, as a member of his kingdom, as a child of God, and so it has a place for the concept of sin. But in any system of concepts in which the true self is simply the organismic valuing process, there cannot be a concept of sin. The same is even more obviously true of the *imago dei,* the image of God in human persons. How can one have the concept of the *imago dei* in a psychology that doesn't involve the concept of God in any way? The same is also true of the concept of salvation. "For Rogers," says Oden, "*the saving event is the mediation of unconditional positive regard through a congruent and empathetic person.*"[5] There would of course be nothing wrong with Rogers using the term "saving event" or "salvation" to refer to what happens when the client encounters the unconditional positive regard of the therapist (although, as far as I know, Rogers never does this). But to suggest by such language that what happens in Rogerian therapy is what *Christians* refer to as "salvation" is to mislead horribly and to set the stage for the corruption of Christian psychology and thus the corruption of Christian people who

5. Ibid., p. 95, his emphasis.

feed on the "word" of this psychology. The concept of salvation is systematically connected to other concepts. To be saved in the Christian sense is to be reconciled to God (and not just to one's organismic valuing process), and to be saved from sin is to be saved from alienation from God, not just from incongruence with one's organismic valuing process.

Oddly enough, after spending the first twenty-five pages of his chapter asserting that Rogerian terms and analogous Christian terms have the same meaning, Oden spends the last five pages pointing out that Rogers's psychology differs from Christianity in that it has no concepts of God, creation, acts of God in history, the law of God, the church, and so on. Indeed, after commending Rogers so heartily, Oden seems equally hearty in his criticism of him. But if my comments about the interconnectedness of the concepts within a psychology (be it Christian, Rogerian, Jungian, or whatever) are correct, then Oden's criticisms undermine his claims about the meaning of Rogerian terms. There are, in fact, only similarities between the concepts of Rogerian psychology and those of Christian psychology, not identities. It is the critical task of the Christian psychologist to note, as precisely as possible, where the discontinuities lie. If it is true, as I have been arguing, that human beings are verbivorous, that they nourish and shape themselves by the ideas in terms of which they understand themselves, then nothing less than the distinctive character of the Christian life and personality is at stake.

Self-Actualization and Self-Centeredness

I asked some pastors about the influence of humanistic psychology on their congregations, and their responses seem to bear out my assessment that people under the shaping influence of Rogerian ideas will tend to focus on their individual "organisms" while letting "external" realities like God, other people, and the authority of the church get out of focus. The

Rogerian ideal of congruence militates against the idea of authority and submission to it and discipline by it. Church people have come to see pastors, youth leaders, and Christian educators less as authorities with a teaching to be accepted in obedient gratitude, and more as "facilitators," enablers, individuals who can "draw us out" and "bring out the best in us" (something that's presumably already there inside us).

One pastor I spoke with had started his ministry in a Rogerian style. "The Rogerian notion [of not imposing one's beliefs on others but simply reflecting their feelings back to them] got me off the hook early in my ministry," he explained. "It clouded over the necessity to clarify my own belief system and apply it to life." After a few years, however, this sort of ministry began to seem empty to him. "I began to think that I was wasting my time and theirs if all I did was read back people's feelings all day."

But wrenching himself free from Rogers was not easy, because the spirit of radical toleration and freedom was intimidating and oppressive: "I was afraid to believe or to share with people that there was an objective truth. Whatever people could live with — that was their truth. And that was sacrosanct, something I shouldn't meddle with. But there was also something in me that said I should believe in something and communicate that belief to others." I said to him, "When you feel constrained to deal with people not in terms of your beliefs but only as a facilitator of their feelings, you can't really be yourself. You have to become abstract and in a way lose your identity." He replied, "I *was* feeling like 'nobody.'"

The Bible as well as the pastor is used to get us in touch with our organisms. As one of the pastors remarked, "There is a move to say, 'Let's get together for a Bible study *without anyone reading a commentary*. Let's not do a lot of study; let's just read Scripture and share what it means *to us*.' I appreciate people wanting to apply Scripture themselves. But if we don't have any disciplined way of studying it, it just becomes part of the process of self-understanding and has no meaning independent of what we feel we need. Whatever it says to us at this moment, that's what it means." In this way the Bible is demoted to the status of Rogerian "facilitator."

This helps to explain the difference that one of the pastors noted between the prayer concerns typical of Christians today and those of an earlier generation: "Today the theme is always our personal needs: getting a new car, finding a better job, selling our house, going to this school or that school. Very seldom do you hear someone saying, 'I'd like to grow in patience and love and holiness.' We talk about prayer and say God wants to answer our prayer, but we don't pray for the things God calls us to search for. We pray about things God's Word doesn't mention: the better job, the higher wage."

One of the pastors I talked with mentioned a seminary course in "evangelism" in which the participants analyzed movies in an effort to discern the underlying philosophy of their culture. Evangelism was supposed to occur during discussion, when the pastors would reflect this basic philosophy back to those participants whose lives were governed by it, facilitating self-understanding and thus helping them to "grow" into congruence with the philosophy they already adhered to. But such "evangelism" has nothing to do with delivering any *news* or attempting to change anybody's orientation. It is simply a matter of "values clarification."

"I think there's also a desire for preaching to be targeted to meet very specific human needs," commented one of the pastors. "And when someone is hurting and comes to church on Sunday morning, there's a growing desire to have that need met and less desire to discipline oneself in worship, to come under God's Word with the understanding that as we grow in God, other areas will be addressed. I think the church has a rough time worshiping because often people come to see what they can get out of a service. Sometimes they will say, 'My needs aren't being met here, so I'll go somewhere else.' They have no concept of worship as glorifying God. And if something happens in one church and they don't like it, they go someplace else, moving around, always looking to have their needs met. So we have a real lack of commitment to the Lord and to worshiping him."

A youth pastor told about a discussion preparatory to forming a youth group: "I talked a little about commitment, and one of the young women said, 'If we make it a group that we need to attend, that will take all the joy out of it.' I said, 'What do you mean?' and she said, 'Well, some day or evening I just may not feel like coming. And if I come then because I have to, there won't be any joy in it.'"

"The thing most lacking is an understanding of responsibility," said the pastor of a midwestern suburban church. "Nobody feels responsible to anyone else — only to themselves. It's tough as nails to get people to feel responsible for others." Another pastor mentioned a man whose wife had been dying of a degenerative disease for the last three or four years. The man felt like "bailing out of the marriage" because it gave him no opportunity for sex and for the kind of communication with his wife that would meet his needs.

The Christian emphasis is very different. Christians are called to bear one another's burdens and to stand by marriage partners in plenty and in want, in joy and in sorrow, in health and in sickness. *That's* what it means to be congruent with one's true self, to be an integrated, whole person. Christian teaching emphasizes that living *through* one's trials with God's help makes one into a mature person, builds Christian character. This life is not supposed to be a setting for the satisfaction of the immediately obvious needs of the "organism"; it is a preparatory school for God's kingdom. So if the Christian's "needs" are not met, the Christian won't be surprised or feel he's being cheated. If he is frustrated, he will as likely conclude that he is being given an opportunity for growth — in patience, forbearance, self-control, forgiveness, and kindness.

Conclusion

Let me review the main points of this chapter. Christian psychology can use Rogers's schema of the four selves and the related concept of congruence because the schema is abstract enough to encompass both Christian psychology and Rogerian psychology (as well as many others). The Rogerian stress on the self-concept parallels Christian psychology's commitment to the idea that people are shaped by a "word" — that what they actually *are* is to a large degree determined by what they *take* themselves to be. This is why much of Christian ministry aims to shape people's self-concept in the terms of the gospel. Although any psychology of the self requires *some* concept of the true self, the schema of the four selves does not in itself dictate any particular one. So the Christian concept of the true self as a member of the kingdom of God, in relationships of dependence and love with God and neighbor, fits the schema. But the distinctively Rogerian concept of the true self as the organismic valuing process differs fundamentally from the Christian one; Rogerian congruence is a very different virtue from Christian congruence. Likewise, the "finished product" — the Rogerian self, the person who is "fully functioning" by Rogerian standards — is a person with a character very different from that of the mature Christian. "Rogerian" theologians and pastors thus run the distinct risk of training people to be spiritual in a Rogerian way rather than a Christian way. The impression of some pastors and theologians that Rogers is either covertly or unconsciously a Christian thinker is a consequence of their failing to notice the systematic, interconnected character of concepts. Christian psychology cannot be pursued without the full range of concepts constitutive of the Christian view of the world. Christian psychology is inextricable from Christian theology.

CHAPTER THREE

The Truth Will Make You Free

Believing the Truth and Being Whole

Christians put a premium on right believing. Of course, it is important to *do* Christian things — feed the hungry, nurture the downcast, heal the sick, witness to the gospel. And the Holy Spirit will enable us to have Christian *feelings* — to rejoice in God, to feel compassion for sufferers, and to experience the peace that passes understanding. But neither Christian works nor Christian emotions will be possible if our *beliefs* are off target. So we work hard at Bible study, insist that the pastor anchor sermons in the Word of truth, and drill our children in the catechism. We believe that it isn't possible to be mature and healthy if the mind is twisted by falsehood.

The psychology of Carl Rogers became a folk philosophy among Christians because of its emphasis on nonjudgmental acceptance and warm empathy, which to the untrained eye look like the heart of Christian grace and love freed from the rigidities of institution and dogma. The therapy we now turn to attracts Christians for rather different reasons, but again ones that bear on the formation of the Christian heart.

Like the Christian faith, this therapy proposes to improve your life by changing your beliefs and to give you peace by detaching you from objects of worldly care. If you are anxious and upset, don't blame your circumstances. You don't need a change of scenery, a new job, or a new spouse; you need a *conversion*, a renovation of your mind and heart. If you are anxious and depressed, says this therapy, it is because your head is full of lies. If you can't get along with your spouse or the folks at work, you need to figure out which falsehoods you're believing, then root them out and replace them with truth.

The therapy in question is known as "rational emotive therapy" (RET). It was developed by a salty, secular New Yorker named Albert Ellis, who thinks Christianity is a fabric of falsehoods that more often makes people neurotic than healthy. Of late, however, some Christian counselors are trying to take captive for Christ the thoughts of Ellis and other psychologists like him. Let's first look at Ellis to see what he stands for and note some pitfalls that any Christian should beware of in adapting RET for Christian purposes. Then we'll look at the work of a Christian therapist who is deeply indebted to RET — William Backus of the Center for Christian Psychological Services in St. Paul, Minnesota.

The Therapy of Albert Ellis

According to Ellis's therapy, it isn't bad situations that make us depressed, anxious, and angry; it is what we irrationally *believe* about them that upsets us. It's not a woman's nagging husband that makes her life miserable. She herself causes her misery by choosing to believe that his nagging is "awful," that he "ought" not to do it, that she "can't stand it," that the world "owes" her a decent husband and that she "must" have one to be happy. If she can stop believing such falsehoods about his nagging, the dark clouds of misery will break up and sunbeams of happiness will start poking through. She may still find his nagging inconvenient and somewhat annoying, but it won't be catastrophic or drop her into a depression.

Such beliefs about what "must" or "ought to" be and about

what one "can't stand" are all false, according to Ellis. It's not catastrophic to have a nagging husband, nor does the world owe us a pleasant spouse. The truth is that nothing is horrible or awful, and the world owes us nothing. If we can get these truths into our heads, most of our more severe emotional problems will be over.

Another mistake is bad reasoning about our value as persons. A great deal of depression and anxiety comes from thinking that because your *performances* are substandard, therefore *you* are a crumb, a louse, or a jerk. But, says Ellis, the latter statement doesn't follow from the former. Depression and anxiety are caused by bad logic!

Take Gettum Grubbs of the Tiptop Roofing Company. The health of Tiptop is a near-perfect barometer of Gettum's self-concept. He likes himself when business is good. If the profits flow in, his self feels robust and tall and rosy-cheeked. But one stupid mistake in a deal and Gettum's self shrinks and stoops in shame and takes on a greenish pallor. "I'm a stupid, rotten person," he says in his heart. "I'm a failure." Then he gets depressed and makes himself jittery about future business deals — after all, his value as a person is on the line. With the world looking so threatening, he's more likely to make more blunders and thus get further "evidence" that he's an incompetent saphead and an all-around boob. Ellis calls this mistake "overgeneralization": "Some of my performances stink; therefore, I stink" is bad logic.

Self-hatred, depression, and anxiety can also result from false beliefs about *other* people. If I think it's terrible when others think I'm lazy, ugly, stupid, weird, malodorous, sinful, or even a bad housekeeper, then I'm in for a lot of anxiety because other people are controlling my life. There's no way I'm going to please everybody, and I need to see that it isn't terrible if people think ill of me. I need to declare emotional independence, to tell myself that while it may be inconvenient if someone thinks I'm a slob, it certainly won't be a disaster. It may be annoying if someone rejects me, but not horrible. If people try to control my life, I need to take the truth to heart: Your life is yours and mine is mine, and I don't need to meet anybody's expectations. According to Ellis, the key to social relations is "You scratch my back and I'll scratch yours, but for the most part let's just live and let live."

Rational emotive therapy, then, is a process of first figuring out what false and irrational beliefs lie behind your emotional upset or undesirable behavior, and then "disputing" these beliefs, pointing out how they're upsetting you and showing you how irrational they are. The rational therapist's style differs from the Rogerian's. The Rogerian is nondirective: she gives you no counseling but instead asks questions and reflects back your feelings so you can get in touch with the "real you." As we have seen, she does have a doctrine to teach about what the "real you" is like, but the Rogerian "word" comes across gradually, being absorbed by psychological osmosis. By contrast, the rational therapist forthrightly smacks you between the eyes with his word: the Doctrine of Truth and Rationality. He will take you on, dispute with you until you see the light; he will try to convert you to his viewpoint. When you start admitting that the beliefs which are upsetting you are "nutty," you are on the way to giving them up. And when you do give them up, you are free from your emotional and behavioral problems. Speaking of nuts, here is the RET "word" in a nutshell:

> Having a pleasant and relatively undisturbed life is the purpose of my existence, and such a life is within my grasp. Most disturbances in life are due to false beliefs and bad logic. The truth is that nothing I can do or suffer is awful or catastrophic. I am neither good nor bad, though I may have good and bad *traits* and *perform* well and badly. Relationships with others are important, and it is rational to cultivate them, doing what I can to make others like me and be pleasant to me; but if they do not cooperate, I shall not be disturbed, because I know that it is not horrible to lose friends or family.

The virtues that grow in the soil of this word are rationality, self-transparency, mutuality in relationships, responsibility, self-acceptance, equanimity, and a sense of humor — all, of course, in their special RET versions, for we will see shortly that there are also Christian versions of these virtues. RET RATIONALITY is a disposition to believe only propositions that can be backed up empirically, not to commit logical fallacies such as overgeneralization when deriving beliefs from evidence, and generally to seek to have beliefs that promote in yourself such other virtues as mutuality, self-acceptance, and equanimity. Ellis's ideal person is roughly a logically consistent empiricist and a pragmatic, enlightened hedonist. To be SELF-TRANSPARENT is to be aware of the influence that your beliefs have on your emotions and behavior. So it's the capacity to do psychotherapeutic troubleshooting for yourself, a capacity basic to responsibility. RESPONSIBILITY, as an RET virtue, is the disposition not to blame your emotions, behavior, and beliefs on other people or on your circumstances but to take responsibility for them and thus to undertake strategies for self-improvement. MUTUALITY is the ability to maximize your satisfactions, insofar as they depend on other people's attitudes and behavior, by maximizing the satisfactions that others experience in relation to you.[1] To be SELF-ACCEPTING is to refuse to rate yourself globally — that is, to take ratings of your particular performances, attitudes, and traits and make them into general ratings of your "self." EQUANIMITY is the ability to remain relatively undisturbed and emotionally level in a wide variety of potentially upsetting circumstances. A SENSE OF HUMOR is the ability to see and appreciate, from the perspective of RET rationality, the comical character of one's own nutty beliefs.

We can see, even from this brief overview, that the RET virtues form an interconnected "package," a structure of personality dependent on a philosophy of life with an internal

---

1. I don't discuss RET mutuality at length in this chapter, but I do discuss it in Chapter Five, where I contrast it with a very different kind of mutuality.

integrity similar to that of the Rogerian and Christian philosophies which we considered in the previous chapter. The RET virtues thus differ markedly from other traits, lodged in other systems of thought, which may go by the same or similar names. Now let's take a closer look at three of these virtues, comparing them in each case with their Christian counterparts.

Musturbation and Equanimity

According to Ellis, much of emotional disturbance comes from making unreasonable demands on oneself, one's associates, and one's environment: "What we normally call 'emotional disturbance,' 'neurosis,' or 'mental illness,' then, largely consists of demandingness — or what I now refer to as *musturbation.*"[2] Thus if I believe that I *must* succeed at lovemaking, or I *must* get the job I'm interviewing for, or I *must* not make a fool of myself in the seminar, I set myself up for experiencing failure as horrible, awful, terrible, catastrophic, and unbearable. I make myself anxious about the prospect of lovemaking or job hunting or seminar participation, thus increasing my chances of failure. Then when I do fail I experience despair and loss of self-esteem. It would be much healthier, says Ellis, to believe that while it would be nice to succeed in these areas, it is certainly not required; and while it is no doubt disappointing to fail, it is hardly catastrophic. Ellis advises that we adopt a generally non-musturbating view of ourselves and the world:

> *All* awfulness or awfulizing, as far as I can see, makes . . . nonsense — because it goes *beyond* empirical reality and invents a *surplus* badness or greater-than-badness to add to the obnoxious element in human living that, because of our

2. *Handbook of Rational-Emotive Therapy*, ed. A. Ellis and R. Grieger (New York: Springer, 1977), p. 27.

choice of basic values (again, surviving and remaining reasonably happy while surviving), actually exist[s].[3]

If we can learn to see all our goals as attractive and even important but not required, then we will have the RET virtue of equanimity. We will be emotionally flexible and adaptable, relatively content regardless of what happens.

Another virtue that can be called equanimity is evident in the writings of the apostle Paul. It too is an adaptability to varied and potentially distressing circumstances.

> Give thanks in all circumstances. (1 Thess. 5:18)

> I have learned, in whatever state I am, to be content. I know how to be abased, and I know how to abound; in any and all circumstances I have learned the secret of facing plenty and hunger, abundance and want. (Phil. 4:11-12)

> We are afflicted in every way, but not crushed; perplexed, but not driven to despair; persecuted, but not forsaken; struck down, but not destroyed. . . . So we do not lose heart. Though our outer nature is wasting away, our inner nature is being renewed every day. For this slight momentary affliction is preparing for us an eternal weight of glory beyond all comparison, because we look not to the things that are seen but to the things that are unseen. (2 Cor. 4:8-9, 16-18)

One can detect in these utterances a trait contrary to what Ellis calls "can't-stand-it-itis." Paul has in his psychological repertoire the capacity to "stand" a great deal of adversity and suffering, to tolerate numerous setbacks and failures without losing his "cool" — indeed, without losing his joy! And an element of this is a kind of nonmusturbation: he does not demand that things go his way.

Demandingness is both a source of unpleasant emotions and, for the Christian, spiritually inappropriate in many cases.

3. Ibid., p. 25.

In the Christian view, it is unhealthy to ascribe ultimate significance to sexual performance, success in a job interview, or making a good impression in a seminar. One ought to be able to put these goals in proper perspective, out of respect for a more appropriate order of priorities. And Christianity even parallels RET in explaining *how* such attitudes are distortions. The Christian can agree that it is just silly (irrational) to give ultimate importance to success in a seminar.

So the Christian and the RET therapist can agree that musturbating in such contexts is irrational. But their reasons are only analogous, not the same. Ellis's rationale is that catastrophes don't exist, that nothing is of ultimate value and thus nothing is ultimately appalling:

> The very worst thing that could happen to me or any other person would presumably consist of our getting tortured to death very slowly. But even that would not be 100% badness — for we could always get tortured to death *even slower!* . . . No matter what you desire, even the moon, you can always conclude in the end, "Well, I just don't seem to get what I want, and maybe I'll never get it. Too bad! I'll just have to live without it, for now and probably forever."[4]

By contrast, the Christian's main rationale for not musturbating is not that nothing is of ultimate value but that something is so much more wonderful and important than seminars and orgasms. Something else is of such great importance that success in earthly terms pales to insignificance by comparison and thus gets decisively put in its place. For one with the eternal destiny of a child of God, to catastrophize over a job interview is to get things out of perspective, to say the least. For somebody who stands in the noble line of apostles, prophets, saints, and martyrs, awfulizing over failure to get an erection is more embarrassing than the failure itself. For one who seeks first the kingdom of heaven — who has only one master

4. Ibid., pp. 23, 26.

whom he loves with all his heart — musturbating over a seminar looks downright comical!

Christianity raises the stakes by conceiving life as an arena in which a person's acceptability before God is at issue; life is a matter of life and death. Such a view of life is strenuous, with the potential for producing or heightening disturbing emotions like anxiety and despair as well as the happy emotions of faith — joy, hope, gratitude, peace. In therapy, Ellis teaches his clients to avoid anxiety and despair by lowering the stakes, by adopting a less strenuous view of life, by making our highest goal not heaven and the love of God and neighbor but "surviving and remaining reasonably happy while surviving."[5]

RET equanimity is thus very different from Christian equanimity. Although both virtues are dispositions not to be "disturbed" by a certain range of things, the goals or ultimate values projected in them are mutually inconsistent, and in consequence the attitudes themselves have a different grammar. Christian equanimity has its background in a Christian "heroism," a passionate pursuit of "the prize of the upward call of God in Christ Jesus" (Phil. 3:14), a transcendent valuing of human life. RET contentment is achieved by eschewing all prizes of upward calls and reducing one's life goals to manageable, obviously attainable ones. The Christian who is clear about RET equanimity will judge that to possess this "virtue" is a matter not of triumph and health but of spiritual defeat.

Self-Acceptance

Another main source of upset, according to Ellis, is self-evaluation and self-justification. This he sharply distinguishes from rating one's *performances*, which is a legitimate activity necessary to lead a "rational" life. The problem is that people have a strong tendency to let their evaluation of their perfor-

5. Ibid., p. 25.

mances stain their evaluation of their selves. (Ellis believes this tendency has a biological basis.) Thus if I perform an awkward act, I tend to think of myself as an awkward person; if I commit a culpable act, I tend to think of myself as a guilty person, thus feeling generally guilty and depressed. People get emotionally upset not as a result of believing they have performed badly but as a result of the further belief that they are therefore bad people. So if we can get them to stop holding the latter kind of belief, thus leaving their "selves" a complete evaluative blank, we will eradicate a lot of anxiety and depression.

Ellis contrasts self-acceptance and self-esteem. Whereas self-esteem "means that the individual values himself because he has behaved intelligently, correctly, or competently,"

> self-acceptance means that the individual fully and unconditionally accepts himself whether or not he behaves intelligently, correctly, or competently and whether or not other people approve, respect, or love him. Whereas, therefore, only well-behaving (not to mention perfectly behaving) individuals can merit and feel self-esteem, virtually all humans are capable of feeling self-acceptance.[6]

Here Ellis needs help understanding his own position. He refers to the "feeling" of self-acceptance as though it is something positive, not just an evaluational blankness about oneself. And if I read his therapy correctly, he does want people to feel good about themselves. It would not really be human flourishing to feel nothing one way or the other about ourselves but only to have feelings about our performances. And yet, according to Ellis, we "accept ourselves" by eschewing all global evaluations of ourselves. On this issue, Carl Rogers's intuitions about selfhood are more on the mark than Ellis's. The self-concept is both global (not just about traits and performances) and evaluative (not blank or noncommittal about the value of the self).

6. Ibid., pp. 101-2.

According to Ellis's view, a feeling is a function of a belief or self-statement. But Ellis has instructed us not to believe anything one way or the other about the value of our "selves." So how can one have a feeling of self-acceptance? If Ellis wants to retain his implicit and commonsense view that self-acceptance is a positive feeling, he must give up his blanket rejection of self-esteem, and if he wishes to deny that this feeling is based on any belief about our selves, he must give up his assertion that feelings are all grounded in beliefs.

One kind of self-esteem is a function of the belief that one is performing well or has good traits, and Ellis is right that a person with this kind of self-esteem risks hating himself if the conditions of his self-regard cease to be fulfilled. But there is another kind of self-esteem that Ellis should not reject. This is a precognitive sense of identity or feeling of personal security that derives not from anything one *believes* about oneself but instead from experiences of being unconditionally regarded by significant others, such as parents (largely long ago in forgotten childhood) and friends. One strongly *construes* oneself as having worth but without this construal being based on any particular beliefs about oneself. So there is a self-acceptance that is a positive feeling of worth but is not based on any fallacious (or valid) inference from beliefs about one's performances. I speculate that Ellis has this concept, though he is not disposed to admit it because of his strongly cognitive orientation. The "self-acceptance" he officially countenances, which involves erasing all evaluative beliefs from one's self-concept, actually feeds parasitically on this precognitive self-esteem. It is only because a person already has some precognitive self-esteem that the process of abandoning self-evaluative beliefs can bring about the feeling of self-acceptance that Ellis mentions in the preceding quote. What then is RET self-acceptance? It would seem to be *a precognitive self-esteem protected against the overlay of cognitive self-rejection or self-condemnation by a systematic abstinence from all propositions of global self-assessment.*

When we turn to the New Testament for a virtue resembling self-acceptance, we find nothing named. Our modern preoccupation with issues of self-love/self-hate, self-acceptance/self-rejection, self-esteem/self-downing (to use Ellis's term) seems strangely absent. The thought world of the New Testament is not a world without selves, but it is short on self-preoccupation. In an address to the American Psychological Association in 1961, biblical scholar Krister Stendahl argued that, contrary to the Western interpretation standard since Augustine, the apostle Paul did not struggle with a guilty conscience, nor did he think of the gospel as an answer to any such "subjective" or "psychological" problems as self-rejection, self-hatred, or self-condemnation.[7] In the Gospels we find some examples of self-condemnation, but it is this, rather than a subsequent self-acceptance, that is commended (see Luke 7:36-50 and 18:9-14). It appears that self-condemnation is recommended in these cases not as a stage in the process toward fully liking or accepting oneself but as a recognition of sin for what it is and thus a certain clarity about what the kingdom of God is and what acceptance or forgiveness by God is. In the New Testament we find a great deal about God's acceptance of sinners at the same time that we find nothing about their acceptance of themselves.

It would be hopeless for us, as twentieth-century Christians, to be so rigidly biblicist as to reject any virtue in the family of self-acceptance just because the New Testament mentions none. Whether or not the concern is biblical, issues of self-esteem are inescapable for us. Furthermore, although there is abundant biblical warrant for self-condemnation, in the redemptive light of the gospel it is incredible to think that self-condemnation should be the last word. The New Testament contains psychologically relevant concepts — such as forgiveness, reconciliation, the love of God, being a child of God,

7. Stendahl, "The Apostle Paul and the Introspective Conscience of the West," *Harvard Theological Review* 56 (1963): 199-215.

and others — that have a clear bearing on Christian self-acceptance. So it seems right to construct a virtue-concept along these lines. Still, if we do not eschew self-esteem as a virtue, what are we to make of the fact that the New Testament never directly applies the gospel, or concepts like God's love and being a child of God, to issues of self-esteem? I think this fact should caution us against giving self-esteem a *central* place in a Christian psychology. A *psychology* is necessarily about the self, its health, its formation, and its relationships, but in a Christian psychology the stress will be less on what the self thinks or feels about itself and more on what it thinks and feels about others — God and the neighbor.

The concepts involved will be beliefs and images concerning who the believer is and what the believer's relationship to God is. These beliefs will be evaluative ones such as that I am a sinner, that I have rebelled against God and am helpless apart from grace, that God loves me and nothing can separate me from his love, that he has adopted me along with these others to be his child, and that I am destined for an eternal weight of glory. That the person accepts himself *in these terms* is what makes the Christian virtue of self-acceptance distinctive.

In the New Testament are two different modes of self-evaluation, which we might call the imputation mode and the responsibility mode. In the imputation mode a person is evaluated, apart from her performances, by her relationship to someone else. A sinner is justified not by works (which would constitute the sinner's own righteousness), but by the imputation of Christ's righteousness (1 Cor. 1:30). In the responsibility mode a person is evaluated on the basis of her performances. Because she has scorned some of God's children, refused them succor in time of need, and committed other identifiable sins, she is a sinner. The more deeply a self-condemning person comes to construe herself in these terms and at the same time to rejoice in the imputed positive evaluation (righteous, accepted, adopted as daughter or son), the more Christianly self-accepting she is.

Thus we see a stark difference between Christian self-acceptance and RET self-acceptance. According to the RET model, to accept oneself is to avoid all terms of self-evaluation so that the only feeling of self-acceptance left is whatever precognitive self-esteem one possesses; according to the Christian model, to accept oneself is to adopt some definite *terms* of self-evaluation and consequently to feel a variety of "rejoicing" emotions such as gratitude, hope, and peace, now focused, in a way somewhat different from New Testament examples, on *oneself.* A therapist who succeeded in Ellis's strategy of getting the client to forswear all global self-evaluations would also have precluded the client's development of Christian self-acceptance. However, some particular RET disputations of self-evaluations will be compatible with Christian therapy. If the client insists on deprecating himself because he makes insignificant social mistakes, the Christian therapist too may find it useful to point out that such mistakes hardly make him a complete jerk. Much of the therapy undertaken with a particular client might turn out to involve correcting this sort of mistake. The difference will be that in addition to this ground-clearing, the Christian therapist will have some global self-conceptualizations to promote that will be central to the formation of self-acceptance in the client.

A Sense of Humor

A striking thing about RET is its use of humor to pry clients loose from their irrational beliefs. Ellis's humor is sometimes little more than playfulness, as when he puns or pokes fun at psychoanalysis. Even this has the therapeutic effect of causing people to relax. But the more essentially therapeutic humor consists in getting his clients to see *themselves* (strictly speaking, their behavior, beliefs, and emotions) in a comic light from the RET perspective. In this way Ellis drives a little wedge between them and their worldview, viscerally recommending to them, by the pleasure of amusement, his own "rational" worldview to replace their "nutty" one.

Perhaps the simplest way that Ellis does this is through a comic RET vocabulary — some of which we've heard already — in which he describes the client's beliefs and self-talk: this belief is a case of "musturbating"; that one is "awfulizing" or "horribilizing" or "catastrophizing"; and that attitude is "can't-stand-it-itis." The comedy in these words makes the client more willing to be drawn into the RET view of himself and thus to abandon his own viewpoint, which he now more or less laughs at as a case of musturbating or horribilizing. While the client may be expecting the therapist to tell him he is suffering from an involutional psychotic reaction, or something equally deep and dire, Ellis tells him his problem is his "nutty ideas." Not only does the client dissociate himself from his problem by enjoying the comedy, but the homeliness of the diagnosis brings the problem within the arena of things the client can do something about. Insofar as this humor amuses him, he is in the process of accepting responsibility for his problems (another RET virtue).

Ellis uses comic exaggeration to reflect back to clients their low self-esteem and to underline its "irrationality": "If I keep referring to their slobhood, their wormhood . . . , they not only realize how they keep rating themselves but also laugh at their own self-downing and tend to help themselves give it up."[8] To promote self-acceptance by discouraging perfectionism, Ellis says to a member of his therapy group, "You mean you only repeated that idiotic act five times this week? I don't see how we can let you remain in a crummy group like this one. Now don't you think you'd better go out next week and do it at least ten times more, so that you can remain a worthy member of this group?"[9] This humorous approach is a palatable way of saying to her, "Your belief that you need

---

8. *Handbook of Rational-Emotive Therapy,* p. 266.
9. Ibid., p. 265.

to be perfect is one of your nutty ideas." It also says unsentimentally, "We accept you, warts and all." Perceiving the comedy in her perfectionism, the client sees herself from the perspective of Ellis's beliefs about what is valuable, appropriate, and rational, and thus dissociates herself from her perfectionism.

Soren Kierkegaard's writings are peppered both with examples of a Christian therapeutic use of humor and with reflections on the Christian significance of humor. He calls Christianity "the most humorous view of life in world-history."[10] He seems to view the humorist as an individual with a special calling and role, that of seeing human behavior in the comic dimension apparent to a Christian perspective and of devising ways to make this comic perception available to others. His humorist is a very serious comedian in the service of Christianity, a therapist and liberator to an age that locks itself into unhealthy and un-Christian patterns of self-assessment and world assessment.

He describes the comic power of the new view of things brought about by the advent of the Christian gospel:

> Everything which hitherto had asserted itself in the world and continued to do so was placed in relation to the presumably single truth of the Christians, and therefore to the Christians the kings and the princes, enemies and persecutors, etc., etc., appeared to be nothing and to be laughable because of their opinions of their own greatness.[11]

As long as there was no higher viewpoint from which to see the pretensions of kings and princes, poets and philosophers, there was nothing humorous in their claims to greatness: If this is not greatness, what is? But in the light of an eternal God, infinitely greater than any king, the pretensions of these

---

10. *Søren Kierkegaard's Journals and Papers*, vol. 2, trans. H. Hong and E. Hong (Bloomington: Indiana University Press, 1970), entry #1681.

11. Ibid., entry #1674.

mortals to deific grandeur begin to look incongruous. The incongruity is heightened immeasurably by the fact that this eternal Ruler of the universe humbled himself, became a man, ministered largely to the poor and outcast, and then died the ignominious death of criminal execution for the sins of people like kings and philosophers. This leaves the kings and philosophers looking a little silly if they strut about as though they are great. Pretentiousness among Christians also becomes laughable, along with a worldly ordering of values to which Christians sometimes fall prey. And when this worldly ordering gets focused in a comic light (probably only with the help of a skilled humorist), it tends to lose its vaunted importance; thus humor becomes "therapeutic" in the Christian context as well — it becomes a confederate of conversion first, and then of sanctification.

It is not difficult to imagine a Christian art of therapeutic humor in which, taking as her viewpoint the fact that God has entered history and died for sinners, the humorist-therapist skillfully casts in a comic light the musturbating, catastrophizing, horribilizing, and self-downing — as well as the rejoicing, pride-taking, hoping, and equanimity — of those who are oriented in these attitudes by the "secular worldview." Just as Ellis's humor is a device for "converting" clients from one set of beliefs about themselves and the world and what matters to *his* set of beliefs, thus nurturing them in the RET virtues of equanimity and self-acceptance, so the Christian therapist might use humor as a device for "converting" people from their set of (pathological) character-shaping beliefs to the Christian set, thus nurturing them in the Christian virtues.

My point is that humor, as a therapeutic expedient for engendering equanimity and self-acceptance, works by moving people from one "viewpoint" to another "viewpoint" inconsistent with the first. But just as there is no such thing as equanimity or self-acceptance *as such* but only equanimity or self-acceptance as supported by one or another web of concepts, so also this therapeutic expedient is inevitably a matter of moving the client from one set of "ideas" to another quite particular set of ideas. A Christian sense of humor founded on the Christian viewpoint is very different from secular counterparts of this virtue such as the RET sense of humor that is founded on Ellis's viewpoint. Accordingly, when the Christian therapist uses some of the techniques of RET, with its very different basic beliefs, she must beware of slackening her hold on those particular beliefs that lie behind the Christian virtues of equanimity and self-acceptance.

Misbelief Therapy

I turn now to William Backus's Christian adaptation of RET, which he calls "Misbelief Therapy," as developed in his influential book *Telling Yourself the Truth*.[12] Does Backus avoid the pitfalls of Christianizing Ellis's therapy?

An important difference between Misbelief Therapy and standard RET comes out in Backus's treatment of anxiety. Like Ellis, he traces anxiety to false beliefs about what is "awful" or "horrible." If Gettum Grubbs believes it would be awful to cut a bad deal, he sets himself up for anxiety, which in turn leads him to be overcautious, avoiding risky situations and venturesome actions. This avoidance only increases his anxiety and decreases the quality of his life and work. He needs to face reality, and to do this he must get rid of the false belief that cutting a bad deal would be awful. "The mistaken belief that life should be sweetsey, nicey, and without problems will make you quite miserable," says Backus. "With these ideas in your mind, you will seek to avoid or run from trouble rather than overcome it."[13]

Up to this point Ellis and Backus agree. But if Ellis is

---

12. Backus, *Telling Yourself the Truth* (Minneapolis: Bethany House Publishers, 1985).

13. Ibid., p. 76.

asked *why* we should believe that it's not awful to make bad deals or even lose our fortune, he will tell us that no matter how bad things get, they could always be worse. This is a pretty grim way to get rid of anxiety. It really amounts to saying that we'd better just resign ourselves to the potential nastiness of life; when we do, we'll find we can stand anything. If we don't ask much from life, we won't be disappointed. This outlook, which is a component of the mature RET virtue of equanimity, is light-years away from that of Backus:

> Jesus tells us quite clearly that we will encounter negatives in this world and that there will be problems, trials, and temptations of all sorts. He said, "In the world you shall have tribulation." He warned us of a devil, the enemy of God who seeks to destroy man; but then He said triumphantly, "But be of good cheer; I have overcome the world." We can be free of crippling anxiety when we rest in this beautiful fact: In Christ, we are safe, loved, protected, watched over, and one day bound for eternal glory.[14]

Christian equanimity is based not on the grim fact that no matter how bad things get they can always get worse, but on the beautiful fact that God loves us and has forgiven us and placed us on the path to glory.

Like Ellis, Backus traces much mental distress to people's failure to "accept" themselves, and he traces this in turn to false beliefs. But the two therapists differ in the *kind* of self-acceptance they promote. In RET, the client is trained to believe that there is no such thing as his overall value: if Ellis is convincing, the client will no longer reject himself, making himself depressed and anxious, because he has become evaluatively blank to himself. For Backus, on the other hand, the gospel is the belief on which self-acceptance is based: "You love and respect yourself because you belong to the Lord Jesus. Your life is His and the Holy Spirit lives in the temple of your being.

14. Ibid., p. 76.

The Lord has wonderfully created and designed you, as He has those around you. You love yourself; therefore you can love others."[15] Christian self-acceptance has this element of positive respect and appreciation for the beauty of what God has made. Backus's therapy attempts to train persons in this self-evaluative joy. We can see that the choice of whether to go to Ellis or to Backus for therapy might be a choice with deep consequences for a person's character.

In these two respects, then, Backus has altered Ellis's therapy to take it captive for Christ. But there are also a few respects in which Ellis's influence has been less fortunate from a Christian perspective. One has to do with our relations to other people, the other with Backus's concept of blessedness.

One way Ellis promotes equanimity and self-acceptance in his clients is by making them emotionally independent of other people. We are not to let other people impose their values on us or lay burdens of obligation on us, nor are we to blame our anxiety and sadness on other people. By contrast, Christianity teaches that we are knit together, as members of a body, with other Christians, that we are to bear one another's burdens, that it is sometimes healthy to reach out to others and take responsibility for them. It teaches us that our very identity as individuals is determined by our membership in the church, which is the earthly foretaste of God's kingdom. If asked "Who are you, really?" a fundamental answer is "I am a member of the people of God." So Christianity contains a number of virtues of bonding, including compassion, brotherly/sisterly love, loyalty, gratitude, trust, humility, truthfulness, tenderhearted-ness, kindness, forgiveness, forbearance, respect, gentleness, and patience.

Backus emphasizes that we shouldn't demand that others fulfill our expectations, such as that our spouse carry out the garbage, fix up the house, or fold our socks. We shouldn't manipulate other people by trying to make them feel "obliged"

15. Ibid., p. 112.

to us in small matters. He is right that there is no Christian warrant for such demands. It is more in the style of Christian love to be flexible in these areas. But Backus seems to push this "live-and-let-live" philosophy to an extreme reminiscent of Ellis: "LOVE SAYS: You are under no obligation to me whatsoever. I love you without strings attached."[16] But surely Christian love sometimes says, "You are under obligation to me. You promised, and it would be contrary to God's will for me to deny your obligation to me." In such cases (say, that of marital unfaithfulness), the fact that we are "demanding" something may cause us enormous emotional upset. (Think of the agony of Hosea.) But to say "You are under no obligation to me whatsoever" would be to abandon the Christian vision of the good life, and our emotional upset is the price we pay for our faithfulness to that vision.

In fact, our emotional upset in such cases may be taken as a sign of our "blessedness." For Ellis, happiness is the same as feeling good, and Backus seems to follow him in defining it as "a continuing sense of well-being, a state of feeling good about life, others, and self. We could also define happiness as the absence of mental and emotional discomfort and pain."[17] According to Backus, "Persistent painful feelings are contrary to God's will. *God does not want His children to suffer depression, worry, and intractable anger.*"[18]

But Christian blessedness is not the same as feeling good; it is instead the mark of an *appropriate* life, for which the kingdom of God is the standard. Sometimes it is joyful, but sometimes the blessed suffer. "Blessed are those who mourn," says Jesus (Matt. 5:4). "If one member suffers, all suffer together," says the apostle Paul (1 Cor. 12:26), who also distinguishes "godly grief" from "worldly grief" (2 Cor. 7:9-10). If these forms of emotional suffering were rooted out by changing

---

16. Ibid., p. 147, Backus's capitals.
17. Ibid., pp. 9-10.
18. Ibid., p. 19, Backus's italics.

a person's beliefs, the change would be a significant abandonment of Christianity.

At no place in Backus's book do we find him trying to rid people of godly grief, or empathic suffering, or mourning over the plight of the unconverted. But neither do we find him carefully affirming these painful emotions as a part of Christian blessedness. The whole thrust and tone of Misbelief Therapy seems to bypass this darker side of the Christian life. One suspects the influence of Ellis's concept of "rationality": to be rational is to believe and behave only in ways that promote feeling good.

It requires delicate surgery to adapt a secular therapy for Christian purposes. Unless we are very watchful, the benefits may be accompanied by influences that for Christians are less happy. Our verdict on Misbelief Therapy is mixed. The bare framework of RET is that emotions depend on beliefs and can be changed by "disputing" the beliefs they depend on. Although RET overgeneralizes this insight, it is certainly, within appropriate limits, an essential one for Christian psychology, and it can be the basis for a Christian therapy. But the particular beliefs about self, world, others, and happiness that RET proposes to "dispute" its clients into are almost all at odds with the Christian Word. Backus has made a good effort, and he has rejected some of the RET beliefs for distinctively Christian ones. But his concepts of human relations and of happiness seem to have been misshapen under the influence of Albert Ellis.

CHAPTER FOUR

Assert Yourself!

Behavior, Behavior Therapy, and the Psyche

The therapy to which we now turn, called assertiveness training, is not quite a full-fledged psychotherapy in the manner of the others discussed in this section of the book. Although among some practitioners it does verge on being a psychotherapy in its own right, it is a technique typically included in the tool kit of behavior therapists.

Some behavior therapists hesitate to call what they do *psycho*therapy; they deal not in psyches but in behavior. The recoil from *psyche* (the Greek word for "soul") and insistence on *behavior* goes back to the forebears of behavior therapy, behaviorists like John Watson and B. F. Skinner, even though behavior therapy, as practiced today, is a far cry from the behavior*ism* that begat it. The behaviorists wanted to set the study of human beings on a firmly scientific footing, and they thought that real science could deal only in facts that are publicly observable — things that can be seen and heard. (They mistakenly thought that sciences like chemistry and physics deal only in matters which are observable in this sense.) But psychology isn't just physiology — the study of the human body as an organism. So if we restrict psychology to what is physically observable in human beings, what can it be about?

The behaviorists' answer was that psychology is about behavior — that is, movements of the body (face, tongue, larynx, arms, legs, etc.) in response to "stimuli" from the physical environment. Behavior and the stimuli that give rise to it can be seen with the eyes or heard with the ears of the investigating scientist, and so are quite different from what supposedly goes on in the privacy of the "mind" or "soul" or "psyche" — thoughts, emotions, intentions, beliefs, desires, mental images, and the like.

Some behaviorists thought that mental phenomena are *nothing but* our tendency to behave in certain ways. Thus my belief that black widow spiders inhabit the outhouse is not a proposition lodged in my "mind" but simply my behavioral tendency to avoid the outhouse or behave very cautiously in there when I can avoid using it no longer. Other behaviorists found it hard to swallow the idea that people's thoughts, emotions, and so on are nothing mental, but are just tendencies to physical behavior; but they still thought that as long as they were doing science, they had no business mentioning anything but behavior.

Behaviorists would be unfriendly to a basic thesis of this book — that humans necessarily interpret themselves in terms of their beliefs about themselves and others, the nature of the universe, the purpose and meaning of their lives, and concepts about good and evil. In the Christian psychology that I am proposing, people do not merely have habits of response to stimuli; they have concepts, stories, images, metaphors, and beliefs in terms of which they make sense of their world and choose their courses of action. Not only does a psychology like mine make "the mental" central to human life; the kind of beliefs that I say are unavoidable are ones that cannot be established by the kind of science that behaviorists believe in. What I'm calling unavoidable is that disreputable, intuitive, speculative, partially unverifiable, tradition-bound thing: a philosophy of life. Of course behaviorism, despite itself, was an "ethic" and a worldview; it was certainly not establishable by the kind of science that it endorsed. Like other psychologies, it was a "philosophy of life," though an exceptionally cramped and humanly unsatisfying one.

I am happy to report that behaviorism has died, though it still twitches now and then, like a frog's leg detached from its central nervous system. In implicit repudiation of its mother, the behavior therapy to which assertiveness training belongs makes rich and systematic reference to emotions, mental imagery, and beliefs. It has gone decidedly "cognitive." Some assertiveness training even makes much of the ethical concept of rights, though the more orthodox behavior therapists tend to be squeamish about this (an example of the twitching I mentioned). If asked why a certain person is not assertive enough, an answer common among even the most orthodox of behavior therapists is that she is *anxious* in certain social situations; no self-respecting behaviorist would explain behavior by reference to an emotion. Albert Ellis, the star of the last chapter, is often included in textbooks on behavior therapy (though he is thought to be a bit on the fringe — another twitch). As we saw, beliefs are central to his diagnosis and therapy: people's emotional problems are traced to their wacky beliefs, and they are cured by replacing these wacky beliefs with "rational" ones. It's hard to get farther from behaviorism than that!

Another technique in the behavior therapists' tool kit is systematic desensitization, which is used to help people get over phobias like fear of flying, fear of rabbits, and fear of sex organs. The therapist induces the client to get very relaxed and then "presents" the feared object, first in a very unthreatening way and then in gradually more threatening ways so that the client becomes "desensitized" to the feared object. For example, a person with a phobia about rabbits might be asked to imagine a woman on the street wearing a rabbit coat. Then, when she starts feeling comfortable with that image, she is asked to imagine a rabbit in a cage fifty feet away, and then, after further intermediate stages, to imagine holding a rabbit and stroking its fur. My point is that much of systematic desensitization makes its "presentations" of the feared object using *mental imagery*, something that behaviorists once regarded as having about the same scientific respectability as goblins and poltergeists.

If behavior therapy has eschewed in practice the basic tenet of behaviorism — the rejection of the mental — does it bear any resemblance at all to its parent? The answer is yes. For one thing, it focuses rather sharply on behavior. It is pragmatic in that if a client comes asking for help with a particular problem — say, the inability to ask women for dates — the behavior therapist will be more willing than other therapists simply to help the client change his date-requesting behavior without probing his deeper psychopathology or trying to restructure his personality. Behavior therapy also tends to take the position that emotional problems have a behavioral basis. As we will see, training in assertive behavior is seen as a way to overcome much depression, anxiety, anger, and low self-esteem. Behavior therapists have also retained from behaviorism a high esteem for scientific research, and they tend to continue thinking that psychological research can be modeled on research in the physical sciences.

In the rest of this chapter we'll take a look at assertiveness training in three versions, which differ from one another in the cognitive training that they include — that is, the understanding of self and other. In one, the relationship is construed in terms of the gratification of the client; in another, in terms of the rights of both the client and the one he or she interacts with; Christian assertiveness trades on the vision of self and other as (at least potential) children of God, members of Christ. Although assertiveness training focuses on behavior more than many therapies do, it is a technique of *psycho*therapy. It aims to transform not just the client's behavior but his understanding of himself and others, his ethical beliefs, and his emotional experience of the world. It is a training in personhood, in integrity, in self-definition.

Two Kinds of Assertiveness

Over two thousand years ago, Aristotle wrote that virtues are on a mean between two extremes, each of the extremes being a vice. For example, courage is found at a midpoint between the vice of cowardice on the one extreme and the vice of rashness on the other. The coward is afraid of too much and the rash person afraid of too little; the courageous person is cautious and wise, but fearless enough to act in dangerous situations when she needs to.

Assertiveness is the virtue that assertiveness training aims to instill in clients, and one of the very first things a therapist does with a client is to explain what assertiveness is. Here the therapist quite explicitly and didactically shares his philosophy of relationships with the client. He explains this by contrasting assertiveness with two vices: nonassertiveness on the one extreme and aggressiveness on the other. We might say that the nonassertive person comes on too weak, the aggressive person comes on too strong, and the assertive person comes on just right.

The nonassertive person tends to keep his feelings to himself — both negative ones, like resentment and anger, and positive ones, such as affection and admiration. He also tends not to assert his rights. A favorite example in the literature is of somebody standing in line when another cuts in front of him. The nonassertive person will tend just to let it go without saying anything, but may feel angry nevertheless. He may also feel weak and impotent and even self-condemning in a vague sort of way for not having protested. The nonassertive person tends to let other people walk all over him, so while others may like to have him on hand when there's something that needs doing, they lack respect for him, and he is short on true, reciprocal friendships. When the situation calls for him to assert himself — to ask for a raise, to make overtures to someone of the opposite sex, to complain to the neighbors about their barking dogs — he feels anxious and incompetent and doesn't like himself very much. He may also have trouble expressing himself when he loves someone or admires another's work. Instead of saying so, he keeps quiet, with the result that he is not much noticed, and opportunities to cultivate positive relationships pass him by.

In describing the nonassertive person for the client, the therapist not only raises the client's consciousness of himself — for the client may now see himself in the light of these descriptions — but also motivates the client to cooperate in a therapy that may require some courage to pursue. Like any other therapy, this one is not "value neutral" but projects a picture of what it is to be a healthy, flourishing person and to live a worthwhile life. According to the assertiveness training model, to be healthy is to be an *agent,* one who acts, instead of a patient, who is *acted upon.* It is to have a sense of self, of competency, of being one's own person, one who must be reckoned with by others. This ideal of selfhood-as-agency comes across clearly in therapy sessions, because assertiveness trainers are not at all abashed about conveying their values in explicit speech. In the version espoused by Robert Alberti and Michael Emmons,[1] this ideal of selfhood is developed in terms of individual rights: you have the right to express your feelings, and you have the right not to be stepped on by others.

Alberti and Emmons could have followed other behavior therapists and couched the ideal of selfhood-as-agency not in terms of rights but in more ethically neutral value terms. For example, they might have suggested motivating the client simply by telling him that he will be less anxious and have more friends if he is assertive: in other words, assertiveness is just a matter of self-interest. But doing this would produce a different self-understanding in the client (assuming that the client takes the therapist's words to heart — really "internalizes"

---

1. Alberti and Emmons, *Your Perfect Right: A Guide to Assertive Behavior* (San Luis Obispo, Calif.: Impact Press, 1978). This is a widely used handbook on assertiveness training.

them). The talk about rights accomplishes three things. First, it lends authority and sanction to acts of self-assertion. The client who comes to understand his assertiveness as his right construes himself as set in a larger universe of which he is not the center, containing a moral authority of which he is not the source. Being a right, assertiveness is not just a convenience that makes his life more gratifying; it is something sanctioned by morality. In being assertive, he is not only serving himself but also bowing to the moral law. This is quite a different self-understanding from the hedonistic every-man-for-him-selfism that we saw in Albert Ellis, and that might be fostered by a more "pragmatic" version of assertiveness training. Second, it will not be lost on the client that a being with rights is a being with dignity. (One assertiveness-training handbook is subtitled *A Humanistic-Behavioral Guide to Self-Dignity.*) To pursue the noble cause of one's own dignity is to understand oneself as having a *self* in a way that pursuing pleasure and convenience does not. The third consequence of presenting assertiveness as a right bears on the other vice in terms of which assertiveness is defined — aggressiveness.

In his initial therapeutic explanation of the philosophy of assertiveness, the therapist cautions the client against confusing assertiveness with aggressiveness. Aggressiveness, like nonassertiveness, is often motivated by anxiety in social situations, but the aggressive person expresses himself in ways that needlessly hurt the other person. Aggressiveness is often hostile or punitive and fails to take due consideration of the other person's point of view. To go back to the example of one person cutting in front of another, the assertive person might say to the offender, "Pardon me, but I'd appreciate your starting at the back of the line," while the aggressive response might be, "Look, you SOB, get your fat butt to the back of the line before I give you a knuckle sandwich." The aggressive response may sometimes get positive results, but as a rule it is less effective than assertiveness as a way to win friends and influence people.

This may be the basic rationale that the therapist offers the aggressive client for becoming assertive instead: assertiveness is a better way to get what you want. This is no doubt correct advice, but it leaves the client with a basically selfish rationale for avoiding aggressiveness: he may have no real respect for the other person, but he *displays* respect in order to reap the benefits of its effectiveness. He becomes a genteel manipulator of others. Of course the therapist is only one source of ethical training for the client, who may very well have some other, more respectful way to understand his assertiveness. In a number of traditions, including the Christian one, a person who is only looking out for Number One and has no real respect for others is not only submoral but also pathological, or at least extremely immature. It seems ironic that some forms of therapy actually promote such immaturity.

If the therapist presents assertiveness in terms of rights, he has a way of teaching the client genuine ethical self-transcendence rather than enlightened egoism. The right to be treated with respect has the odd property that if you claim it for yourself, you have to ascribe it to other people too. Alberti and Emmons offer their clients a philosophy of life in which all people are regarded as having equal dignity, a philosophy that stands opposed to the impression our society may give us, which suggests this kind of hierarchy:

– adults are better than children
– bosses are better than employees
– men are better than women
– whites are better than blacks
– physicians are better than plumbers . . .
– winners are better than losers.[2]

If the belief in universal human equality is the rationale for being assertive (that is, being gentle and respectful in one's

2. Ibid., p. 3.

self-expression) rather than aggressive with people, then the virtue of assertiveness is a form of self-transcendence and not just a more judicious and effective way to satisfy ourselves.

We can see that "assertiveness" is not the name of a single virtue, even among behavior therapists. The reason is that "assertiveness" is not just the name for a kind of behavior — straightforward, self-expressive behavior that does not hurt the other — but also includes the *attitudes* that one takes toward oneself and the other. It is a matter of behavior, but behavior *understood* in one way or another. In the practice of some behavior therapists, assertive behavior is understood (by the therapist, but eventually also by the client if the therapist's training is effective) simply as a way of getting what one wants: respect from others, self-confidence, and whatever particular things one may be asserting oneself on behalf of. In the practice of Alberti and Emmons, by contrast, assertive behavior is understood as behavior directed toward a being who has, in himself, a personal dignity that requires reverent respect. Assertive behavior in Alberti and Emmons' view also has all the nice payoffs that other behavior therapists claim for it, but it has this self-transcending purpose as well, and this makes, as the saying goes, "all the difference in the world" for the character of the person with this virtue.

Assertiveness is not just a behavioral disposition but a form of understanding of that behavior and a set of attitudes toward self and others. This is true not only for moralists like Alberti and Emmons but even for the most orthodox behavior therapists. The evidence for this is twofold. First, as we have seen, an important part of the therapy is explaining to the client what assertiveness is, how it differs from aggressiveness, and the reasons for being assertive. Behavior therapy isn't just a therapist popping M & M's into the mouth of a client when he exhibits desired behavior and giving him an electric jolt when he misbehaves! The behavior therapist does a lot of *talking* to the client, and much of it conveys a philosophy of life that the therapist takes to be healthy. Second, all the assertiveness literature that I have read points out that you can *be* assertive without *behaving* assertively. There are times to behave assertively, and there are times to keep your mouth shut, let an insult pass, suffer the fool. The important thing, says the behavior therapist, is to be *able* to assert yourself when the time comes. If you understand yourself as assertive, then you will have that self-confidence, that sense of agency, that freedom from anxiety characteristic of the assertive person, whether or not you happen to be behaving assertively at the moment. In this way assertiveness fits the classical model of a virtue: it is always proper to have it but not always proper to exercise it.

Behavior Rehearsal

So far we have looked at the first main stage in assertiveness training, in which the client is instructed in the concept of assertiveness and persuaded of the importance of becoming more assertive. This process of conceptual clarification will no doubt recur and receive confirmation in the midst of the next, more properly "behavioral" stage of therapy, to which we now turn. This stage is called behavior rehearsal, and its name is apt because it resembles rehearsing for a play, with the client as actor and the therapist as coach.

As we have noted, the behavior therapist tends to address rather specific problems, such as the client's inability to approach her boss for a raise or to deal effectively with an overbearing husband. Behavior rehearsal aims to equip her with a repertoire of responses that will allow her to behave assertively in one or another interpersonal context. The therapist begins by asking her to demonstrate how she typically responds when her husband calls her from work in the middle of the afternoon and announces that he will be bringing two important business associates to dinner, and that he would like her to have the table set with an impressive meal for them when he gets home:

Therapist (playing the husband, phoning): "Hello, darling. Sims and Postema are in town from Milwaukee, and it's terribly important that we make a good impression. Do you think you could make a roast and use the good china tonight?"

Client (playing herself): "Well [long pause], I'm awfully tired, but I suppose I could arrange something . . ." (end of role playing). And then I get so angry and think of how I'd like to tell him off, and my head aches, but somehow I pull it together and smile sweetly through the evening. I'd like to be more assertive, but ever since we got married he's "worn the pants," and I just can't bring myself to say no.

Therapist: It sounds like you want to be a good team player, but you don't get across to Steve what his demands are putting you through. Now you be Steve, and let's see if we can come up with a more assertive response.

Client: "Hello, sweetheart. Sims and Postema are in town tonight, and we've really got to impress them. Could you make something special?"

Therapist: "Well, Steve, I love you and I understand you're in a bind. But I'm afraid you haven't given me enough advance notice. You'll have to make do with taking them to a restaurant. I hope it goes well for you" (end of role playing). Now I'll be Steve and you give it a try.

Therapist: "Hello, darling. Remember Sims and Postema? Well, they're in town just for tonight, and I was wondering if you could whip up one of your special dinners."

Client: "No, I don't think so. It's awfully short notice, and it makes me mad that you always dump this sort of thing on me. What do you think I am, your slave?"

Therapist: You've got the idea of being direct and expressing your feelings, and that's definitely progress. But words like *dump* and *always* and *slave* are kind of aggressive. If I were Steve, I would feel sort of ambushed. You've been sweet and compliant all these years, and then suddenly the bazooka! Can you be more sympathetic to Steve's position, but still be firm? Let's try it again.

Therapist: "Hello, sweetheart. Sims and Postema are in town, and I'd like you to make a real nice meal for them tonight."

Client: "You know, Steve, I understand your concern to make a good impression on Sims and Postema, and if I could have a few days' notice so I could plan carefully and not feel too pressured, I'd be glad to do my part. But the pressure really gets to me, so I'm going to ask you to take them to a restaurant instead. I hope your talk with them goes very well."

Therapist: That was excellent! By letting Steve know that you're "for" him, you kept him from being too hurt, but at the same time you were firm and managed to gently communicate your feelings. Now let's see what you might say if Steve gets angry or starts pressuring you to change your mind. . . .

We can see that assertiveness training is very concrete. The client is trained in quite specific behaviors for quite specific types of situations.

The advantage of the stress on concrete behaviors comes from the fact that human beings are by nature agents, actors, behavers, doers of things. Our self-perceptions, our perceptions of others, and our emotions and feelings are intimately tied up with how we act and thus with what kind of interpersonal skills we possess. We will see ourselves as less threatened in interaction with others if we know ourselves to be behaviorally competent in those contexts. This is why assertiveness (which, behaviorally speaking, is simply an interpersonal skill) tends to reduce anxiety, increase self-confidence, and help build a positive self-image. Behavior therapists never tire of pointing out that positive emotions and attitudes depend on appropriate behavior as much as appropriate behavior depends on positive emotions and attitudes, and this is something the Christian psychologist can heartily affirm. I don't think it is an overstatement to say that our very selfhood (to use a not-very-behavioristic concept) is gradually consolidated by our actions.

We may have the most perfect person-forming worldview in the world (and we do have that in Christianity), but it won't form *us* into proper persons unless we act on it. That is an important part of what it is to take the Word to heart. Behavior therapy more than any other kind of therapy capitalizes on this fact of human nature.

The disadvantage of behavior rehearsal is that it is in danger of being too concrete to affect the client's selfhood significantly. Behavior therapists note this fact when they point out that assertiveness training does not "generalize" very well. That is, our client may learn to be assertive with her husband in contexts where he is making a certain kind of demand on her, but this training may do little to make her generally assertive — say, in the grocery store, in conversation with friends, in the workplace, in dealings with her children, or even, perhaps, in other contexts with her husband. According to Alberti and Emmons, assertiveness applies to the expression of admiration and affection for others as well as to expressions of "negative" feelings. But we might expect that training in the expression of anger would not cause one to be more expressive of love and admiration.

David C. Rimm and John C. Masters[3] suggest that assertiveness training may "generalize" better if, toward the end of the course of training, the therapist gradually does less and less modeling of assertive behavior for the client and encourages the client to be more and more resourceful in devising assertive behaviors for herself. This suggestion seems right, given that assertiveness as a virtue is a form of autonomy, of being one's own person, and autonomy is inconsistent with depending heavily on the therapist for knowing how to behave assertively. A therapist who wanted the client to become generally assertive (something most therapists do not aim at) might train the client for a variety of interpersonal contexts. I would

---

3. Rimm and Masters, *Behavior Therapy: Techniques and Empirical Findings* (New York: Academic Press, 1979).

think that the cumulative effect of becoming more skillful in a range of contexts that more or less encompasses the individual's life would be to promote a general sense of competence in the individual and thus consolidate a sense of self-as-agent. Also, as the client's "repertoire" became more diversified, we might expect that she would become more inventive. And finally, the nonbehavioral aspect of assertiveness training that we examined in the previous section, instruction in the "philosophy" of assertiveness, has a general character. So to the extent that something like Alberti and Emmons' conceptual training in assertiveness as respect for rights is systematically integrated with behavior rehearsal, we might expect a greater generalization of assertiveness. However, it should not surprise us that behavioral training does not "generalize" if the client is not deeply trained in a way of conceptualizing her newly learned behavior. Man does not live by behavior alone but by every word with which he *interprets* his behavior.

Self-Denial

Assertiveness trainers often describe the nonassertive person as self-denying and so present assertiveness as promoting (or being a form of) personal integrity. Making a point reminiscent of Carl Rogers's stress on "congruence," assertiveness trainers point out that people who do not express their feelings openly and honestly present to the world (and probably to themselves) a face that is not their own. One who does not stand up for his rights is selling himself short: he is not being "himself." So Alberti and Emmons quite explicitly teach the client *not to deny himself.* This can make assertiveness training seem very much like Rogerian therapy and RET: a philosophy of self-gratification, perhaps even an invitation to "let it all hang out" and "go with the flow" and, "if it feels good, do it." Is it in fact such a philosophy? Usually not, but it depends on the individual therapist. We have seen how behavior therapists differ: some present assertiveness in terms of rights, and others present it in terms of gratification.

These two concepts of self-assertion correspond to two concepts of self and thus two ideas of what it is to deny oneself in the sense of violating one's integrity. It is really the matter we raised in connection with the psychology of Carl Rogers: What is the true self? If the aim of self-assertion is to gratify whatever individual desires one may have, then the true self is defined as the one who desires *whatever* it happens to desire. So the "me" that feels a burning urge for a new Corvette is the real me, and if I deny myself that indulgence I'm denying my true self and thus violating my integrity. Of course, most psychologists don't think that just any desire a client may have expresses the client's true self; they are painfully aware of how perverted and destructive people's desires can be — though Rogerians sometimes give the impression that we ought to indulge just any desire. But even they will distinguish desires that reflect one's organismic valuing process from desires resulting from introjected conditions of worth — and it may very well be that my desire for the new Corvette is really just the voice of my social milieu telling me how to be accepted and looked up to.

Most psychologists who adopt the gratification model of the true self would distinguish true gratification from merely apparent or momentary gratification. We can see this in Albert Ellis's appeal to what is "rational": indulgence of some desires will get you into trouble, so you need to do some calculating about what indulgences are consistent with a long and satisfying life. Given my income, for example, it might be stupid for me to buy that Corvette because, though it would be delicious to tool around town and give rides to all the girls, paying for it would mean moving into a shack by the railroad and eating unadorned soybeans for the next three years, and the beans may drive off the girls. So the gratification model of the true self must reject false gratifications: true gratification is what is "natural" (Rogers) or "rational" (Ellis) or "adaptive" (behavior therapy). It isn't just a matter of satisfying any desire that happens to arise; it requires saying "no" to some of my desires.

But the assertiveness that Alberti and Emmons commend is of a self defined in terms of rights rather than in terms of gratification. As we saw earlier, the logic of rights is that if I claim them for myself, I must also respect them in others. If Alberti and Emmons only taught the client to assert his *own* rights, we might suspect that the language of rights they are using is just a moralistic garment disguising a gratification-self. But this is not what they do. They teach the fundamental equality of all human beings, regardless of social position or physical characteristics, and they teach that the assertive person respects the rights of others as much as he claims his own. So the true self is a being of dignity living among other beings of equal dignity, and that self is most truly itself when its interactions with these others express self-respect and respect of others. Assertiveness is basically an active common respect for self and other. The self that is "asserted" on this model is very different from the self that is asserted on a gratification model, and connected with these two concepts of self are two quite different virtues, though they go by the same name of "assertiveness."

What then do assertiveness trainers mean when they warn a client against denying himself? It seems to me they are discouraging the client from denying his *true* self — the definition of "true self" depending on whether the self being promoted is a gratification-self or a rights-self. Or, as I said earlier, they are warning against the violation of one's integrity. They cannot mean that the client should never forgo gratifying any desire that he feels strongly; even the gratificationists cannot advocate that. The case is similar if one adopts Alberti and Emmons' concept of the true self. Times come when respecting either my own dignity or the dignity of others requires me to resist some intense desire. If I think that a certain sexual encounter is a violation either of my own dignity, or of the dignity of the proposed sex partner, or of someone else (my wife, my children), then I may have to deny "myself" in the interest of my true self.

Christianity agrees that it is never proper to deny oneself if the self being denied is one's true self. *That* would simply be a loss of one's soul, a denial of what God created us to be, a repudiation of God and his kingdom, a loss of Christian integrity. Yet self-denial is an essential part of the discipline by which the Christian comes to full selfhood — indeed, an aspect of the deepest Christian "psychotherapy." That Christian self-denial is not self-violation is clear from the central scriptural text on self-denial. Jesus says,

> If any man would come after me, let him deny himself and take up his cross and follow me. For whoever would save his life [*psyche*, meaning "soul, self"] will lose it, and whoever loses his life [*psyche*] for my sake will find it. For what will it profit a man, if he gains the whole world and forfeits his life [*psyche*]? Or what shall a man give in return for his life [*psyche*]? (Matt. 16:24-26)

The point of denying oneself, of losing one's *psyche*, seems to be to gain one's true self. The self that is lost or denied is therefore either some false self or some lesser self that is to be subordinated to the true self. (For more on this subject, see Chapter Sixteen.)

When Jesus invites the rich ruler to sell all he has and give it to the poor, the self he invites the man to deny is his self-concept or ideal self as wealthy. This is an identity to which the man seems to be inordinately attached. So Jesus invites the man to give up *this* identity in order to find his *true* identity as a follower of Jesus, an adherent of God and lover of his kingdom. In a similar way, Jesus invites each of us to give up, or at least subordinate, our identity as big-shot scholar, teacher, store owner, politician, pastor, artist, inventor, or whatever we may be that is central to our "soul,"[4] so as to find a wholesome identity

4. Alternatively, Jesus invites us to give up our despair at *not* being

in our love and service to him and his kingdom. When the apostle Paul speaks of the death of the old self, he connects it with the resurrection or rebirth of the new self. Death to sin means becoming alive to God in Christ Jesus. (See Romans 6.)

Christian Assertiveness

It should be clear that assertiveness as forthright expression of one's self in words and actions is consistent with a therapy or spiritual discipline that involves self-denial. The self that one expresses in distinctively Christian assertiveness will of course be a different kind of self than that expressed in gratification assertiveness or rights assertiveness. The Christian will assert herself *as* a Christian — that is, as a child of God, a member of Christ's body, one for whom Christ died. (This does not, of course, mean that she will verbally identify herself as such in every self-assertion.) This spiritual status (self-understanding) will have been achieved, in significant part, by self-denial. If we set aside for a moment the social dimension of assertiveness, thinking of it simply as a sense of agency or a competency to act, then we can even imagine acts of self-denial themselves being rather "assertive." That is, one would deny oneself with confidence and a sense of efficacy. This assertiveness would no doubt be born of having achieved a significantly deep Christian sense of self.

A social dimension that is absent from gratification assertiveness and not much stressed even in the rights assertiveness promoted by Alberti and Emmons is assertiveness on someone *else's* behalf. This dimension is particularly salient in Christian assertiveness because of the way in which the vision of the other is shaped by the Christian Word: the other is not just someone with dignity and rights; he or she is my brother

---

much of a scholar, musician, business person, artisan, and so on. Such despair is spiritually equivalent to the self-satisfaction just mentioned.

or sister, someone I love. That person and I are (at least potentially) "one body . . . members one of another" (Rom. 12:5), so there is a very definite rationale for being assertive on his or her behalf. There will be many occasions in the life of the Christian community that call for vigorous, assertive action on behalf of others. In this way, Christian assertiveness is not only a dimension of individual emotional health; the presence of assertive individuals is a condition of "community mental health" in the church.[5]

Assertiveness training originated as an effort to help people "stand up for themselves" vis-à-vis others who might take advantage of them. For this rather narrow purpose the language of rights was handy: you have a right to stand up for yourself. The concept of rights also serves the purpose of distinguishing assertiveness from aggressiveness: in pursuing your own rights, you must respect the rights of others. But even this extension leaves assertiveness applicable only to what Alberti and Emmons call "hard assertions" — ones in which the agent has some adversarial or quasi-adversarial relationship with the "receiver" of the assertion. What about "soft assertions," expressions of affection and admiration for another? Isn't it important to assert oneself in these ways as well? Assertiveness trainers have thought so; like other psychotherapies, assertiveness training has tended to grow into a general philosophy of life. So in the practice of at least some trainers the virtue of assertiveness has come to include behavioral forthrightness about love and other "positive" interpersonal feelings.

This last dimension of assertiveness is less well served than the other two by the language of rights. If a friend of mine builds a particularly beautiful deck on the back of his house and I admire the deck and his work on it, then if I am assertive, I will be disposed to express my admiration to him in words. Such an expression may very well confirm my sense of self

5. I owe the point in this paragraph to my jogging partner, Stan Jones.

and his, and our sense of being in a positive relationship with one another. But it doesn't seem proper to talk here about my *right* to express my admiration or his right to hear my expression. The rights ethic seems to be the wrong ideological support for the expression of admiration and love.

The Christian ethic, on the other hand, gives strong support to all aspects of assertiveness. Our admiration and affection are elicited by the beauty and sheer wonderfulness of the things that God has made. We are made to be attuned to this wonderfulness and thus to be moved to awe and praise. Also, because we are image-bearers of God and are respected and cared for by him, we are beings who should not be ill-used by others, and our claim to assert ourselves against those who fail to respect us or our brothers and sisters can be based on our status of God-likeness. And in demanding this respect, we see the one against whom we assert ourselves as requiring that we treat *him* with respect as well, because he has the same status as we, as a child and image-bearer of God.

We have discussed three kinds of assertiveness, three virtues involving different understandings of self and other: gratification assertiveness, rights assertiveness, and Christian assertiveness. These distinctions can be drawn because, as behavior therapists now implicitly acknowledge, assertiveness is not just a disposition to certain kinds of behavior but a disposition to behaviors in which the individual *understands* himself and the one toward whom he is behaving according to some conception of what a person is. This is clear from the "cognitive" dimension in assertiveness training and the consequent cognitive dimension of the virtue of assertiveness. And I have argued that the concept of personhood offered by Christianity gives support to all the dimensions of the assertiveness that ethically sensitive behavior therapists seek to inculcate in their clients — something that no conception of the person presently native to behavior therapy can do.

CHAPTER FIVE

Between Give and Take

Is Therapy a Bad Influence?

Several authors in the past twenty-five years or so have censured psychotherapy as an unhealthy social influence.[1] Paul Vitz comments that therapy "has created widespread 'social pollution' by its analytical (and also reductionist) emphasis on the isolated individual and its relentless hostility to social bonds as expressed in tradition, community structures, and the family."[2] Speaking of some of the leading concepts in Rogers's theory of therapy, Vitz says, "The encouragement to narcissism, solipsism, and self-indulgence is obvious."[3] Therapy is not ethically neutral; it is an ethical system that subtly subverts traditional values of social obligations, family loyalty, community responsibility, and aggressive justice. Robert Bellah and his colleagues write,

1. Philip Rieff, *The Triumph of the Therapeutic: Uses of Faith after Freud* (New York: Harper & Row, 1966); Christopher Lasch, *The Culture of Narcissism: American Life in an Age of Diminishing Expectations* (New York: W. W. Norton, 1979); Alasdair MacIntyre, *After Virtue* (Notre Dame: University of Notre Dame Press, 1981); Robert Bellah et al., *Habits of the Heart: Individualism and Commitment in American Life* (New York: Harper & Row, 1985).
2. Vitz, *Psychology as Religion: The Cult of Self-Worship* (Grand Rapids: Wm. B. Eerdmans, 1977), p. 89.
3. Ibid., p. 45.

81

While the culture of the manager and therapist does not speak in the language of traditional moralities, it nonetheless proffers a normative order of life, with character ideals, images of the good life, and methods of attaining it. Yet it is an understanding of life generally hostile to older ideas of moral order.[4]

These authors complain that psychotherapy discourages the social virtues. Vitz and Bellah, however, place guarded hope in the ethical promise of family therapy, a kind of therapy that has been developing since the 1950s.

According to family therapists, psychological problems are not diseases residing in individuals, but improper patterns of interaction between family members. The child with an eating disorder, the depressed father, the schizophrenic, or the individual with a phobia is not the real patient, only the "indicated patient." The real patient is the family as a whole; the indicated patient is just the member in whom the family breakdown is manifesting obvious symptoms.

Family therapists like to compare the family with other systems that have mechanisms of self-correction. For example, hunting the wolves in a forest may cause an overpopulation of rabbits, which results in the rabbits' not getting enough to eat, which results in their contracting disease and dying off, which in turn corrects for the overpopulation of rabbits. The disease acts as a substitute for the missing wolves. To the untrained eye the rabbits' disease looks like just the rabbits' problem — something we might want to "cure" by immunizing the rabbits — but the ecologist knows it is only a sign of a problem with many echoes in the larger ecosystem: the dwindling number of rabbit predators. Also, the untrained eye sees the disease as simply bad, but the expert knows it is really for the good of the forest system as a whole. It is a pathological solution to a defect in the system, but it is still a solution. In an attempt to develop a systemically

4. Bellah et al., *Habits of the Heart*, p. 47.

apppropriate solution to the problem, the ecologist works to increase the wolf population.

In the same way, according to family therapists, psychological problems in an individual are often correctives for something that has gone wrong in the family system. Johnny's delinquency may be a subconscious strategy to save his family by drawing his estranged parents together in a common cause. Seen in this way, the delinquency is not just a child's hostile misbehavior but a perversely ingenious expression of loyalty to his parents. It isn't possible to solve Johnny's problem simply by working with him, any more than the ecologist can rid the rabbits of disease by vaccinating them. One doesn't touch the root of Johnny's problem by floating him in a warm vat of professional empathy and unconditional acceptance, or by disputing the false beliefs that have led to the anger he is now "acting out." Nor is there much point in training Johnny to behave "assertively" rather than "aggressively," if his aggressive behavior is serving an important ecological function in his family system. Instead, the family therapist will try to help Johnny's parents overcome their alienation from one another, just as the ecologist does what he can to build up the wolf population. In each case, one intervenes at that point or those points in the system that are throwing the system most out of balance.

Family therapy comes in several versions. Some of them go to extremes in comparing families to self-correcting mechanisms such as cybernetic machines, homeostatic organisms, and ecological niches. The danger of these comparisons is that the individual person may seem to disappear into the "system." In Christian psychology, persons are responsible actors, not cogs in machines. The therapist whose concepts I will look at in this chapter, however, does not lean heavily on the mechanical images. He is an immigrant to the United States from Hungary; his name is Ivan Boszormenyi-Nagy. ("Nagy" is pronounced "nodge.") He calls his approach "contextual therapy" or sometimes "intergenerational therapy." Contextual therapy is not presently the most influential version of family therapy, but Nagy is regarded as one of the fathers of the movement, and the influence of contextual therapy is growing.

Like the other therapies we've been exploring, contextual therapy is clearly a philosophy of life; its distinguishing characteristic is that Nagy sees human beings as strongly connected to others in the context of the family. This makes his diagnostic and therapeutic vocabulary forthrightly ethical and relational: he speaks the language of justice, fairness, loyalty, trust, trustworthiness, gratitude, merit, entitlement, courage, generosity, responsibility, integrity, mutuality, reliability, and accountability. The Nagyan virtues that I will examine are trust, mutuality, gratitude, and justice. But before we turn to them, let's look briefly at Nagy's theory of human nature, his diagnostic concepts and theory of pathology, and the central strategy of his therapy.

Contextual Therapy

As our opening quotations from Vitz and Bellah suggest, many therapies attempt to dissociate issues concerning the client's obligations or ethical merits from the issues of mental health. Contextual therapy, by contrast, is a return of the ancient Greek and Judeo-Christian view that to be ethical is to be well, and to be well is to be "righteous" (*dikaios*, "just"). To become ethical — to have loyalty, justice, gratitude, trust, trustworthiness, and accountability as virtues — is to have developed in a mature form dispositions for which human beings have a natural teleology. According to Nagy, at a very early age children already have — in a pre-ethical form and independent of training — loyalty, gratitude, trust, and generosity toward their parents. It would be incorrect to say that little children or people with severe problems of relating to others have the *virtues* of loyalty, justice, and the like. But they do have a (sometimes "invisible") attachment to their families that, if properly formed, becomes true loyalty, a sense for give-and-take that in the healthy person becomes justice, a need to give to others that in the mature individual blooms as the virtue of generosity.

This nonnegotiable attachment of family members to one another Nagy calls "ontological relatedness." The word *onto-logical* comes from the Greek word for being and suggests that the relatedness of a father and son, for example, is fundamentally different from the relatedness of an employer and an employee or any other merely circumstantial relatedness. The son is, as it were, part of the very being of the father, and the father is part of the son's being. They are separate individuals, but the identity of each is tied up with that of the other in a way that the identity of an employee is not tied up with the identity of his employer. A man can sever his relationship to his employer without doing any damage to his being as a person, but he cannot cease to be the son of his father, and if he tries to do so, he damages himself.

To be a human being is to be "between give-and-take," which is, most importantly, to be a member of a generation. To be a mature person is to understand oneself as being between one's children, to whom one chiefly gives, and one's parents, from whom one chiefly took (though there is both give and take in both of these relationships). Because this placement between generations is fundamental to our deepest self-understanding, we will not be "satisfied" or complete unless we are both rich recipients of the giving of the preceding generation and abundant givers to the upcoming one. Furthermore, our ability to give the next generation its due is a function of whether the preceding one gave us our due. Thus the human being is in the profoundest sense "relational." We do not just band together for efficiency and survival. Nor are we simply a social product — for example, inheritors of a language and culture that are necessarily communal, and formed by a family "background." The product that we are (if one wishes so to speak) itself functions at its deepest as giver to and taker from close others; this is the most basic form of our most distinctively human activities. And our nature dictates that this giving and taking must — on pain of the deepest personal troubles — occur according to rules of fairness.

If our pre-ethical loyalty is frustrated and our need for justice (reciprocity) is thus contravened, stunted growth and personal ineffectiveness result. Indeed, it is our nature as ethical beings that both largely explains our psychopathology and provides "leverages" or "relational resources" for therapy. Let me describe briefly three basic patterns in which frustration of loyalty and contravention of justice result in pathology.

Split Loyalty

Since by a fact of nature parents come in pairs, the filial loyalty by which the child is bound to them is at risk of being split. If the parents present a united front to which the child's generous responses can be presented, he develops an appropriate sense of personal efficaciousness in relationships (self-delineation). The "world" is trustworthy, and the child develops basic trust. But if the parents' conflict requires that loyalty to one be disloyalty to the other, the child is put in a bind in which the need to perform loyal (grateful) actions is inevitably frustrated, with the result that the child cannot develop basic trust. Out of this frustration, loyalty is likely to take the form of "parenting" the parents. The child tries — probably failing dismally — to mediate the differences between them. If the rift between the parents is unbridgeable, the bind in which the child is put can lead him to deep despair, loss of a sense of the unity and delineation of self, and even suicide.

Parentification

Since the natural order of the family is that the child primarily "takes" from his or her parents, the individual who has been neglected or "parentified" in childhood is left with an unbalanced ledger. He is "owed" something. Feeling this subconsciously, the adult who was parentified as a child may seek redress by being "parented" by his or her own child. Because the child is instinctually loyal to his parents, he easily becomes party to this pattern of parenting his parent. Since the child parents the parent by a failure to grow up, leave home, and take on an independent life, various pathologies that are patterned on the failure to grow up can result: anorexia nervosa, schizophrenia, delinquency, a phobia of school.

Destructive Entitlement

Other pathologies take the form of irresponsible, negligent, and destructive behavior, often engaged in without any sense of guilt. According to Nagy, people who have been neglected or abused or parentified as children are "entitled" to be destructive and selfish. Spouse and child abuse, rape, vandalism, and murder can be motivated by a deep sense of not having been given one's due. One takes out on others the unfairnesses that one has suffered. This diagnosis says that criminal behavior is often deeply motivated by a sense of justice. This explanation reinforces Nagy's thesis that ethical motives are basic to human nature and are ineradicable. Obviously, however, such "justice" is also *unfair*, since the ones who suffer the revenge are not typically the ones to whom it is owed. So injustice begets injustice, and such "legacies" of injustice can create chains of pathology from generation to generation.

In a nutshell, we can say that Nagy believes that *fairness heals*. The purpose of contextual therapy is "restoration of a balanced reciprocity of fairness"[5] among family members. This is accomplished through a process that he calls "crediting" and by an attitude/policy on the part of the therapist that he calls "multidirectional partiality." With the family gathered together

---

5. Boszormenyi-Nagy, *Foundations of Contextual Therapy* (New York: Brunner/Mazel, 1987), p. 131.

in a comfortable room, the therapist becomes "partial" first to one member and then to another, taking his or her side, as it were, often against one or more of the other family members, on issues of imbalance in the family ledger. But this partiality is entirely fair because it is multidirectional. Each person in the family is given his or her due. Often the crediting takes the form of pointing out the invisible loyalty, generosity, and goodwill that is the deeper motivation for some outwardly disruptive behavior — for example, a juvenile delinquent may use his troublesome behavior to try to catalyze agreement between his mutually distrustful parents. Or the crediting may take the form of acknowledging the injustice that someone — an abusive parent, for example — suffered in the past from her own parent, and which has "entitled" her to behave unjustly (Nagy calls this kind of crediting "exoneration"). Since, according to contextual thought, the pathology can be traced back to an imbalance in the family ledger, giving a person his or her due begins to remove the motive for the pathological behavior.

Nagy carefully points out that what finally restores justice in the family is not the therapist's crediting, but the family members' giving *one another* their due. Through multi-directional partiality the therapist can model fair acknowledgment for the family members and can start to break down the self-defensive/other-accusatory patterns of thought and action that Nagy calls "ethical stagnation." After all, it is to one another that these individuals are fundamentally loyal, not to the therapist, and it is these bonds, distorted by injustice, that have led to the present pathology. So the therapist's essential goal is to facilitate active and overt acknowledgments by the family members themselves of their fellows' "merits." By fairly acknowledging one another, each accomplishes something for himself as well, which Nagy calls "self-delineation." By fairly acknowledging you who are in close relationship with me, I assert and define myself; I become more of a "self," more of an "individual." This process of self-delineation through ethical acknowledgment of close others Nagy calls "rejunction."

Rejunction is the opposite of "disjunction," the rugged individualism governed by the "ethic" of (often subtle and covert) manipulation and power.

Bellah's Objection to Therapy

According to Bellah, it is largely the relationship between client and therapist that explains the pernicious influence of therapy: "Therapy is a special kind of relationship . . ." that "more and more becomes a model for all relationships."[6] The therapist is a professional intimate. Because she is *professional*, hired for her expertise, the intimacy is disconnected and unnatural, unlike that with a family member, where trust is set in the context of commitment, loyalty, and mutuality. Because she has been hired, the therapist can also be fired if she doesn't come across with the goods. (Family members can't be fired.) And yet she is a professional *intimate*, one with whom the client develops a special bond through sharing secret thoughts and emotions. The therapeutic character of the relationship comes from this intimacy, which helps the client get in touch with himself and learn what "relating" is really about:

> The therapeutic relationship underscores the intersubjective nature of reality. It alerts the participants to discrepant definitions of the situation stemming from different personal histories. It cautions them against projecting their feelings on others and overgeneralizing their own views of what is going on between them.[7]

This paradox of intimacy and instrumentality, which makes therapy so powerful, is also what makes it morally devastating if it is taken as a model for all relationships. For as a hired intimacy, it is devoid of loyalty and genuine indebtedness; as

6. Bellah et al., *Habits of the Heart*, pp. 121-22.
7. Ibid., p. 122.

an instrumental and one-way intimacy, it is devoid of mutuality. Such a moral ideal tends to dissociate intimacy from commitment and to produce people overly focused on their "psychology," preoccupied with their feelings and "needs," and disposed to use the techniques of intimacy (e.g., empathic listening) as subtle new instruments of power.

Bellah's frightening picture fits some therapies better than others. It is truer of Rogerian and Freudian therapy than of RET, in which intimacy is less central as an instrument of therapeutic change. (In RET, curling up with a self-help book may be as close as the client gets to intimacy with a therapist.) But it does not fit contextual therapy at all. The central resource in contextual therapy is not the artificial, transferred[8] relationship with the therapist but the real relationships with one's family members. Contextual therapy tries to respect and use therapeutically the client's natural loyalty to his parents; it sees in transference the danger of pressing the client into filial disloyalty. The therapist is to become not a substitute parent for the client but rather an ally to him or her in the common project of helping the whole family. Because the partiality of the therapist is multidirectional, the individuals in the family are repeatedly pressed to transcend their own psychology (their feelings, needs, problems, etc.) and to place themselves more and more fairly (objectively) in the context of their close relationships. This therapeutic move is obviously designed to avoid the kind of "narcissism" that seems to be produced in clients of those therapists who follow Rogers and Ellis.

What are we human beings, most essentially? We aren't just individuals on the prowl for pleasures and comforts

---

8. In Freudian thinking, transference occurs when the client begins to feel toward the therapist as he would toward some significant other, such as one of his parents — for example, dependent, loyal, angry, loving. The idea is that these feelings have been "transferred" from the parent to the therapist, that they are in some sense still directed toward the parent, but with the therapist as a stand-in.

stretched out over as long a life as possible, with a need to become more "rational" in our pursuit of these things. We aren't promiscuous relaters for whom an empathic therapist or encounter group is a good substitute for (or even an improvement over) our own family. We are not even free-floating individuals with rights of our own and obligations to respect the rights of others (though this comes somewhat closer to Nagy's idea). We are, instead, individuals embedded in a web of close relationships, connected to certain others by an indestructible loyalty. It is not an incidental fact about us that we belong to families: at our deepest we are "members one of another," and the name for this tie is loyalty.

Rogers and Ellis aim to develop in the client such traits as self-acceptance, being in touch with one's feelings, congruency with oneself, rational calculation of one's best interest, and a resistance to letting other people run one's life. In contrast, Nagy aims to form such traits as fairness, trust, trustworthiness, gratitude, generosity, and mutuality. This constitution of the heart corresponds to a word that is its shape and its rule, a word we can express this way:

> As a child of our parents and a parent of our children, each of us is a link in the generations. We can't avoid having special loyalty to our families, and it's entirely proper that we do. We are like filaments in a web; cut some filament nearby, and we begin to sag. We thrive on giving to and taking from our family members, on crediting them for their contributions and receiving credit from them for ours. Our loyalty flowers into personal maturity when we give and take, in a balanced and fair way, in our intergenerational family.

Christianity too sees persons as inseparable from a "context," and yet at the same time as actively contributing, responsible, self-delineated individuals. That context is the kingdom of God, and the historical church is a more or less faint foretoken of it. Saint Paul sometimes describes the church in familial images, of brotherhood/sisterhood under the father-hood of God. He describes the communal and interdependent character of the church with the metaphor of a body, of which the members are the organic parts. How close are Christianity and the Nagyan philosophy of relationships? Let's look now at some of the Nagyan virtues.

Trust

Some virtues can be traits not just of individuals but of rela-tionships. When we say, "There's a lot of trust in that family," we're speaking of a circle of trust and trustworthiness: because the members are trustworthy to one another, they tend to trust one another, and because each knows that the other is trusting him, each tends to rise to trustworthiness. But a family is not just a homeostatic, or self-regulating, system. If there is any health at all in it, it will contain individuals with enough understanding and moral strength to be able to transcend the system and initiate change: You can "venture" trusting some-one who is not very trustworthy (and this is important, because trusting him may elicit trustworthiness from him); also, it is possible to be trustworthy without being trusted.

What is trust? The contextual therapist endeavors to build trust in distrustful family members by crediting first one member and then another and by encouraging the members themselves to give one another their due. So they come to see each other in a new light: they focus on the real contributions that each member makes or has made and acknowledge the victim in the victimizer, and when they see the "justice" in the victimizer's behavior, he assumes a more human face. This approach indicates what trust is: it is seeing the other as a contributor, as a person of goodwill. It is the absence of anxiety — about being hurt, manipulated, used without credit, or let down. As contextual therapy shows, trust can be enhanced without any change in the "object" of trust; the therapist fosters it by getting one family member to focus on features of another member's behavior and history that have not been salient to him before. Contextual work shows the power of positive viewing to heal relationships.

Take the situation between Andy and Beth. Andy's trust involves a relative lack of anxiety with respect to Beth in situations where something Andy cares about is in Beth's hands (for example, Andy's self-esteem). And this lack of anxiety means that certain defensive behaviors and attitudes, which in turn create distrust in others, will be absent. If Andy is afraid of being ridiculed or betrayed by Beth, he will keep his distance, either by physical separation or by a superficiality that keeps him from being vulnerable. Trust is Andy's disposition to entrust himself to Beth in some way, to place himself in a position of dependency. Mutual dependency is so vital to close relationships that without the virtue of trust, one will never know the joys of love and friendship.

In trusting Beth, Andy lacks anxiety, but this is not the same as not caring what Beth does. Indeed, trust is Andy's ability to be relatively anxiety-free while caring deeply about what Beth does. On this point it is instructive to compare contextual therapy with rational emotive therapy. RET fosters what I called "equanimity," which is also a lack of anxiety that can apply to relationships. But RET equanimity is almost the contrary of Nagyan trust. The difference is that RET aims to reduce anxiety by teaching the client that ultimately it doesn't matter what the other person does or thinks, while contextual therapy aims to create a situation in which one can realistically *both* care what the other does and thinks *and* be relatively free of anxiety. The price one pays for learning one's ethics from Albert Ellis is an excision from one's life of what Christians call fellowship, of true spiritual intercourse marked by vulnerability and interdependence. Without trust one cannot be connected with others in the give-and-take that constitutes the communal life.

I have indicated my sympathy with Nagyan trust, a sympathy that has a Christian background. But contextual therapy is not itself Christian. What then might be distinctive about Christian trust, and how might it relate to Nagyan trust? The most obvious point is that Christianity enlarges the context. Our close relationships are not just human, for we have an Eternal Parent. Since Christianity regards human nature not just as relational but as God-related, we are freed to acknowledge that there is much in life to be anxious and distrustful about, even if our family members are as trustworthy as humans can be expected to be. Christian realism about the likelihood of finding security within the bounds of earthly relationships reveals the need for a trusting relationship with one who is trustworthy even when all else in life has fallen apart. Trust of God is facilitated in the Christian community in much the way that trust of family members is facilitated in contextual therapy: by "crediting" God, by preaching God's trustworthiness, by telling stories of God's faithfulness, by praising God's goodness, and then by acting as though God can be trusted. This crediting must be accompanied by the spiritual discipline of a realism about earthly prospects, an assignment into God's hands of all the earthly things we hold most dear. The Christian then acquires the emotional disposition called peace.

I have mentioned venturing trust and claimed that facilitating trust in a family may require that an individual with a certain degree of understanding and courage undertake to trust another family member whose trustworthiness would not itself warrant that trust. Thus through individual initiative a cycle of mistrust can be broken down. In less than deeply pathological families, this sort of thing happens frequently (for example, a parent trusting a child just a little beyond the child's trustworthiness). It seems to me that contextual therapy in a Christian context has a "relational resource" not otherwise available for facilitating venturesome trust. Entrusting oneself and the other and the relationship to God's care reduces anxiety and defensiveness in relationships and thus facilitates trust of people. Christian contextual therapists will credit God in therapy, right along with crediting other members of the family.

Mutuality

When the critics complain that therapies promote atomistic individualism, they are not denying that therapies provide the client with resources for establishing and maintaining relationships (though the maintaining is more in question than the establishing). Instead, they are complaining about the ethical quality of the relationships that the therapies promote. For example, Bellah and company speak of a "utilitarian conception of community" and "the 'giving-getting' model of therapeutic contractualism."[9] Such social skills as friendliness, communication, and empathy are "promoted" by therapists as useful tools for personal satisfaction and success. In Chapter Three I discerned a social virtue promoted by the RET therapist that I called mutuality, which I defined as "the ability to maximize your satisfactions, insofar as they depend on other people's attitudes and behavior, by maximizing the satisfactions that others experience in relation to you" (see p. 43). Such therapists have no difficulty talking about "love," says Bellah:

> "You need to get to know people," counsel these therapists, since "well-connected" persons live longer, healthier lives. On the grounds of interpersonally enlightened self-interest, therefore, such therapists advocate "love and closeness" over the "noncaring, self-actualizing pursuits" encouraged by therapies whose individualism relies on naïve ideas of self-sufficiency.[10]

Despite the talk of love, the individualism of such a conception is obvious. It is clear that each person is out for her own satisfaction, self-actualization, and health, and it just happens that as humans we do better if we have good relationships. The relationships are treated, at bottom, as means to our private ends. Our commitment to others is based on the con-

9. Bellah et al., *Habits of the Heart*, pp. 134, 136.
10. Ibid., p. 135.

dition that they give us what we want or need (thus Bellah's word *contractualism*). So we might think this virtue is called mutuality only by courtesy. It is not really a concern for fair give-and-take, though it may superficially appear to be such; it is a concern for *my* well-being, and yours insofar as it serves mine. A pragmatic recognition that you, like me, have relational needs and are in a position to make relational demands means that I will have to "give" if I want to "get."

By contrast, the kind of mutuality that contextual therapy promotes is based on the recognition that *you and I are in this together*, that my treating you fairly is not just a means to get you to treat me fairly, but that we together constitute a kind of unity — of father and son, husband and wife, parents of these children. To use biblical phrases, we are "members one of another," perhaps even "one flesh." The relationship is not just instrumental to my satisfaction; it is somehow fundamental to my *being*. If we could call the mutuality of the preceding paragraph "contractual mutuality," we might call the present kind "communal mutuality." The difference may be elusive; one of the charms of contractual mutuality is its superficial similarity to communal mutuality (recognizing contractual mutuality for what it is tends to reduce the "satisfaction" it aims at). But the difference between the two virtues is enormous and fundamental. It is a difference in popular ontology, in how we see ourselves and others.

Nagy's "give and take" sounds similar to the individualist and utilitarian "give and get" that Bellah criticizes. But it would be wrong to confuse these ideas. Nagy's idea is that unless we are given our due by our parents, we will not give our children their due. Being generously and justly given to is a necessary condition of human psychological/moral development, not a price that mature people consciously or subconsciously exact for behaving "generously." If this condition of moral development is met, then we have the psychological wherewithal to be truly generous — to give to our children although what they give us in return does not even begin to approach an equitable repayment. The fact that Nagy believes that we pay our debt to our parents by nurturing our children (rather than by paying our parents) and that this ethic is based on ontological relationships and not mere agreement (even implicit) removes his concept of justice quite far from any contractual conception.

Nagy sometimes insists that he is not advocating altruism. By this he doesn't mean that he isn't interested in helping his clients desire someone else's well-being without viewing it as instrumental to their own. Altruism in that sense is essential to communal mutuality, and Nagy does advocate it, most clearly when he insists on the importance of doing justice to as yet unborn generations (whose well-being certainly cannot be instrumental to our own).[11] Since those future generations partake of the larger context that constitutes our being, to do justice to them is in a sense to do justice to ourselves. But doing well by unborn generations is not a *means* for getting something for ourselves; it would be better to say that in the Nagyan intergenerational vision of who we are, to do well by future generations just *is* to do well by ourselves. The "altruism" that Nagy censures is a martyr-like, unstable, and self-deceptive attitude in which the individual attempts to "give" without "take" in contexts (such as a marriage) where give *and* take are clearly demanded by the rules of contextual justice.

One might think that if Nagy is right, and we are all unavoidably loyal to our families of origin, then there could not be any people with the moral formation that I have called RET mutuality. RET mutuality would have to be an inauthentically espoused ideology, not a real character trait. I think there is some truth in this. If somebody like Ellis claims that all our relationships are characterized only or at best by contractual mutuality, then strictly speaking he is wrong about everybody, for however distorted or covered up our familial loyalties are,

---

11. Boszormenyi-Nagy and Barbara R. Krasner, *Between Give and Take: A Clinical Guide to Contextual Therapy* (New York: Brunner/Mazel, 1986), pp. 419-20.

at some level we all care noninstrumentally about somebody else's well-being. But this is just one side of the matter. The other is that the critics of therapy are right in claiming that therapeutic ideologies affect people's moral character. Our familial loyalties can go underground or become "invisible," to use Nagy's expression;[12] an ideology like RET can beget a character that behaves and thinks in terms of contractual mutuality, and the altruism of communal mutuality can be effectively lost. (For example, RET can bring me to think of my marriage primarily in terms of what I "get" out of it.)

Christianity is clearly on Nagy's side in advocating a communal mutuality as contrasted with a contractual one. The commandment "Love your neighbor as yourself" may be plausibly read as, "Love your neighbor because you and he are both members of the kingdom, children of the one Creator." Since the most momentous thing about you is that you are a member of that kingdom, ontologically related to your fellow children of God, loving your neighbor *is* in a strong sense loving yourself. Because persons are bound by kingdom ties, someone who does not love his neighbor is at odds with himself, just as, according to Nagy, a person who is unconcerned about the well-being of future generations is in friction with something fundamental about his own nature as an intergenerational being.

Again, the difference between the contextual view and Christianity is that the latter broadens the context. In addition, it connects mutuality with hope — for the kingdom of God is to a large extent something hoped for rather than presently visible. Whereas Nagyan mutuality, in the relatively narrow context of the intergenerational family, arises out of the biological fact of blood relatedness and its extension in in-law relationships, Christian mutuality, extended ideally to anyone who becomes a neighbor, arises out of the historical fact that

12. Boszormenyi-Nagy and Geraldine M. Spark, *Invisible Loyalties: Reciprocity in Intergenerational Therapy* (New York: Brunner/Mazel, 1984).

God in Christ has reconciled all things to himself and will one day consummate this reconciliation in an eternal kingdom.

It will come as no surprise that Christian mutuality depends more on doctrinal teaching than does its Nagyan counterpart. The Christian rationale for construing self and neighbor as being in the same boat depends on the particular story about Christ. For this reason the Christian contextual therapist will make sure that the client has some rudimentary acquaintance with the Christian doctrine of reconciliation. By contrast, the contextual therapist can emphasize facts of familial relatedness that can be teased out of a family independently of any special teaching, by trading on ethical concepts that are available in the society at large. Yet we should not underestimate the extent to which contextual therapy is also a teaching. In many of the interview transcriptions included in Nagy's writings, it is evident that the clients have picked up quite a bit of contextual jargon and are using Nagy's conceptual scheme for understanding themselves and their problems.

Gratitude

Because we are inescapably bound to our parents by pre-ethical loyalty, it can never be healthy for our primary attitudes toward them to be resentment, anger, and hostility. This is why contextual therapy seeks to bring the client to exonerate the "bad" parent: to credit the parent for his own victimization and for whatever goodwill can be discerned in his past transactions, as well as to facilitate present parental behaviors that are a credit to him. Ideally, a person's settled and basic attitude toward his parents is gratitude, a glad, voluntary, and active acknowledgment of the important gifts for which he is indebted to them.

Gratitude serves a peculiar sort of justice, since it is a way of repaying debts for which no payment in kind may be possible. If I am grateful to my parents for feeding me, changing my diapers, introducing me to God, holding me when I was afraid, comforting me when I was distraught, and housing and educating me for twenty years, then I acknowledge gladly that there is no way I can give back to them in the measure that they have given to me. If I nurse my father for the last two weeks of his life or do a few repair jobs around the house for my mother, these acts can only by some grotesque distraction of mind be considered repayment for their gifts. Instead, they are tokens, expressions of appreciation, symbols of acknowledgment that say, "I gladly admit that my debt to you is unrepayable."

And yet in "saying" this again and again I do them justice and in a sense repay the debt; I do what is appropriate in my position of son vis-à-vis them in their position of parents. Because of the generosity with which they gave to me, this attitude with which I gladly recognize my indebtedness to them is all they require in the way of repayment. If I tried to repay them for twenty years of food and clothes and housing and inconvenience by writing a check, computed with interest, this would count not as repayment but as a devaluation of their gift, an affront to them as parents. Attempting to pay my debt would count as an effort to dissolve our child-parent relationship. What is wanted is not that the debt be wiped out, as in everyday contractual relationships, but instead that it be retained so that this glad acknowledgment of it can cement and validate the filial relationship. Thus pre-ethical loyalty comes to mature fruition in filial gratitude, which is at the same time ethical appropriateness (fairness) and relational health.

In a less momentous way, the paradox of gratitude is characteristic of relations between friends. It is clear that when a friend gives a gift, the recipient owes his friend something, and yet it is an offense to the friend and a threat to the relationship if this debt is too literally or too quickly disposed of by repayment. Nagy quotes the Seneca Indians as saying, "A person who wants to repay a gift too quickly with a gift in return is an unwilling debtor and an ungrateful person."[13] Another Seneca, this time the Roman philosopher, said, "One who is anxious to make speedy repayment is unwilling to be under obligations to another, and this is to be ungrateful." Indebtedness in close relationships is not just something to be repaid; it is an important part of what ties us together.

Nagy also points out that crediting another delineates the self of the creditor. Thinking in terms of a rugged and heroic individualism, it might seem that the way to define myself is to dissociate myself — in all essential ways, at any rate — from you. But if we are interdependent beings, this is an unrealistic strategy. By showing forthright gratitude to my creditors, I align myself emotionally with reality and thus become freer. I gain in autonomy by taking "responsibility" for (that is, affirming) my indebtedness.

Naturally the freedom of my gratitude is also in part a function of my parents' attitude toward me. If they impose on me what Nagy calls a "captively owed gratitude,"[14] then real gratitude and the free self-delineation it involves become difficult if not impossible. Gratitude is not goods delivered in response to payment. It is a response to a gift. A "gift" that is given as payment for goods to be delivered is not a gift but an act of attempted purchase, and someone who makes the paradoxical attempt to purchase gratitude puts the recipient of his payment in a bind. A gift must be given in the spirit of generosity without too keen an eye for the return. Gratitude, as a response to a gift, is also a form of generosity, of graciously crediting the other for something that was not strictly owed. Thus again we see the importance of the contextual strategy of working with the whole familial context, of rearranging the real balance of reciprocity and not trying to generate new attitudes just by manipulating the consciousness or behavior of individuals. Gratitude is a relational virtue

13. Ibid., p. 59.
14. Ibid., p. 62.

and cannot be wholly managed from just one side of the relationship.

Like trust and mutuality, Christian gratitude differs from its Nagyan counterpart in the scope of its context. Christians not only have earthly parents to whom they owe much that is of enormous importance to them and can "repay" only with glad acknowledgment of their indebtedness; they also have a gracious Creator to whom they owe literally everything they have and are and can "repay" only with grateful praises. And they have a Savior to thank for their rescue from sin and their hope for the world to come.

Christian psychology disagrees with contextual therapy in affirming that it is more central to our nature to be God's children than to be children of our biological parents or primary caretakers. Christianity ranks loyalty to family lower than loyalty to God and his kingdom (Matt. 10:37). So a family that would be regarded as relationally healthy by contextual standards might be idolatrously loyal by Christian standards and thus quite far from ultimate relational health. Christian psychology affirms that gratitude to one's biological parents is important for mental health, while insisting that this not be the primary gratitude.

Apart from this important difference, however, Christian gratitude and Nagyan gratitude have much in common. Christian gratitude is simultaneously a state of well-being and a state of righteousness, since it is a happy and proper acknowledgment of our indebtedness to our Creator and Savior. It is an emotional adjustment to the way things are and thus a contemplative realization of our nature as dependent and begifted beings. As a matter of giving due credit, it is connected with justice but differs from paradigmatic justice in being a response to freely given gifts. The "repayment" for the gift is largely in the attitude of thankful acknowledgment itself, the acts of repayment (acts of worship and service) being chiefly tokens of this. The repayment involved in Christian gratitude does not even come close to disposing of the debt. Christian gratitude as a glad acknowledgment of Another's generosity frees us and motivates us to show generosity toward others, not just our children and parents but also our "neighbor." Christian gratitude individuates the self just as filial gratitude does. A chief importance of Christian gratitude, as of filial gratitude, is that it binds us in love to the one to whom we are indebted.

Justice

The centrality of justice in the contextual view of human nature and character ideal is indicated by the therapeutic strategies of crediting, multidirectional partiality, and exoneration, and by the central diagnostic concept of destructive entitlement. Basically, pathology is traced to injustice in the intergenerational context, and therapy is an effort to restore justice in that context.

The fact that in Christianity justice does not occupy such a centrally exclusive place and is in fact often contravened in the interest of relational and individual well-being suggests a need to alter contextual strategies and diagnosis. This is particularly clear when we consider exoneration and destructive entitlement. The very word *exoneration* should be a red flag because it suggests that the offender's "reasons" for his malice and destructiveness — say, the parentification or abuse he suffered from his parents — really do "entitle" him to his behavior. Nagyan exoneration occurs when the offender's family members openly acknowledge this entitlement. But in Christian therapy it would rarely be fitting to explain away an offender's guilt by reference to injustices done to him. The Christian therapist will make the plausible assumption that in all but the most deeply pathological cases the offender both knows that his destructiveness is unjust and has enough resources of self-control not to be emotionally compelled to the destructive behavior. That is, the offender is really guilty and cannot be exonerated. This is not to rule out the kind of acknowledgments of the offender's suffering that result in Nagyan exoneration. They will, however, be conceptualized for the family not as exonerating but rather as extenuating, as softening the offender's guilt.

But the Christian therapist's goal will be similar to Nagy's: she will aim to restore the offender to full dignity, to generate respect for and acceptance of him on the part of the other family members and make the offender into an honestly contributing member of the family. The obvious counterpart of Nagyan exoneration is Christian forgiveness. Forgiveness is the means by which Christians reintegrate offenders into the community while fully acknowledging their guilt — that is, *without* exonerating them. As such it is a contravention of strict justice: the community (or victim) says, as it were, "You have some demerits against your account, so that you do not deserve to be accorded full dignity. But we declare that, as God has forgiven us, so we forgive you. Thus, despite justice, we accept you and accord you full dignity." (For a more thorough discussion of forgiveness, see Chapter Ten.)

Strict contextual therapists will probably feel that forgiveness is not likely to achieve reconciliation, precisely because it retains the ascription of guilt to the offender. How can the offender be made to feel accepted and reintegrated into family patterns of reciprocity if the other members continue to ascribe to him an unpaid, and now unpayable, debt of guilt? Surely what is needed for therapy is exoneration rather than forgiveness, even if exoneration has somewhat the status of a pious fiction? Our response is that in Christian therapy the other members of the family will be encouraged to express their solidarity with the offender, despite his guilt, by acknowledging their own need for forgiveness. He will not be singled out as guilty and thus kept at arm's length by the family; he will be welcomed into a community of the guilty, all of whom are covered by the forgiveness of God and thus freed for interactions more closely approximating justice. One can well imagine a form of multidirectional partiality in which the therapist elicits not only acknowledgments of the suffering the offender has caused but also the victim's confessions of offenses against the offender. Thus, while the therapist facilitates the forgiveness of the offender by the other family members, he also facilitates the offender's forgiveness of the other family members. This multidirectional rotation of forgiveness and confession within the family would, it seems, be a staple strategy of Christian contextual therapy.

Conclusion

Our analysis of Nagyan trust, mutuality, gratitude, and justice shows contextual therapy to be immune to the ethical-sociological critique of therapy waged by recent critics. Large areas of compatibility suggest that contextual therapy can instruct us in our development of a Christian psychology. The idea of ontological relatedness, the goal of getting each client to transcend his individual "needs," and the therapeutic strategy of multidirectional partiality are promising. However, in contextual therapy, loyalty to the intergenerational family is primary, while in Christianity one's loyalty to family is always secondary to loyalty to God and God's kingdom. God's sovereignty and the primacy of the relationship to him are basic in Christian psychology. So, while contextual therapy and Christianity share a communitarian vision, the contextual view differs basically from the Christian view of human nature and well-being. Finally, the sovereignty of justice in contextual therapy is inconsistent with Christianity and requires an alteration of the concept of destructive entitlement and of therapy. In particular, exoneration must be replaced with forgiveness as a central therapeutic strategy.

CHAPTER SIX

Healing from the Eternal

Carl Jung's Theology

I have been saying that the major psychotherapies are spiritualities that are more or less in competition with Christianity. To call Ellis and Rogers purveyors of spirituality may have sounded bizarre at first, since both reject Christianity and since Ellis, at any rate, rejects all forms of religion. But we've seen that none of the psychotherapists under examination are simply practicing medicine. What they do is less like removing an appendix or prescribing a sedative and more like teaching Sunday school: they draw us to their creed, telling us how to live, how to think and feel about ourselves and others; they proclaim the meaning of life and aim to shape our character and our relationships accordingly. And by a process of conceptual seepage, they color our social world and shape us in ways beyond our knowing and beyond our ability to resist, doing on a small scale what Christianity has done on a large scale — they soak into the pores of our culture.

The claim that Carl Jung is proposing a spirituality will seem less surprising. He oozes "religion." He revels in mystery, and believes that we all belong at least as much to another, nonmaterial world as we do to this visible one. Much of Jung's prescription for our growth and mental health consists in training our sensitivities to the mystery and depth of our life, putting us in touch with a world of spirit, much in the way that Christianity puts us in touch with God and Christ through the Holy Spirit and teaches us to see ourselves and our neighbors in spiritual terms, as children of God. So Jung's ideas have been attractive to some Christians, especially liberal (and some not so liberal) Episcopalians. And he speaks to non-Christians as well. To many sensitive people, the picture of the universe as nothing but molecules in space fails to satisfy their sense of themselves as persons. Jung taps into a religious need in the human breast, the need to believe that the universe is something more personal, more spiritual, something more like a home.

In a much-quoted passage, Jung says,

> During the past thirty years, people from all the civilized countries of the earth have consulted me. I have treated many hundreds of patients, the larger number being Protestants, a smaller number Jews, and not more than five or six believing Catholics. Among all my patients in the second half of life — that is to say, over thirty-five — there has not been one whose problem in the last resort was not that of finding a religious outlook on life. It is safe to say that every one of them fell ill because he had lost that which the living religions of every age have given to their followers, and none of them has been really healed who did not regain his religious outlook.[1]

Jung's anti-Protestant sentiment stems from his conviction that Protestantism is seldom a "living religion." With its emphasis on blind faith, it does not give us *experience* of a larger reality beyond this world and so cannot minister to our deepest longings and heal us of our deepest distresses. Why is Protestantism therapeutically impotent? Because it has become "ra-

---

1. Jung, *Modern Man in Search of a Soul*, trans. W. S. Dell (London: Routledge & Kegan Paul, 1933), p. 229.

tionalistic": it has clung to formulas, propositions, and theological dogmas, and it has neglected to open up channels of living contact with the world of spirit. Jung thinks Catholicism is much more a resource of mental health because it has retained a place for mystery, intuition, and symbols. (Symbols, especially mythological imagery, are not in Jung's view "rational" — and thus not contrary to experience — in the way that propositions are.)

For Jung, the paradigm of Protestantism's power to stunt personality is his own father:

> Once I heard [my father] praying. He struggled desperately to keep his faith. I was shaken and outraged at once, because I saw how hopelessly he was entrapped by the Church and its theological thinking. They had blocked all avenues by which he might have reached God directly, and then faithlessly abandoned him. Now I understood the deepest meaning of my earlier experience: God Himself had disavowed theology and the Church founded upon it. . . . I was equally sure that none of the theologians I knew had ever seen "the light that shineth in the darkness" with his own eyes, for if they had they would not have been able to teach a "theological religion," which seemed quite inadequate to me, since there was nothing to do with it but believe it without hope. . . . The arch sin of faith, it seemed to me, was that it forestalled experience.[2]

No doubt Jung had a bad experience with theological religion. But his implicit definition of faith — faith is believing things you haven't experienced to be true — is itself a piece of bad moral psychology. Nothing about religious doctrines as such prevents experience (though there is a way of "intellectualizing" religion that can be quite deadly). The standard Christian view is that the Holy Spirit works in conjunction with doctrinally

---

2. Jung, *Memories, Dreams, Reflections*, ed. Aniela Jaffé, trans. Richard and Clara Winston (New York: Random House, 1961), pp. 93-94.

correct preaching, and the lives of many orthodox believers bear this out. We are creatures shaped and fed by words; we would be incapable of a distinctively human life if we were deprived of our beliefs, our propositions, our concepts. Doctrines shape our experience, and as we've seen in the earlier chapters of this book, psychotherapeutic doctrines too become lenses through which we see ourselves and our world. Jung's own psychology is no exception to this, though he likes to tell us that he bases it not on theory but on experience. I think it is more useful and accurate to distinguish Jung's brand of religion from Christianity, by seeing both of them as "doctrinal" in a broad sense but as *different* and partially *competing* doctrines.

We may distinguish *pure religions of self-exploration* from *religions of historical revelation*. Christianity and Judaism are religions of historical revelation. Essential to the Jew's knowledge of God is the story of the liberation from Egypt: for the Jew, God is *identified* and *experienced* as the one who delivered the people of Israel from Egyptian bondage. The Jew's knowledge of himself is likewise historical. Who is he most essentially, this individual man? He is a member of the people that God delivered from Egypt. He belongs in and gets his identity from that historical lineage. The pious Jew knows God not merely as the one who performed those distant historical actions; he also meets God as a "very present help in trouble," the source of blessings in the here and now. But this present God is experienced *as* the God who delivered his people from bondage long ago.

In the same way, the Christian's knowledge of God is cradled in the story of Christ. She knows God as the Father of Jesus of Nazareth, who was crucified to reconcile the world's sinners to God and was raised by God on the third day. She knows God as the king whose kingdom, inaugurated in the acts of Jesus and furthered in the acts of the apostles and of the disciples in subsequent centuries, will one future day be elaborated before her dazzled eyes. She experiences herself as a member of that past, present, and future kingdom, and in this way she belongs not just to this present moment but to the ages of God. This does not exclude her meeting God in the here and now; on the contrary, she could not meet *that* God in the here and now if she did not know him as the one who has that history.

Jung's religion, by contrast, is one of pure self-exploration. God is known not by reference to any acts that God may have performed in the past (or any "doctrines" that report and interpret such historical data) but purely by a process in which the individual explores the goings-on within his own psyche. The individual finds God *only* in the depths of his own being. The first principle of this theology is this: There is nothing in true religion that was not first in the psyche.

This does not rule out our getting help from "history," for human history casts up artifacts of religious experience — symbols in art, mythology, and dreams — that reflect the self-exploration of earlier individuals and communities. (It is a corollary of Jungian theology that all testimonies about God, insofar as they are genuine and useful, are symbols of psychic transformation.) Such historical symbols may be of use to the individual in interpreting what's going on in his own psyche, for the process of bringing into consciousness what is going on within oneself is an essential part of the religious quest, and other people's symbols can aid that process. Thus Jung spent a lot of effort on historical research, especially the study of mythology, Gnosticism, and the symbolism of alchemy.

But the abundance of Jung's interest in history should not hide from us the difference between his religion and religions of historical revelation. It is important to see how history functions in Jung's theology. His many historical studies all aim to provide us with ways of understanding what is already going on inside us and would be going on inside us even if, say, we knew nothing of the Exodus or the gospel history. By showing us historical parallels to our own dreams and fantasies, these historical studies give us keys to unlock the secrets of our minds, thus bringing to consciousness religious truths that are there but might otherwise remain hidden. History and the doctrines about God and man which derive from that history do not function to identify God by his deeds and consequently to identify us as members of his people. For Jung, history functions instead to "reveal" to us what we already are, quite independent of that history. (Notice that the Jungian too has a use for the word *revelation*, but that it carries a very different concept than the Christian one.)

By reinterpreting Christian claims as symbols of psychic transformation with parallels in other mythologies and religions, Jung can affirm Christianity:

> Not only do I leave the door open for the Christian message, but I consider it of central importance for Western man. It needs, however, to be seen in a new light, in accordance with the changes wrought by the contemporary spirit. Otherwise, it stands apart from the times, and has no effect on man's wholeness. I have endeavored to show this in my writings. I have given a psychological interpretation of the dogma of the Trinity and of the text of the Mass — which, moreover, I compared with the visions described by Zosimos of Panopolis, a third-century alchemist and Gnostic. My attempt to bring analytical psychology into relation with Christianity ultimately led to the question of Christ as a psychological figure. As early as 1944, in *Psychology and Alchemy*, I had been able to demonstrate the parallelism betwen the Christ figure and the central concept of the alchemists, the *lapis*, or stone.[3]

Christians should know that Jung affirms Christianity only on the assumption that it can be reinterpreted as a religion of a different kind than original Christianity — as a pure religion of self-exploration.

But religions of historical revelation do not necessarily rule out our gaining insights from consulting what is going on within

3. Ibid., p. 210.

us. After all, Christianity and Judaism do not say that God's only attributes are the ones he derives from his historical actions, or that our only attributes are the ones we derive from God's historical actions toward us — however crucial those actions of God may be for our identity and his. There will be room within a religion of historical revelation for some of what makes up the entirety of a religion of self-exploration. It may be possible for Christians to integrate some insights from Carl Jung. In this chapter we are particularly interested in the extent to which Jung's psychotherapy can be adapted by persons who wish to remain faithful to the central Christian tradition. Let us begin by considering the source from which Jung says religious insights and ultimate psychological healing — as well as some rather terrifying experiences — spring.

The Unconscious

I can begin to explain Jung's idea of the unconscious by describing an experience most of my readers have had — or could have by undertaking a simple exercise. When I was reading books by Jung in preparation for writing this chapter, I was sometimes sleepy. As I read along, my mind would lose contact with the text, and in that drowsy state somewhere between waking and sleeping, visual and auditory images quite unrelated to what I was reading would come before my mind, sometimes vividly. They were like snippets of dreams, and they would occur in just a second or two, after which I would catch myself dreaming and snap back to reality. On a couple of occasions when this was happening, I recorded these images before they escaped. (If you don't write them down or talk about them, they are irretrievable within a few seconds.) Here is what I "saw" and "heard" (within a space of an hour or two total, on two separate occasions; some of the images did escape me because I was not quick enough or energetic enough in my attempt to articulate them):

1. A can of scouring powder
2. Something about my friend Steve Evans
3. A scene in the food line of a cafeteria, probably at a university, maybe Harvard
4. Something about my thesis supervisor, and maybe his wife; there seemed to be some scolding, or at least animated talk
5. A scene from a Wheaton College philosophy conference, in the hallway of the east wing of Edman Chapel
6. Something to do with negotiating about a book
7. A scene of a basement stairway; something or someone was being pushed down
8. Somebody in trouble saying, "Help me just a little bit"
9. A scene in a pizza parlor in New Haven
10. A scene in the dining room at 1829 Mifflin (a house my family and I lived in for nine months in Huntingdon, PA), with my daughter Maria
11. A sister-in-law, seemingly dismayed
12. I am entering a large, barnlike building on the west side of Wichita, where the 4-H county fair was held in the late 1950s; this cavernous building is filled with tables displaying 4-H projects
13. A very distinct voice saying, "I would get a microscope . . ."
14. Parking meters near the bike path a half mile from my house in Wheaton, and something else, which I missed
15. A street scene in New Orleans
16. A voice saying, "And that would give you the whole story"
17. A road on the way to the water spigot in an Ontario provincial park where my family and I camped a few weeks earlier
18. The body of a dead dog lying on a junk pile in the yard of the house neighboring my childhood home
19. A voice saying, "Don't take my word for . . ."
20. Somebody with his hands on the antlers of a mature buck

deer, wrestling it, and a voice (from behind, I think) saying, "Well, what do you know!"
21. Two men trying to sell me something
22. A large eyebrow, viewed partly from behind, being scratched rather violently by what looked like one of the hind feet of a mouse, and a voice saying, ". . . get some people to your door" (with the verb not in the imperative mood).

I suppose that most of us think we dream only now and then, and certainly only when we are asleep. According to Jung, we are dreaming all the time, day and night, but we are unaware of it because when we are awake the light of consciousness blocks it out, and we don't remember most of our dreams. Only on the edges of sleep do we become aware of what is going on in the unconscious: there the light of consciousness is dim enough to allow the contents of the unconscious to appear, but we are conscious enough for the contents of the unconscious to "register" in consciousness. Thus drowsiness is ideal, or the moment when one has just woken up and thus still is experiencing traces of the images of sleep. Or a special technique like Jung's association test or active imagination can be used to bring out what is in the unconscious. If consciousness is like daylight (as opposed to the darkness of night), then the contents of the unconscious are like the stars in the sky. They are always there but become visible only when the light of day is sufficiently dimmed.

In Jung's view the human psyche or mind is really an inhabitant of two distinct worlds, the world of consciousness and the world of the unconscious. These worlds are equally essential to full human life, and neither should be slighted. But as we have seen, the two worlds tend to remain separate. When we are deep in sleep, the stars of our unconscious are out in their full glory, but the waking ego has no access to them. When we are awake, our consciousness is accessing many things — in particular the physical and the social world (what we prejudicially call the "real world") — but it is cut off from the world of the unconscious. So we tend to be divided creatures, beings of "two minds" that do not communicate very well and do not create a single whole individual.

Jung pretty much identifies the world of spirit with the unconscious. It is a world of larger meanings that speaks to our need for a significance that goes beyond the molecules-in-motion of our physical world. It is a world of sheer possibility, of imagination not limited by restrictions of time and space in the way that our conscious world is. So it can be thought of as eternal and infinite. By contrast, the world of consciousness is "down to earth." It is delimited and concrete. Not just anything goes; this is reality! If the unconscious is the world of possibility, then consciousness is the world of actuality. Jung thought that to be fully human, one had to bring these two worlds together, to live in both of them somehow at the same time — to soar in the infinite with the unconscious, but to do so as a concrete individual in the conscious world of actuality. One can see here a certain similarity with Christianity, which holds that we are neither angels nor beasts but have a dual nature, akin to the beasts in many ways but at the same time made in the image of God and created for fellowship with him.

All of the images that I recorded from my unconscious can be traced to earlier conscious experiences. Some of them seem to be memories of actual scenes from my past, others more or less fantastic constructions out of past experiences. However, Jung argues that if we look closely at people's dreams and also study the world's mythologies, we find patterns of imagery that cannot be accounted for simply by reference to experiences people have had as individuals. The unconscious already has a structure of its own, independent of our individual histories. Universally across cultures we find recurrent themes that are best accounted for on the supposition that there is an "objective" or "collective" unconscious. The collective unconscious is formed not of actual images but of forms of images, or themes, that Jung calls "archetypes."

Jung points to his own earliest remembered dream as a clear example of how material that cannot have come from individual experience can be present in the unconscious. He was three or four years old when he dreamt of a giant penis enthroned in an underground vault; its urethral orifice was an eye with a light source above it. He notes that the light and the eye point to the etymology of *phallus* (*falós*, meaning "shining, bright"), and that the anatomical correctness of the penis and the architectural detail of the vault cannot have been individual memories.[4] Later, when he was twelve or so, Jung fashioned a manikin that he placed in a pencil box along with an oblong stone, the upper and lower halves of which he painted in different colors. He had no idea at the time why he did this, but he had a sense that what he was doing was important to his own identity.[5] Later he noticed the similarity of his stone to those in a cache of ancient soul-stones discovered near Arlesheim and to the Australian *churingas*, and the resemblance of his manikin to the Telesphoroi that stand on monuments to the ancient Greek god Asklepios and read to the god from a scroll. His conclusion is that the dream and the behavior had their sources in an objective reality different from, beyond, and larger than the world of his conscious individual experience.

Prominent among the archetypes are quasi-personal "figures" that are significant in the development and constitution of the individual psyche. For example, each man has his anima, an archetypal feminine figure that is the unconscious psychic complement of his masculine personality:

Every man carries within him the eternal image of woman, not the image of this or that particular woman, but a definitive feminine image. This image is fundamentally uncon-

4. Ibid., p. 13.
5. Ibid., pp. 22-23.

scious, an hereditary factor of primordial origin engraved in the living organic system of the man, an imprint or "archetype" of all the ancestral experiences of the female, a deposit, as it were, of all the impressions ever made by woman. . . . Since this image is unconscious, it is always unconsciously projected upon the person of the beloved, and is one of the chief reasons for passionate attraction or aversion.[6]

An exactly analogous remark can be made about the animus present in the unconscious of every woman. The idea seems to be that every person is psychically both male and female, but normal development involves "detachment from the hermaphroditic archetype"[7] so that one pole of our sexuality becomes unconscious and we become sexually one-sided. But the presence of the opposite-sex archetype causes a sense of personal incompleteness such that we find a part of ourselves in members of the opposite sex through projecting on them our unconscious anima or animus. Thus sexual attraction is not just "animal lust" but is part of the quest for psychic wholeness.

Other archetypes are the Wise Old Man, the Hero and the Monster, the Mother, the Maiden, the Child, and the Trickster (a kind of fool-savior). In each case the archetype is a legitimate aspect of the psyche and thus something that needs to be dealt with in the fundamental human project of synthesizing the conscious and the unconscious. All the archetypes have a broadly religious significance — they all come from the "other world" and have a numinous character, being surrounded by the mystery inherent in the unconscious.[8] Also, like God as he is conceived in Judaism and Christianity, the

6. Jung, *Collected Works*, vol. 17, trans. R. F. C. Hull (New York: Pantheon Books, 1954), p. 198.

7. Jung, *Collected Works*, vol. 9, 1, trans. R. F. C. Hull (New York: Pantheon Books, 1959), p. 71.

8. Jung, *Dreams*, trans. R. F. C. Hull (Princeton: Princeton University Press, 1974), pp. 256-57.

unconscious cannot be manipulated or "trained."[9] When Jung speaks of the therapeutic significance of religious experience and of finding a religious outlook on life, he is speaking of the unconscious as a whole and all the archetypes as a class, and the importance of being in touch with them, integrating them into one's conscious life.

But there is one archetype that has particularly powerful religious and healing significance, and that is the archetype of the Self, symbolized by the mandala — a circle, usually divided into four parts, that recurs often in people's dreams and in the religious symbolism of virtually all cultures. The Self (in German "das Selbst" — literally, "the Itself") is a representation, in the unconscious, of the whole psyche, both conscious and unconscious. Jung warns us again and again not to confuse the Self with the ego. The ego is the center of consciousness, but the Self is the center of the entire psyche. As such, the Self is itself the synthesis of consciousness and the unconscious — or, better, as an archetype, it is the *representation* of that synthesis.

It is true of all the archetypes that they have a "life of their own." They affect us — our behavior, our fantasies, our dreams, our relationships with others. There they are, whether we like it or not. We do not create them, nor is there anything we can do to eliminate them. (We can of course try to deny them — for example, many "macho" men try to deny the existence of their anima — but this is to no avail, for when they are denied, they just come out in perverse ways rather than in natural ones.) This independence of the archetypes from our conscious control is part of what Jung means when he describes them as "objective" and suggests that they constitute a "world," a realm of existing things. He does not mean that they exist independently of the psyche *as a whole;* they are, after all, psychic realities. But they do exist independently of the *conscious* psyche.

But the Self archetype is "especially objective," so to

9. Ibid., p. 120.

speak. As the figure of the synthesis of the conscious and the unconscious, the Self archetype represents the psyche in its proleptic wholeness. Thus it transcends even the unconscious. It is wise beyond anything we could expect from the conscious ego, having the character of a Suprapersonality that corrects for the foolishness of the ego, guiding the individual to wholeness — all the more if the individual can manage to set up some communication with the Self through opening himself to the world of the unconscious. Jung notes that in many cultures the mandala is both a symbol of the Self and a symbol of the divine, and this, along with the Self's wisdom, transcendence, uncontrollability, and commitment to wholeness, suggests that the Self and God are really not distinguishable.

Kelsey's Use of Jung

Morton Kelsey is probably the best-known Christian counselor making use of Jung's thought. He regularly identifies the Self as "the risen Christ." This practice is confusing, because the question is never quite answered whether we are to understand "the risen Christ" in a Christian way or in a Jungian way. We saw earlier that the Christian understands phrases like "the risen Christ" as having an essentially historical reference — the risen Christ, in terms of whom we are to understand both God and ourselves, is Jesus of Nazareth. But Jung understands such phrases as symbols (pretty much on a par with the alchemists' Philosopher's Stone and Navajo mandalas), symbols of nontemporal facts about the unconscious psyche. So when a Jungian uses the phrase "the risen Christ," it has a completely different reference than when a Christian uses it.

I am convinced that Kelsey understands Christianity as a religion of historical revelation,[10] and so we must assume

10. See, for example, *Christianity as Psychology: The Healing Power of the Christian Message* (Minneapolis: Augsburg, 1986), pp. 78-79.

that he is seriously revising the meaning of "the Self" when he identifies the Self as the risen Christ. This historical use of the phrase is one that Jung would have to reject in the most decisive terms. This can be illustrated with an anecdote from Kelsey:

> Jung was asked by a study group in Los Angeles why he never dealt with the subject of Jesus' resurrection. His answer is to be found in vol. 18 of The Collected Works, entitled "The Symbolic Life," pp. 692-696, written February 19, 1954. His treatment of the subject is weak and rationalistic. He did not see how the event could have been a historical event, so he treated it as only a psychological event. He did not even consider that it could have been a synchronistic event, both psychological and physical. That Jung did not apply this principle to the resurrection suggests to me that he had an emotional block on the subject.[11]

Kelsey is puzzled by Jung's "emotional block," and he seems to suggest that Jung is being irrational in refusing to apply his own concept of synchronistic event to Jesus' resurrection. Jung's autobiography does give us reason to think that Jung had an irrational resistance to Jesus engendered by early childhood experiences. But Jung also had a more rational reason for denying the historicity of Jesus' resurrection, and this is one that Kelsey fails systematically to see. If we put together the fact that the Jungian religion is a pure religion of self-exploration and the fact that in Christianity the resurrection of Jesus is regarded as vindicating his claims to be the unique historical redeemer (and thus far more than one more symbol of the contents of the collective unconscious), we see that Jung's refusal is quite consistent. As a cornerstone of Christianity's status as a religion of historical revelation, Jesus' resurrection threatens the cornerstone of Jung's theology — namely, the proposition that there is nothing in genuine religion that was

11. Ibid., p. 126.

not first in the psyche. Synchronistic events certainly happen, in Jung's view, but if Jung was to accept Jesus' resurrection as one of these, he would have had to detach it from the often indirect yet unmistakable claims of Jesus in the Gospels to be the unique son of God. Perhaps Jung thought (plausibly, in my view) that he would not be able to make a convincing case for this separation.

I do think that Christians can make some use of Jung's insights about people's psychological needs for religion and about the symbols that well up out of the unconscious. But we need to do this with an initial clarity that Jung is a theologian, not just an empirical psychologist reporting in a theologically neutral way the data that his research has uncovered; and we must be clear that the theology to which he is committed is inconsistent with Christian theology. Once we have started correctly, then we may *reinterpret* some of his findings in Christian terms. We may, for example, say that the yearnings for wholeness-in-the-eternal that Jung finds universally in humankind are dim premonitions of a filial relationship with the God of Abraham, Isaac, and Jacob, through Jesus Christ his Son. And we might say with Kelsey that the voice of "the Self," calling us to a health that our ordinary modes of thought cannot imagine, is in reality (contrary to Jung's convictions) the voice of the risen Christ, the voice of Jesus of Nazareth, a voice which cannot be correctly identified apart from that historical revelation on which Christianity is built. In saying these things we must be clear how radically our psychology has departed from Jung's. We will become clearer about this if we now look more closely at the Jungian character ideal.

Individuation

The "individuation process" is the process of becoming the Self that one already is potentially. The state of character of someone well along in this process — the central Jungian virtue — is called "individuation." What is the individuated person like? How does he or she relate to other persons? How does this Jungian virtue compare with some Christian virtues?

We may begin by asking why Jung calls his character ideal "individuation." What we have said so far about mental health à la Jung does not quite prepare us for this. We have seen that Jung believes that the psyche has a dual nature, a conscious and an unconscious side, a temporal and an "eternal" side. The conscious ego is just one aspect of the psyche, a small light in a large, real, and structured darkness. The light and the darkness *together* are the Self, and human wholeness is achieved when the separation and conflict between these two are overcome, when the two parts are integrated or synthesized into an actual whole in which the conscious ego fully taps the "numinous" resources of the unconscious. So we might have expected Jung to call his character ideal *synthesis* or *integration* rather than *individuation*. Jung does use these other words on occasion, but I think it is significant that his preferred term is *individuation*.

We are not prepared for the term *individuation* because so far we have emphasized the unconscious in Jung's psychology. We have not yet appreciated the importance he gives to consciousness. Consciousness makes us individuals in the sense of being centered, integral, and distinct from others. Insofar as we are unconscious we are without responsibility for what we do; we are not "agents," initiators of genuine action. We are not fully persons, or selves. Instead, we are just channels for collective human tendencies, mere pawns of the archetypes. So the process of becoming a self, of synthesizing the two dimensions of the psyche, is a process of taking those mental contents that belong to the *collective* unconscious and personalizing or concretizing or individualizing them, making the infinite finite, as it were, or the eternal temporal.

That is one aspect of the meaning of individuation. The other trades on the etymology of the word, which means "not divisible." The individuated person is very "whole," "self-contained," "self-sufficient," "independent," "invulnerable," "impassive." She is "above the fray," not subject to environmental vicissitudes, not dependent on other people, emotionally detached. She is of one mind, not divided in her loyalties, and not "torn up" by attachments to things that pass away. In this way, too, the mature Self is like God, for these are attributes that philosophers have traditionally ascribed to God.

We began this chapter by noting a stark contrast between Jungian theology and Christian theology — the difference between a religion of self-exploration and a religion of historical revelation. A consideration of Jungian virtue will show an analogous and related contrast between a Jungian psychology and a Christian psychology: that between an internalist character-ideal and a relational character-ideal. The essential point is that Jungian virtue is conceived most fundamentally as *wholeness* and is wholly a matter of the right relating of aspects of the psyche. The Jungian paragon, in other words, is in a harmonious or proper relationship with *himself.* Thus the term "internalist": virtue is entirely internal to the psyche, and troubles of "relating" all have the form of intrapsychic "conflicts." (Remember the male [p. 118] whose problems relating to females are traceable to his failure to integrate his anima, something internal to his psyche; it is as though the actual females to whom he relates are just external stimuli to a process going on inside him.) Insofar as Jungian virtues fit us for relationships with other beings, the relationship is most fundamentally *detachment.* By contrast, the Christian virtues relate us to *other beings* — in particular, to other human beings and to God conceived as a different being than ourselves. And the relationship is not detachment but *attachment:* the double commandment to love God and neighbor sums up the Christian calling to virtue, and this relational conception of our well-being (mental health) is captured in the Christian hope for the kingdom of God, that society in which God is honored as God and our fellow humans are cherished as his children and our sisters and brothers. The centrality of attachment and relation to Christian virtue is also captured by the apostle Paul's image of the church as the body of Christ. One can hardly be more "attached" than to one's head and other body parts! A Christian psychology will be a psychology of attachments and thus will not be internalist.

Like other individualist psychotherapists such as Rogers and Ellis, Jung is confident that his therapy will improve your relations with others, but it will do so indirectly, by straightening out your relation to yourself. Unlike Nagy, he does not think of your psyche as *essentially* ("ontologically") related to the others. Improved relations with others are a bonus, almost a felicitous side-benefit, of getting your psychic house in order. It is true that Jung's therapy makes essential reference to the collective unconscious, and so it puts you in touch with something far larger than your individual psyche. But two points must be made: first, it is *in* your individual psyche that the collective unconscious is found; and second, the collective unconscious is not a society of *individuals* with whom you are to live and interact. The collective unconscious contains humanity, in a sense, but it doesn't contain any people; it does contain (or is identical with) "God," but this "God" is not a being other than yourSelf. The social world, both with God and with other human beings, remains misty and peripheral for the Jungian paragon. Jung suggests that individual persons had significance for him only to the extent that they were occasions for his own self-discovery: "Other people are established inalienably in my memories only if their names were entered in the scrolls of my destiny from the beginning, so that encountering them was at the same time a kind of recollection."[12] By contrast, Christianity, with its concept of the neighbor, and Nagy's psychotherapy, with his notion of the ontological relatedness of the intergenerational family, define human nature essentially by reference to a context of concrete others. As a consequence, the linea-

12. Jung, *Memories, Dreams, Reflections*, p. 5.

ments of character that they recommend differ fundamentally from Jungian individuation.

Let's look at a Christian virtue that is a counterpart of Jungian individuation to bring out the contrast I have been claiming.

Humility

Like Jungian individuation, Christian humility is an abandonment of the egocentric perspective. It is a loss of self in the interest of gaining a holier and truer and healthier self. The immature or "proud" person is one whose egoistic self-concept prevents him from recognizing God and neighbor. He cannot recognize God as Lord because he sees himself as lord, and he cannot recognize his neighbor as brother or sister because he sees them as either threats or opportunities in a deadly struggle for self-worth. Humility is the joyful recognition of God as Lord and thus of oneself as his subject, and of the neighbor as brother or sister and thus as one's equal. As contrasted with "pride," Christian humility is the gaining of a new and better self because it puts one in a proper and healthy relationship with God and neighbor, and because, on Christian assumptions, to *be* a self is to be a member of the kingdom of God and thus to stand in these relations with God and neighbor.

As we have seen, Jungian individuation is also a form of humility (we might call it "Jungian humility"), but it has an internalist rather than a relational logic. As a person grows in Jungian humility, his conscious ego becomes more and more aware that it is not his true self, just as the Christian becomes aware that his egoistically oriented self is not his true self. But if we ask, *Before what* is the Jungian humble? the answer is, The Self, the unconscious, the vast dark side of his own psyche, his own "infinite" or "eternal" dimension. In humility, he discovers that his Self is much larger than his ego, and that his ego must in a sense die and be reborn as a mere aspect of the psyche. In other words, the "relationship" in which humility puts him is a relationship with *himself*, not with another being, as in Christianity. For the Jungian, humility is not a form of community, as in Christianity, but a rearrangement entirely internal to the larger, dual-sided psyche.

In a sense the person with Jungian humility sees all humans as equal because they are all partakers of the collective unconscious, and so in the human-human dimension Jungian humility bears a formal resemblance to Christian humility. Even so, however, the particular *experience* of others as equal to oneself because of the collective unconscious is quite different from the experience of others as brothers and sisters beloved of a common Parent. We see again the importance of our earlier point that Jung has a theology and that it shapes experience just as much as Christian doctrine does.

But to say that Jungian humility sees all persons as *equal* already bends this Jungian concept too far in the direction of Christianity. It is perhaps more accurate to say that Jungian humility blurs the distinction between oneself and others. As Jung says, "The self comprises infinitely more than a mere ego. . . . It is as much one's self, *and all other selves*, as the ego. Individuation does not shut one out from the world, but gathers the world to oneself."[13] Just as the Jungian God is gathered into the Self and is thus not another being with whom one can enter into a relationship, so the Self gathers all other selves into itself. The experience of Jungian humility, then, is not that of real others who are equal to oneself but that of apparent others who are in reality identical with oneself. Accordingly, the "relation" to others, just like the "relation" to God, is not really a relation but an ordering of elements internal to the psyche. This is not a Buddhistic loss of individuality, a loss of centeredness in the conscious ego; such would be incompatible with Jungian individuation. But it does seem very

13. Jung, *Collected Works*, vol. 8 (New York: Pantheon Books, 1960), p. 226 (my italics).

close to solipsism — the identification of one's own standpoint as the totality of what is, the denial that there is anything outside one's own psyche.

The internalist character of Jungian individuation is also evident in the fact that it involves detachment from other persons. During and after a near-death experience in 1944, Jung had visions and dreams in which he experienced emotional detachment (or "objectivity," as he also calls it) that he takes to be characteristic of the last stages of the individuation process. One of the dreams featured an image of his wife of 53 years (who by this time was dead):

> The objectivity which I experienced in this dream and in the visions is part of a completed individuation. It signifies detachment from valuations and from what we call emotional ties. In general, emotional ties are very important to human beings. But they still contain projections, and it is essential to withdraw these projections in order to attain to oneself and to objectivity. Emotional relationships are relationships of desire, tainted by coercion and constraint; something is expected from the other person, and that makes him and ourselves unfree. Objective cognition lies hidden behind the attraction of the emotional relationship; it seems to be the central secret. Only through objective cognition is the real *coniunctio* [uniting — as of the disconnected aspects of the psyche] possible.[14]

In advanced individuation emotional ties are cut because they are an enemy of independence and freedom:

> [The goal is] to detach consciousness from the object so that the individual no longer places the guarantee of his happiness, or of his life even, in factors outside himself, whether they be persons, ideas, or circumstances, but comes to realize that everything depends on whether he holds the treasure

14. Jung, *Memories, Dreams, Reflections*, pp. 296-97.

or not. If the possession of that gold is realized, then the centre of gravity is *in* the individual and no longer in an object on which he depends. To reach such a condition of detachment is the aim of Eastern practices, and it is also the aim of all the teachings of the Church.[15]

But the apostle Paul says that "if one member suffers, all suffer together; if one member is honored, all rejoice together" (1 Cor. 12:26). And he instructs the Romans, "Rejoice with those who rejoice, weep with those who weep" (12:15). Such sayings suggest the very opposite of emotional detachment as a feature of Christian maturity and mental health. According to the Christian view, the person who is not touched by the well-being or ill-being of his fellows is the one who is lacking in true selfhood and true individuality. Jung betrays his tendency to reinterpret Christian teachings in terms of his own psychology when he says that all the teachings of the church aim at emotional detachment.

What Jung calls "projections" are construals of the other as one whose destiny and well-being are essentially tied to one's own: they are "confusions" of one's own issues with the issues of other people. If one assumes an internalist view of individuation, such projections are obviously mistakes and a source of psychological distortion. But for a relational view, which says that to be a true individual is to be fit to live in community with God and neighbor, such "projections" may be genuine perceptions — just what the Doctor ordered. It is fitting that other people make demands on us and that we make demands on them. According to a relational view of individuation, another's burdens may very well *be* my burdens, and to be a mature individual is to feel these demands emotionally.

A kind of detachment does have a place in Christian practice. Take the virtue of humility, with which we began this

15. Jung, *Analytical Psychology: Its Theory and Practice* (New York: Random House, 1968), p. 186.

section. To become a person who honors God as God, you must be "detached" from honors to yourself. You must respond to honors (or their absence) with a kind of "objectivity," a certain emotional indifference. If being honored is a big issue to you, then to that extent you lack Christian humility. But this does not mean that the person with Christian humility is *generally* emotionally detached. For she will be emotionally exercised over another issue: whether God is honored as God.

What Shall We Make of Jung?

It is encouraging for Christians to see a psychologist who takes as seriously as Jung does the role of religion in mental health — so encouraging, in fact, that some Christians have latched onto Jung as a force of spiritual renewal in the church. My account of him should caution us, to say the least. Jungian theology and its corresponding psychology contrast starkly with Christian theology and psychology. His theology is a flat rejection of Christianity's character as a religion of historical revelation, and the character ideal of his psychology, which is internalist, contradicts something fundamental about the Christian virtues — namely, their relational or communal character. Let me now try to sketch how I think Christians might profit from Jung.

It seems to me that Jung's formal schema of human nature and thus of mental health — that the human psyche is a synthesis of the temporal and the eternal, the finite and the infinite — is something the Christian will affirm wholeheartedly, though with a rather different interpretation than Jung gives to it. The Christian psychologist will look for features of human nature and experience that suggest we are made for a *relationship* with God. Not that we have a divine "side" which needs to be developed, but that we are so constituted as to need God — need to love him, to trust him, to obey him, to be grateful to him, and to receive love and support and guidance from him. That we are a synthesis of the temporal and the eternal will mean that this relationship to God will have to be worked out in our finite daily life. It will need to take the form of virtues that are traits of our individual concrete personalities and that relate us to other individual human beings.

To our search for features of human nature that suggest our need for God, Jung's studies of the unconscious, of dreams, of schizophrenic imagery, of mythology, and so forth may provide rich sources. Our attitude toward these sources should be like that of C. S. Lewis, who proposes that we read pre-Christian myths of dying and rising savior figures as "a divine hinting in poetic and ritual form at the same central truth which was later focussed and (so to speak) historicized in the Incarnation."[16] In this way we can hold firmly to Christianity's character as a religion of historical revelation while affirming that Christianity has some characteristics of a religion of self-exploration. The unconscious will be interpreted as a human organ into which God whispers, ambiguously, things that he makes much clearer in historical revelation and in the doctrines of the church that derive from that revelation. Apart from God's historical revelation, it may not be crystal clear that it is he, an existing being different from our unconscious, who is speaking to us through it. That is why the deliverances of the unconscious *can* be interpreted in a Jungian fashion. But in retrospect, in light of God's self-revelation in Jesus Christ, we can look back and interpret what the unconscious was seeming to tell us as the voice of God whispering to us in anticipation of what he would do and let us know.

Often we will be able to make some such Christian sense of the deliverances of the unconscious. For example, as a boy Jung had a vision of God defecating on a cathedral. He was shocked at this thought, and interpreted the dream as a

---

16. Lewis, *God in the Dock: Essays on Theology and Ethics*, ed. Walter Hooper (Grand Rapids: Wm. B. Eerdmans, 1970), p. 132.

blasphemous departure from traditional Christianity. But the dream is really quite consistent with biblical revelation. One need only read the Old Testament prophets or Jesus' comments about the religious establishment of his day to know how characteristic it is of God to poop on religion.

When he was about sixty-five, Jung had a vision of Christ: "One night I awoke and saw, bathed in bright light at the foot of my bed, the figure of Christ on the Cross. It was not quite life-size, but extremely distinct; and I saw that his body was made of greenish gold. The vision was marvelously beautiful, and yet I was profoundly shaken by it."[17] Presumably Jung was shaken by the possibility that God was telling him that he had been too hasty in his rejection of traditional Christianity. Jung regained his equanimity by interpreting the greenish goldness of Christ in the vision as an indication that the true Christ is the alchemical (symbolic) Christ, not the historical Jesus who is the unique Son of God. A Christian who believes that God was speaking to Jung through the unconscious might agree with Morton Kelsey[18] that here Jung misinterpreted the data of his unconscious. Or, alternatively, we might say that Jung's unconscious was sinfully blocking God's message by presenting Christ in the colors of alchemy. When we encounter an element in a dream or myth that seems uninterpretable as the voice of the Father of Jesus Christ, we do not need to take the attitude that Jung so often does and say that the unconscious doesn't lie, that this is unavoidable "data." We can allow, with C. S. Lewis, that the supernatural sources of mythology and dreams may include the diabolical as well as the divine. Furthermore, as believers in the corruption of sin, we have no reason to think that the unconscious must always be right. We will not "deify" the unconscious as Jung does. We may say, "This is what the unconscious seems to be telling us, but we know better." My point is simply that Christians will have

---

17. Jung, *Memories, Dreams, Reflections*, p. 210.
18. See Kelsey, *Christianity as Psychology*, p. 44.

their own ways of interpreting the deliverances of the unconscious and do not need to accept Jungian ones.

In utilizing Jung's thought and data in the construction of a Christian psychology, we will follow the aggressive policy of the apostle Paul, "taking every thought captive to obey Christ" (2 Cor. 10:5). And we will no doubt find that Jung's thoughts have grown rather un-Jungian by the time they've been in captivity for a while.

CHAPTER SEVEN

Empathy and the Formation of a Self

Like Jung's psychology, Heinz Kohut's descends from Sigmund Freud's psychoanalysis. But both Jung and Kohut have departed from Freud's theory in ways that make them more charming to Christians. For Freud, the basic agenda of a human life was to deal successfully with biological instincts — in particular the sexual urge, the drive for pleasure, and also, in his later theorizing, the drive for destruction or the death instinct. Since the real world — the social world, that is — does not let us follow our instincts freely and so always ends up frustrating us, we are beings in conflict, wanting what we cannot have and trying to find passable civilized substitutes for the aspirations of our genitals. Pathology is the deeply engrained use of maladaptive ways of dealing with our frustrations, while mental health, or virtue, is the deeply engrained use of appropriate ways of dealing with the same frustrations.

Jung and Kohut agree that the agenda of a human life is something more exalted — more "spiritual," if you will — than to deal successfully with our biological drives. For Jung, as we have seen, the agenda is essentially religious, that of affiliating with the eternal aspect of our Self. Kohut too thinks the central human task is to become a self, and though he does not see this goal in religious terms, the more personal and even spiritual character of the self as he conceives of it has made his psychology attractive to a growing number of Christians.

Selfhood

In the last chapter we saw that Jung diverges from Christianity in conceiving the maturity of the self as an intrapsychic rather than a relational matter. Other persons — God, conceived as a being distinct from oneself, as well as other human beings — seem incidental to being a self or to the process of becoming one. According to Kohut's view, by contrast, the self is more embedded in a context of other persons. This is especially clear in Kohut's account of the *development* of the self, an account that is central to his whole theory.

Having a consolidated self does not come automatically with being born human. It is an achievement accomplished by a close cooperation between the individual and others who are significant to him — in the usual case, his parents. To have a self is in large part to have a *sense* of being a self, and this in turn is a deep kind of emotional orientation to one's own identity. By "deep" I mean an orientation that is maintained despite more superficial emotional ups and downs caused by changes in one's environment — for example, personal failures or disapproval by others. A real self, on Kohut's view, is a person who in this deeply underlying way sees himself as admirable, capable, and going somewhere (that is, he has orienting goals or ideals), despite various "injuries" that the world may inflict on his sense of being admirable, capable, and oriented.

How is a healthy self created? We all start out with what Kohut calls "narcissistic libido," a drive to become a self — to be "somebody" admirable, capable, and oriented by ideals. The primitive need to be valued is satisfied in the infant by the admiration of his parents, especially their admiration of what he does. Here they function as "mirroring self-objects" — it is as though the child sees his value (and thus an important ingredient of his selfhood) mirrored in their joy in him and their concern for him. Thus they create in him a sense both of his own value and of his ability to accomplish things, a sense of agency. For example, when he says "goo-goo," his parents smile and kiss him and hug him and dance around the room. But the child must sense that his parents admire him not only for what he does; he must sense that they have regard for *him* — that they do not confuse him with his accomplishments. Kohut calls this parental capacity *empathy*, and it is perhaps most salient at moments when the child is a less-than-successful performer or is in some way hurt. At that point the parents hug him and comfort him and let him know that it hurts them too that he is hurt. One or more of the parents also models ideals for the child (moral, intellectual, athletic, aesthetic, religious, etc.), and the child finds his own admirability and agency by identifying himself with this ideal-bearing parent (the ideal self-object). The ideals serve to focus the child's sense of himself, giving coherence to the things he does and meaning to his life as a whole. His life is oriented, for example, by the fact that intellectual achievement is an ideal for him; the ideal unifies the incipient narrative of his life by providing it with a theme.

In each of these ways the parents function as "self objects" for the child; that is, the child, in receiving admiration or in identifying himself with the ideal-bearing parent, is using the parent to satisfy his narcissistic libido, his need to be a valuable, capable, and coherent person. Up to this point the child's self is parasitic on his parents' capacity to admire him and to be consistent ideal-bearers. He does not yet have *within* him the resources for a solid sense of his own value, capability, and coherency. If his parents did not supply his "selfhood," he would not at this point have any. As long as the child remains parasitically dependent on his parents, he is not yet a real self. He must internalize his sense of his own value, power, and coherency; he must become his own self.

According to Kohut, this process of individuation happens quite naturally by virtue of the inevitable occasional failures of the parent to admire, empathize with, and bear ideals for her child. When the child feels himself "let down" by his parent in one of these ways, then if he is for the most part getting plenty of support for his self, he will respond with an attitudinal adjustment that Kohut calls "transmuting internalization." It is as though he says to himself, "Well, if she won't admire my coloring job right now, that's her tough luck. I know it's good; I'll just admire it myself." Or, "I'm hurt, and she didn't really comfort me enough, but I can handle that; I'm tough." Or, "I can see from Daddy's embarrassment that he doesn't always do the right thing, but that doesn't mean that there *isn't* a right thing to do." Such responses to disillusionment can be called transmuting internalization because they transmute resources for self-esteem, a sense of agency, and a commitment to ideals that were originally external to the child into resources in himself. Of course, he would not be able to take on the role of self-comforter, self-admirer,[1] and self-committer had he not been comforted and admired by his parents and been allowed to identify with them as bearers of ideals, so in this sense he continues to carry within him his original self objects. But if he is acquiring a healthy self, these are being transmuted into his own self.

Illness and Therapy

Toward the end of his life, Kohut thought that the most fundamental form of psychopathology could be traced to defective development of the self — that is, to sustained and systematic

---

1. In relation to the self as agent, this perhaps translates into "self-starter." He does not require the prospect of others' admiration as a condition of undertaking difficult tasks, but out of his own self-confidence, ambition to achieve, and commitment to ideals, finds himself "intrinsically motivated."

frustration of narcissistic libido. His own therapeutic work was with patients who had what he called narcissistic behavior disorders and narcissistic personality disorders. These were not the severest forms of mental illness but problems of perverse, delinquent, and addictive behavior or problems of depression, anxiety, hypochondria, hypersensitivity to slights, and lack of zest. The deeper damage to the self evidenced in psychoses and the borderline states (schizophrenia, empty depression, mania, and guilt-depression) was not "analyzable." Psychotherapy — at least the kind that Kohut practiced — would not help here because the self in these cases was too fragile to stand the exposure of therapy or too undeveloped to present a self to be analyzed.

The mentally ill person is one in whom the development we traced in the last section went awry. In particular, his self objects failed to form in him a deep sense of being valuable, capable, and oriented. Imagine that the following two scenes are *typical* — not just occasional — for some child.[2]

A little girl comes home from school, eager to tell her mother about making the winning goal in a soccer game. She wants to experience her own value and capability mirrored in her mother's joy. But instead of listening with pride, the mother deflects the conversation from the child to herself and begins to talk about her own athletic successes, which overshadow those of her daughter. The mother is unable or unwilling to be a mirroring self object for her daughter because her own narcissistic libido is unsatisfied. She feeds her own famished self rather than her daughter's.

A little boy is eager to idealize his father. He wants his father to strut a bit, to tell him about his life, the battles he has won, so that the boy can share the glory ("that's *my* Dad!") and find himself in the ideals his father represents. (He wants

---

2. These scenes are adapted from "The Disorders of the Self and Their Treatment: An Outline" by Heinz Kohut and Ernest S. Wolf, *International Journal of Psycho-Analysis* 59 (1978): 418.

his father to cooperate in being an idealized self object for him.) But instead of joyfully parading himself for his son, the father is embarrassed by the request. He feels tired and bored and, leaving the house, finds a temporary source of vitality for his enfeebled self in the bar, through drink and mutually supportive talk with friends. This father, like the mother in the first illustration, cannot or will not provide for his child's needs because his own are so great. He passes the damage of his own self on to the next generation. Instead of the "healthy narcissism" by which the parent would "forget" himself or herself, out of the resources of self-possession, and would "give" himself or herself to the child as an idealizing or mirroring self object, these parents evince a self-preoccupation, a concern with their own needs to be admired or comforted, and the child's need goes unsatisfied.

When parent-child interactions like the ones in these two scenes are typical in a childhood, we can expect the child to develop a disorder of the self, according to Kohut. The reason is that the child will not have enough capital from his self objects, in the form of self-value, sense of agency, and orientation, to be able to achieve transmuting internalization and thus become an independent self. The result of such a childhood will be an adult who is always narcissistically "hungry." He will seek an ever-elusive selfhood in empty bravado, exhibitionism, substance abuse, sexual promiscuity, relentless pursuit of confirmation and admiration by others, parentification of his children, idealization of hero figures — or he will suffer from depression, hypochondria, anxiety, and rage and bitterness at relatively insignificant slights.

What can be done for a person suffering from a damaged self? Kohut's main strategy is to create a relationship between the therapist and the patient in which the therapist becomes a substitute for the inadequate self objects of the patient's development — a substitute for the patient's parents. This is called a transference because the patient transfers to the therapist the attitudes and emotions she would have toward her parents. The therapist encourages the patient to recall representative episodes of childhood in which her parents let her down, frustrating her narcissistic libido. As the patient recalls these episodes, the therapist takes a deeply empathic attitude toward the patient's pain. He attends closely to what the patient is saying, showing that he understands her distress and predicament, thus communicating a supportive warmth. In particular, he shows empathy by accurate interpretations of what the patient says — ones that seem insightful, at any rate, to the patient. When the recall of the childhood episodes is cradled in this "parenting" by the therapist, the patient regresses (feels like a child again) and so construes the therapist emotionally as a parent figure. But this time, "childhood" feels *good.* With this relationship established, the patient begins to get the narcissistic gratification she missed in real childhood, and so she can begin to achieve a sense of self-value, agency, and meaning. In the course of therapy the therapist, like a good parent, will inevitably "fail" the patient's hunger for narcissistic gratification, and a process of individuation (separation from the therapist) is the natural consequence. When this transmuting internalization is complete (though of course it is seldom *absolutely* complete), the patient's self has been restored.

Healthy Narcissism

A person who has become individuated in the way I have just described — either through a healthy upbringing or through therapy — has what Kohut calls *healthy narcissism.* Just as congruence was the central Rogerian virtue and individuation the central Jungian virtue, healthy narcissism is the principal Kohutian virtue. This would be the central moral-spiritual trait of the best members of a community that took to heart Kohut's philosophy of the person. This is how they would articulate his credo of what it is to be human:

We believe that a human being is destined by nature to become a self — a being confident of his own value and his own ability to achieve, and securely oriented by some set of ideals. We become selves only by the help of others who admire and affirm us and let us attach our selves to theirs. When we have become selves, we are able to stand setbacks, failures, insults, and other blows without serious injury to our selves, and we are able to give selfhood to others by admiring them and letting them attach themselves to us when they need us.

I want to spend some time now taking a close look at healthy narcissism and asking to what extent it corresponds with the Christian virtues. This should allow us to decide how to assess Kohut's psychotherapy and how it might contribute to a Christian psychology.

The name of this virtue is meant to be a shocker. "Narcissistic" usually means self-centered, self-preoccupied, having an exaggerated sense of one's own importance, being insensitive to the rights or concerns of other people, being insecure in one's sense of self. So the suggestion that narcissism might be a virtue is paradoxical. But the self-possession that Kohut has in mind is just the opposite of what is usually called narcissism. He tells us that the inability to take another person's point of view (say, that of someone you are angry at, or someone who is suffering) is one of the chief signs that therapeutic work is still incomplete.[3] The person who has truly achieved healthy narcissism has empathic concern for other people.

So healthy narcissism is a social virtue, not only in its social origins, in the relations to one's parents or therapist, but also in its social consequences. The healthy narcissist is so self-possessed, so self-confident, so self-affirming that she can forget herself and get involved in the lives of others. There are

3. Kohut, "Thoughts on Narcissism and Narcissistic Rage," *Psychoanalytic Study of the Child* 27 (1972): 394.

indeed "helpers" who find helping others, especially disadvantaged, weak, dependent people, a source of personal gratification because they "need to feel needed" or because they enjoy the sense of power they can exercise (very benevolently, of course) over their charges. But the healthy narcissist does not help out of a need for reassurance and self-affirmation.

What does motivate the empathy, helpfulness, and generosity of the person with healthy narcissism? I have not found an answer to this question in Kohut's writings. It is clear why the healthy narcissist *can* be empathic: she doesn't have the distraction of excessive self-preoccupation that most of us suffer from. However, the question remains, Why *is* she empathic? I think we can appreciate the force of this question by comparing the Kohutian framework with a couple of others — namely, contextual therapy and Christianity. In Chapter Five, I noted that a strong analogy between Nagy's contextual therapy and Christianity is that contextual therapy interprets members of the intergenerational family as ontologically related. This identifies a natural bond between family members. Their well-being is not independent; they have a natural investment in one another's well-being. Part of the power of contextual therapy depends on the therapist's getting family members to accept this way of seeing themselves. If we ask somebody living according to the Nagyan philosophy of life why she has empathy with another member of her family, she answers, "We're ontologically related, and so have a natural loyalty to one another." The Christian is ontologically related not just to his own family members but to all people. If asked why he has empathy with another human being, he answers, "This is a child of God, and thus a brother or sister of mine." In each case, the philosophy of life includes a way of perceiving another person as naturally bound to oneself; accordingly, the prospects of fostering healthy empathy in someone depend on getting him to adopt this "word," this way of seeing himself and the other.

Kohut does not seem to have any comparable way of

conceptualizing the bond between persons. The two relationships in which empathy is especially important are those of parent/child and therapist/patient. In the first case the idea of an ontological bond is very plausible, and maybe Kohut would, if pressed, appeal to this bond to explain why the healthily narcissistic parent actually empathizes with his child. In the case of the therapist, one might (somewhat cynically) cite the fee as motivator, but it seems eminently implausible that money would motivate genuine empathy. The therapist seems to need some sense of bond with his patient. If, as I suspect, Kohut has no way of conceptualizing this motivation within his psychology, this is a weakness. If healthy narcissism implies empathy and not just the possibility of it, there ought to be something in this philosophy of life to motivate it. Perhaps Kohut's psychotherapy is an incomplete philosophy of the person, parasitic on some other ethic, such as (vestigial?) Christianity or Judaism.

It seems to me that healthy narcissism, unlike Jungian individuation or Rogerian congruence, really is a relational virtue, but that there is insufficient support for its relational status in Kohut's account of it. Perhaps it makes sense to speak of a pre-ideological human instinct of concern for others, somewhat in the manner of David Hume's "sentiment of humanity." But even if so, this instinct can be de-activated or covered up by an individualistic ideology like that of Rogers or Ellis, and it needs to be encouraged by a communitarian conceptual scheme such as Christianity or contextual therapy. In this respect, Kohutian self-psychology might be regarded as calling for integration into another philosophy of life, such as Christianity.

Another question that healthy narcissism raises for Christians relates to its "narcissistic" character. The healthy narcissist is comfortable with his enjoyment of being in the spotlight, of being capable and important, of being admired by others. He is not desperately hungry for these things, but still he enjoys them. Healthy narcissism is a disposition to joyful self-assertion. This may seem inconsistent with Christian humility and meekness. Isn't Christian humility a disposition to avoid the limelight, to let others take positions of leadership, or at any rate not to enjoy the position of leadership that is thrust upon you? Isn't Christian humility an inclination to take the seat farthest from the high table and keep your mouth shut?

Well, no. These might be appropriate exercises in humility for someone inclined to *desperate* self-assertion who is short on trust in God. But it is not of the essence of humility (see the discussion of Eric Liddell in the next chapter). Essential to Christian humility is that your self-assertion remain within the bounds of an emotional recognition that you are (1) a creature subject to and dependent on God for all your powers, and (2) a creature not essentially superior to any of your human fellows, despite your incidental superiorities, be they leadership qualities, intellectual abilities, athletic or artistic skills, or beauty. Nothing in healthy narcissism requires an emotional assertion of one's essential superiority to other people. But we'll see in a moment that Kohut's virtue does require one to deny God's perfection, and this requires, for a Christian, denying God. Thus healthy narcissism rules out Christian humility by contradicting its emotional recognition of our subjection to God. Christians who find healthy narcissism an attractive trait will be happy to know that Christian confidence has some of the same attractive features.

Healthy narcissism is a deep strength that provides protection against what Kohut calls "narcissistic injuries" — that is, eventualities that tend to shake a person's sense of his own worth, of his power as an agent, and of his orientation by ideals. For example, just about everyone feels smaller and somewhat impotent when fired, or when rebuffed by someone "important," or when divorced by one's spouse, or when taken hostage by people who do not speak one's language, or when unable to accomplish some significant task. In such situations as these, it is natural to feel depressed and anxious, or even to have a sense of "Gee, who am I, after all?" Even the healthy narcissist may have these feelings temporarily, but he rebounds quickly because his sense of self does not depend on external circumstances; he carries his sense of self within him as a deep disposition.

In this way healthy narcissism is the counterpart of the Christian confidence, which the apostle Paul expresses thus:

> As servants of God we commend ourselves in every way: through great endurance, in afflictions, hardships, calamities, beatings, imprisonments, tumults, labors, watching, hunger; by purity, knowledge, forbearance, kindness, the Holy Spirit, genuine love, truthful speech, and the power of God; with the weapons of righteousness for the right hand and for the left; in honor and dishonor, in ill repute and good repute. We are treated as impostors, and yet are true; as unknown, and yet well known; as dying, and behold we live; as punished, and yet not killed; as sorrowful, yet always rejoicing; as poor, yet making many rich; as having nothing, and yet possessing everything. (2 Cor. 6:4-10)

Christian confidence too is a capacity to withstand attacks on one's selfhood without "losing heart" (2 Cor. 4:16). But a difference between Christian confidence and healthy narcissism is that the transcendence of circumstance, the strength against "attack," comes from *continuing* attachment to *God* as self object. In the midst of adversities that would fragment a weaker person, the Christian remains together because she remembers God: by the Holy Spirit she hears the voice of God's love (mirroring self object) and remembers the hope for his kingdom (ideal-bearing self object). In this living communion with God, the "fellowship of the Holy Spirit," the Christian finds her equilibrium, her sense of self, her power to act. That is why the Christian is said to find her strength in weakness: there is a sense in which, in contrast with the healthy narcissist, the person of Christian confidence is not independent, and the strength of her self against adversity is most in evidence in those situations in which her purely inner resources would be insufficient to carry the day.[4] Through transmuting internalization, the healthy narcissist declares complete independence from the self objects to whom she is indebted for her sense of self, but at the very height of fully mature self-confidence, the Christian remains dependent on and in continuing fellowship with God.

I don't deny that Christian confidence is an "inner strength" like healthy narcissism, nor that it develops through a process something like transmuting internalization. As we have seen, transmuting internalization occurs as the child, empowered by the generally adequate empathic responses of his parents, responds to felt inadequacies in their support of his selfhood. He responds by internalizing that support, detaching it from them. Human parents are inevitably defective in their support of their children, but God is never defective in his support of Christians; he never actually lets us down. But there is in his interactions with us something analogous to letting us down — namely, that he is invisible and his ways are beyond our understanding. Thus Christian growth typically involves being "disappointed" in God, yet not so radically disappointed as to lose faith in him. Through these disappointments we come to a maturer conception of God (an understanding that his ways are not our ways), one that depends

---

4. The healthy narcissist's development is a bit like that of the Stoic, in that it aims to center all the strength (invulnerability to narcissistic injury) *in the self*, to root out all "dependency." By contrast, Christian development is willing to leave the self *in itself* somewhat weak; indeed, it counts such weakness as a virtue that allows for the demonstration of God's power in the person's life. But thought of in another way, the Christian self is just as strong as — maybe stronger than — the Kohutian self. For the Christian self can be thought of as including the God-relationship (the dependency on God), in which case the power of God is *part* of the power of the self. Which interpretation one chooses depends on how much one allows the concept of the self to include. In a relational schema, there is in principle no obstacle to including relations to others — and thus by extension their attributes and powers — in the self. For example, one's relation to one's wife might be conceived as part of oneself. This is of course not to indulge in some form of monism in which the wife is not distinct from oneself.

less on the vicissitudes of external circumstance and is thus more of an "inner" strength. But throughout this development, God is conceived not as an aspect of the self à la Jung, but as an independent, compassionate ("empathic"), demanding ("idealizing") being (Parent) on whom we *depend*. Like healthy narcissism, Christian confidence involves an independence from external vicissitudes; but unlike healthy narcissism, Christian confidence involves a dependence on an external Parent. It is arguable that God is the only parent who could function in just this way in the constitution of the self.

Another difference between healthy narcissism and Christian confidence goes with the one I have just outlined. On Kohut's view, the infant demands both absolute devotion from the mirroring self object and absolute perfection in the idealized self object. Both of these demands, being unrealistic, have to be got over as the individual matures into healthy narcissism. By contrast, Christian confidence not only involves an ongoing dependency on God as self object; it is also "infantile," by Kohut's standard, in not abandoning its archaic insistence on the perfection of the idealized self object. On the Christian view, to demand anything less than perfection from God would be to demote him, blasphemously, from the status of God. And the Christian, whose self is formed and sustained in interaction with God, must also sustain this demand, a demand that we might call "the passion of the infinite." Perhaps we have here a partial explanation of Jesus' saying that unless you become as a little child, you cannot enter the kingdom of heaven (Matt. 18:3; also see Chapter Twelve). The implication would seem to be that the person with healthy narcissism (thus having the characteristic independence of self and "cynicism" about perfection) would not be fit for the kingdom of heaven!

I think that Christian confidence is really quite rare. Many people "believe" in God and even have some personal dealings with him (for example, they may petition him for things). But it is something quite beyond this to take God as a self object, to be his son or daughter in a deeply psychological way: to have the sense of one's own value determined by the perception of his love, to perceive that one's own powers of agency are an ongoing gift from him, to derive the sense of one's deepest identity from the ideals of his promised kingdom.

Kohut points out that the healthy narcissist is able to become angry without "the fanaticism of the need for revenge and the unending compulsion of having to square the account after an offense."[5] This is because healthy narcissism does not see the offense as "infinite." If one's narcissism is infantile, then one sees offenses against one's own person as having ultimate significance, because one's self is "grandiose." If it is not oneself but a moral ideal that has been offended against, fanatical anger results from the infantile insistence on the perfection of the idealized self object. Healthy narcissism moderates anger and makes it rational by cutting both the self and its ideals down to size and thus reducing the perceived severity of the offense. It is easy to find cases of such fanatical, defensive, infantile anger. In the public sphere it can result in senseless wars; in the private sphere it accounts for endless interpersonal conflict and misery. If healthy narcissism spells an end to this kind of anger, it is a virtue and a facet of mental and relational health.

But healthy narcissism is just one way to preclude narcissistic rage; Christian confidence is another. As we have just seen, Christian confidence affirms the perfection of God as the idealized self object and daily renews its sense of dependence on him. Narcissistic rage is precluded by some of the particularities of the relation to the divine self object, especially that he is merciful and forgiving. To construe God as merciful to oneself is to acknowledge one's *need* of mercy and thus to feel contrition. But in the Christian scheme, God's offered mercy is not selective, so both the offended person and the offender are covered by it. Christian confidence, in its identification with the perfect idealized self object, thus construes the offender as a brother or sister in iniquity. If this contrition and solidarity with the offender do

5. Kohut, "Thoughts on Narcissism and Narcissistic Rage," p. 385.

not mitigate the sense of the offender's crime, they certainly reduce the distance between the offender and the angry one, a distance that is essential to narcissistic rage.

If the insistence on the perfection of the idealized self object is not outgrown in Christian confidence, the insistence on one's own grandiosity, omnipotence, and centrality to the universe *is* outgrown. Indeed, the acceptance of one's own finitude (construed now as creatureliness) is the complement of the satisfied passion of the infinite — the recognition in God's face of the perfect idealized self object. By attaching itself to God, the finite self does in a sense become infinite, thus satisfying its archaic grandiosity. So Christian confidence is as connected with humility as it is with contrition, and this too is protection against narcissistic rage.

Kohut and Rogers

Because of the centrality of empathy in Kohut's therapy, some have suggested that he is little more than a Rogerian with a fancier vocabulary. This is unfair to Kohut, and I think our look at healthy narcissism gives us a way to see this. Paul Vitz and others are right in alleging that Rogers's psychology is a perfect ideology for *un*healthy narcissism — for self-centeredness and self-indulgence, for the kind of thing of which the "me generation" is an ugly paradigm. In Rogers's philosophy of life, the human "organism," thought of completely individualistically, is the final arbiter of what is good for it and the ultimate source of its own well-being. It only needs to be freed from (socially imposed) conditions of worth to find itself, and this is the significance of empathy as unconditional positive regard. This is also why Rogers believes that the unfettered spontaneity of early childhood is the ideal of human well-being and virtue.

By contrast, Kohut believes that we don't become solid selves until we are civilized by other human beings. This is particularly evident in the importance he gives to the idealized self object and to ideals. These are a necessary orientation for the coherence of the self, and they are not just read off the "organism." They are passed from one generation to the next. I have noted that Kohut is weak in his conceptualization of the healthy narcissist's positive relations with others, but it is still clear that for him the self is "social" not just in its origins but also in its actions and attitudes: the ability to take the other's point of view is essential to healthy narcissism. And lastly, it is clear that Kohut does not worship change as Rogers does. We hear nothing from Kohut analogous to Rogers's claim that the "organism" is a "process" and that we are dead unless we are constantly changing and quite fundamentally open to new experiences. Kohut's character ideal is closer to that of the central classical traditions which emphasize the virtues of constancy, stability, and integrity. A paragon of Rogerian virtue would be, in Kohut's view, a paradigm of "fragmentation."

Using Kohut's Ideas

We have seen that healthy narcissism has many structural features in common with its Christian counterpart, but that these virtues also diverge at a number of significant points. They agree in endorsing the natural joy of self-display as well as the freedom for empathy with others, but I noted that Kohut's psychology does not seem to provide a positive motive for empathy and behavior directed toward the good of others, as the Christian psychology does. In this respect Kohut's system is less "relational" than Christianity or Nagy's contextual therapy. It seems to need a concept like ontological relatedness. Healthy narcissism and Christian confidence both provide strength that protects against "narcissistic injuries" and thus an independence from external vicissitudes, but Christian confidence is not detached from its self object (God) in the way that healthy narcissism is detached from its original self objects. Unlike healthy narcissism, Christian confidence does not require abandoning the archaic insistence on the perfection of the idealized self object, but instead passionately insists on this perfection and finds selfhood in attachment to the Perfect One. And lastly, Christian confidence and healthy narcissism both preclude narcissistic rage, but their ways of precluding it differ, and in the difference we see again the more strongly relational character of the Christian psychology. It is clear, then, that anyone committed to the Christian ideal of mental health and to the fundamental importance of nurturing people in the Christian virtues will want to exercise caution and make some adaptations in the use of this therapy.

I'm no psychotherapist, and maybe the question of what a Christian therapy informed by Kohut would look like is best left to be answered by the practitioners. But having warned you that I don't know what I'm talking about, let me venture, for your skeptical consideration, some practical implications of this chapter. The therapist will certainly want to help the patient retrieve and work through memories of his parents' failures as self objects, and the therapist's empathic responses will be crucial in facilitating the transference and the recall. But since the aim of Christian therapy will be to lead the patient to Christian confidence rather than to healthy narcissism, the therapist's empathy will also function as a model of God's compassion and mercy, and the patient will be encouraged to be in communion with God through regular prayer and worship, and to recognize his dependence on God. He will be encouraged to find in God the satisfaction of his archaic need for a perfect idealized self object. The importance of God as self object requires that God be central in the therapeutic process, and the Christian relational framework — of God and neighbor, of the fatherhood of God and the siblinghood of humankind — will enter explicitly into the therapist's interpretations. The client's empathy for others and his inoculation against narcissistic rage will be provided conceptual motivation (as they seem not to be in straight Kohutian therapy) by these references to the self's ontological relatedness.

PART TWO

RELATING TO
ONE ANOTHER

In Part One we have looked at six systems of psychology and have assessed them in Christian terms. From each of these, I have argued, Christian psychology can learn something, but none of these systems is completely compatible with Christianity; much less *is* any of these a Christian psychology. In interacting with these psychologies we have learned some things about a Christian psychology. We have seen, for example, that Christians do not get their standards of mental health simply by consulting the organismic valuing process or the unconscious; the standards are "cultural," and in particular they come from the Christian tradition — the Bible and the wisdom of the ages of the church. Christians have their own standards for what is "rational" in behavior and outlook. We have seen that Christian psychology needs to accommodate several emphases and insights from other psychologies: (1) the cognitive emphasis on the place of beliefs and patterns of construal in the formation of character and the maintenance of mental health, (2) the behavioral emphasis on training people in appropriate behaviors and the power of this to change people's attitudes and relationships, (3) the Rogerian emphasis on aiming at congruence of our various "selves," (4) the insight of family therapy that we are not merely individuals but are embedded in and depend on a context of close relationships, (5) the analytic emphasis on the unconscious, and (6) the neo-psychoanalytic insight that our selves are formed in intercourse with "self objects," be these our human parents or God. We have seen that a Christian psychology defines the human person in terms of his or her relationship to God and the destiny to be a citizen of God's kingdom. The healthy self is thus in an important sense "outside itself" or "beyond itself" in its attachment to God and other human beings, and not turned back on itself and preoccupied with its own "needs," as so much of contemporary psychotherapy tends to make us. Christian psychology is equally concerned with forming individuals as definite, concrete, individuated selves, and with their fitness for life in community.

Thus some of the themes that have emerged in the past six chapters. In the chapters that follow, I want to dig a little further by thinking about some themes that are more peculiar to Christianity but have psychological relevance. They are all "relational" issues — issues about how we interact with one another, the attitudes we take toward one another, the influences we have on one another. But they are at the same time issues of individual character, for the question of how we relate to one another cannot be separated from the question of what kind of persons we are as individuals. The themes are highly selected, perhaps even somewhat arbitrarily selected, and I make no pretense here of offering a systematic or complete Christian psychology. These explorations will, I hope, be suggestive for Christian psychologists and persons interested in exploring the psychological dimensions of Christianity, but they are not more than informal excursions into the territory.

Chapters Eight and Nine are about dimensions of competition, a way of relating that can be very destructive and about which Christians should have their own special reservations. What do we do with competition, competitiveness, and its emotional consequences of pride and envy? This topic will allow us to have a look at sin, a concept that must certainly have an important place in a Christian psychology. Chapter Ten is about forgiveness, the reconciliation of parties who have been alienated by some kind of offense. Forgiveness is a basic and distinctive Christian "intervention" for healing relationships and individual psyches. Chapters Eleven and Twelve explore some dimensions of marriage and parenting, two themes that have as much bearing on psychology as they have on Christian ethics. Chapter Thirteen addresses hospitality, an attitude and set of behaviors that Christians direct at strangers. (Because of who we Christians think we are, strangers have a peculiar importance in our philosophy of life.) Chapter Fourteen is about friendship with God, that attitude and relationship which, according to a Christian psychology, is absolutely central and essential to our psychological well-being; and Chapter Fifteen is about the nature and therapeutic power of belonging to the church. In Chapter Sixteen I describe the task that lies before Christian psychologists and begin to set forth some parameters of a Christian psychology: our verbivorousness (that is, the word-eating and word-digesting character of persons), our nature as "indwellable" by God, our need for attachment to God and our human fellows, the concept of sin as the central description of psychic dysfunction, and the place of self-denial in psychological development.

CHAPTER EIGHT

Playing at Competition

The Balloon Stomp

In a commentary aired on "All Things Considered," Jim Roberts, a family therapist in Kansas City, told the following story. He was visiting the fourth-grade class of his son Daniel, where the teacher had organized a "balloon stomp." Each child had a balloon tied on his or her leg, and the object was to obliterate everyone else's balloon without letting anything happen to yours. It was every man for himself and each against all. As soon as somebody stomped you, you were "out," and the child who still had a plump, glistening balloon when everybody else's hung limp and tattered would have the winner's glory.

The teacher gave the signal, and the children leapt ferociously on each other's balloons, doing their best, meanwhile, to protect themselves against the onslaught of others. All, that is, except one or two who lacked the spirit of competition. These were just dismayed by all the hullabaloo, and their balloons were predictably laid waste. In a few seconds all balloons were burst but one.

Then a disturbing thing happened. Another class, this time a class of mentally handicapped children, was brought in and prepared to play the same game. Balloons were tied to their legs and they were briefed on the rules of play. Said Roberts, "I got a sinking feeling in my midsection. I wanted to spare these kids the pressure of a competitive brawl."

They had only the foggiest notion of what this was all about. After a few moments of confusion, the idea got across to one or two of them that the balloons were supposed to be stomped, and gradually it caught on. But as the game got underway, it was clear these kids had missed the spirit of it. They went about methodically getting their balloons stomped. One girl carefully held her own in place so that a boy could pop it, and then he did the same for her. When all the balloons were gone, the entire class cheered in unison.

These children had mistaken the competitive game for a cooperative one, but their error has some advantages. In the original game only one child could win, but they discovered how to make everybody a winner! In normal balloon-stomping, the participants are momentarily alienated from one another (it's you *against* me), but as these children played it, the game was an occasion for camaraderie. Instead of feeling anxious about fellow players, you know the others are there to help you along. In the original game, you wouldn't be likely to learn love, but the play of these children seemed to foster generosity, trust, cooperation, gentleness, and concern for one another.

The Philosophy of Beak and Claw

Some parents and teachers seem to style themselves after managers of fighting cocks. These wild chickens, with their taste for high-stakes competition, remind us of some human beings. The loser in the cocks' "game" may literally lose its life. Nor do the managers temper the birds' inclination to kill each other; in fact, being dissatisfied with the birds' natural armory, they fit them with razor-sharp metal spurs. The parents and teachers I have in mind not only seek athletic and intellectual excellence for the children. They do so in a spirit that views these skills as beaks and spurs for prevailing in the struggle for survival against fellow human beings.

This philosophy of life, which I'll call the PBC (the philosophy of beak and claw), seeps into just about everybody's personality in our culture. It says, in effect,

> The real world is a nasty place where you need to protect yourself and stomp the other guy's balloon before he stomps yours. If you don't learn this, you won't survive. It's all very well to croon sentimentally about the mentally handicapped youngsters cooperating and loving one another, but the world that the normal kids will have to survive in follows the rules the teacher had in mind. Darwin had it right: life is about surviving, and the fittest survive. To be a fully functioning human being, the pride of evolution, you must be on the offensive *and* on the defensive. It's not whether you win or lose in the game of life, but whether you win. People who don't aggressively enter the fray are simply cowards, afraid of defeat, willing to exchange greatness for safety and excellence for comfort. The only way to be valuable and have a worthwhile life is to be *on top.*

Of course not everyone in our culture believes this credo. Christians, for example, do not believe it. But that doesn't mean we are not deeply affected by it. We may know that the lenses through which we see the world are distorting it, and yet keep right on seeing the world in the way these lenses present it to us. "Serious competitiveness" is the name I give to the chief virtue commended by this philosophy of life, and I will subsequently distinguish it from "playful competitiveness," which is the counterpart Christian virtue. Serious competitiveness is the steadfast, even compulsive, disposition to stake one's value as a person on *winning,* where winning means besting other people. The beaks and claws we use on one another are the basic tools of success. The spirit of this philosophy is nicely caught in the classic title of Robert Ringer's book, *Winning through Intimidation.* In the business world, big companies often use the "teeth" of power, influence, and intimidation to bite and chew up weaker ones. When the PBC is active in politics, beaks and claws are made of money and rhetoric and cunning strategy. You "go for the jugular." You collect all sorts of corruption in your mouth by researching the other candidate's moral history so you can spit him in the public eye. Under the influence of the PBS, politics is not so much an arena where individuals can work together for the public good as a jungle in which the fittest claw their way to success by using promises, rhetoric, ingratiating smiles, and connections. Christians call these attitudes, beliefs, and behavior sin, and even non-Christians seem to be uneasy about the PBC, for in all these arenas the underlying philosophy tends to get covered up by subordinating the "winning" to some more noble goal such as "excellence," the good of the company or the public good, or democracy and justice. But the real guiding goal in the bloody business is to be on top.

What would the therapies that we looked at in Part One say about serious competitiveness? To their credit, each one would regard it as pathological, would oppose the PBC, and would try to correct its manifestations in individual clients and families. They would point to the anxiety that serious competitors feel, often chronically; the alienation from others that is generated by making being on top a chief agenda of life; the attack on self-esteem that serious competitiveness promises for all but the few winners, and even for them once they cease to be winners (as inevitably they will); the sense of emptiness that descends on the winner once the crowd has stopped cheering and he is home alone; and the false self-concept involved in investing so much in being on top. According to Robert Bellah, therapy's opposition to competitiveness is embedded in its history: psychotherapy arose in our culture as a response to the emotional problems generated by competitive democracy. If serious competitiveness is sin, it is sin with ill effects palpable enough to be widely recognized.

The PBC establishes (with a vengeance) a "condition of worth" that it would be the business of Rogerian therapy to dispel through empathic, unconditional acceptance. RET would try to convince the serious competitor that the PBC is irrational: it teaches shoulds and oughts and musts ("You must be the best!") that become the basis for awfulizing, catastrophizing, musturbating, and other horrific things; and it specializes in overgeneralization: "If I don't win (at this or that), I'm a loser." Assertiveness training attempts to inculcate in the client behaviors that are neither aggressive nor passive, and aims at amiable relationships; this is an aim very different from and perhaps incompatible with that of being top dog in competitions. The emotional isolation and alienation from others that are characteristic of the PBC are contrary to the kind of close relationships in which, according to Nagy, we find our truest identity; giving someone "credit" seems to be stylistically and motivationally at odds with establishing one's superiority over that individual. Heinz Kohut aims to form a self in the client so strong and confident and firmly established that it will not need the unhealthy narcissistic gratification of being superior to others. And Carl Jung would regard the seriously competitive individual as lacking the emotional detachment, objectivity, and sense of the "eternal" that are characteristic of individuation.

A Christian Diagnosis

Most serious competitors do not think of themselves as neurotic or dysfunctional, though if they are at all sensitive you could probably get them to admit that competitiveness has a dark side, manifested in anxiety about possibly losing, agony of actually losing, blinding obsession to be the best, addiction to glory, and alienation from one's competitors. But to the extent that serious competitors do not see deeply into their own pathology, it is because they are caught up in the PBC and lack a philosophy of mental health that would provide a measure of their pathology. The PBC, after all, tells us not only that serious competitiveness is "OK," but also that it is positively a virtue. Christianity, on the other hand, sides with the retarded philosophy of life, which says we are all in this together. It says that we are all heroes and heroines not because we are victors on the world's terms but because we are created in God's image and are his daughters and sons; we are to be princes and princesses in his kingdom. We gain this prize not by besting each other, but through God's grace and the pursuit of his kingdom's goals. There is no limit to the number who can be "winners" in this sense. To be "somebody" is not to be at the top of a pecking order but to serve faithfully the cause of the kingdom, and that may be done as well at the "bottom" as at the "top." This means that the matters in terms of which competitions are set up — how beautiful, wealthy, or clever you are, how much influence you have over others, how fast you can run, how beautifully you can play the piano or how brilliantly you can argue and write books, and so on — are all of decidedly secondary importance by kingdom standards.

Where does serious competitiveness come from, according to Christian psychology? The story is complex, but let's consider some of its main features.

First, and perhaps most obviously, we are indoctrinated into the PBC. Christian psychology is committed to diagnosing people's psychological dysfunctions in terms of the philosophies of life they have imbibed. We feed spiritually on "words," and one of the persistent words of our culture, passed on to us in subtle and not-so-subtle ways in our schools, in the workplace, on TV, and in our families, is that the way to be somebody is to "get ahead" — that is, ahead of other people. This is not an abstract philosophy but one we are induced daily to *practice* in our balloon-stomps, our exam-taking, our efforts to gain or retain employment, our pursuit of a mate. Our entire culture is set up to seduce us into thinking competitively about ourselves and our neighbors. While anthropologists may exaggerate the noncompetitiveness found in some cultures, it does seem that many other cultures — for example, those of the Zuñi Indians, the Inuit of Canada, the Israeli kibbutz — produce less competitive people than ours does.

But the Christian diagnosis will go beyond merely saying that our culture made us do it. First, it will want to explain why the competitive philosophy of life is so seductive by exploring what the PBC so beguilingly speaks to in our nature. And second, it will hold us individually responsible — to one degree or another — for allowing our culture to corrupt us. If serious competitiveness were completely caused by our culture, making us mere victims, it would be improper to describe it as sin.

In Christian psychology, it is part of the *imago dei* in human beings that we want to "be somebody." We want to be distinct individuals who have *worth* and *efficacy as agents*. Our worth is largely a conferred one, conferred by other persons who cherish us, enjoy our company, approve us, applaud us, respect us, and include us in their lives. It is a premise of Christian psychology that the worth so achieved, while necessary to human development, is never adequate to our selfhood as long as it is conferred only by human persons. We must also know ourselves to be accepted, cherished, and enjoyed by God. We need to see ourselves reflected in God's loving eyes and not merely in the loving eyes of our family members, friends, and colleagues. Earlier we called this need to "find ourselves in God" the passion of the infinite, and we noted that, in contrast with Heinz Kohut's account of narcissistic libido, Christian psychology takes the need for a perfect mirroring and idealizing self object (God) to be not merely infantile or archaic but irrevocable. In this respect we remain forever children, even in our most perfect maturity. We may deny our need for God; we may become unaware of it; we may *think* we have outgrown it. But we do not thereby eradicate it.

We not only need to know that we are loved by God — to see our selves mirrored, as it were, in God's affirming eyes and thus constituted as selves by his approval. If we are to "be somebody," we also need to take the active role of lovers. We must become agent participants in God's cause, actively attaching ourselves to him by working, at his side, toward his goals. We need to take the initiative and ourselves affirm what is most worthy of affirmation in the universe. In a famous prayer, St. Augustine says,

> "Great art thou, O Lord, and greatly to be praised; great is thy power, and infinite is thy wisdom." And man desires to praise thee, for he is a part of thy creation; he bears his mortality about with him and carries the evidence of his sin and the proof that thou dost resist the proud. Still he desires to praise thee, this man who is only a small part of thy creation. Thou hast prompted him, that he should delight to praise thee, for thou hast made us for thyself and restless is our heart until it comes to rest in thee.[1]

Augustine is saying that there is in the human organism a need to praise God, a need that, if it goes unfulfilled, will cause the individual to be "restless." By "praise" Augustine does not just mean singing God's praises or saying prayers of praise, though these things are included. He is speaking of praising God with one's whole life — honoring him in one's attitudes and actions, serving him in word and deed, showing by all that one is and does that one regards God as wonderful, beautiful, great, and glorious. To be a self is to be more than just an *object* of God's admiration; it is to be at the same time a *subject* who actively admires God — or, as we might say, an agent driven by God's ideals.

The need to be related to God in these two ways arises from our capacity to take in, however vaguely, via conceptualization and imagination, the whole universe, the ages before and after our own lives, and the ideas of perfection, of God the perfect parent, and of his kingdom, the perfect society. It is to have some idea of eternity (whether or not one *believes* that anything is eternal) and thus to be able to be dissatisfied

---

1. *Confessions*, trans. Albert C. Outler (Philadelphia: Westminster Press, n.d.), Book One, Chapter I (p. 31).

with merely finite life. According to Christian psychology, these powers "infinitize" the drive of our selves for worth and agency. Or, put in the personal terms more typical of Christianity, these powers enable us to hear the voice of God speaking to us and calling us to himself. Or, to use another theological concept, this need to be not just a self but a self before God is an important aspect of the *imago dei*, the "image of God" in the human being.

The Christian psychologist sees in serious competitiveness an abortive attempt to become a self, a distortion of the need to "be somebody," to be an approved agent. The serious competitor seeks to be glorified for what he does, to see his own glory mirrored in the approving looks of his admirers and the envy of his defeated opponents. Just as the true self finds greatness in attaching itself to God's ideals and working for the kingdom, the serious competitor, wishing to be great, attaches himself to the standards of the competition (beauty, cleverness, speed, skill, and so on) and very likely to some great achievers in his arena. These, like the ideals of God's kingdom, are "values" that only a being with powers of conceptualization and imagination could be oriented by, could define his self by reference to. These standards are of course pseudo-standards if thought of as addressing the passion of the infinite, as Christian psychology diagnoses them as doing. They are a pathetic mockery of true selfhood. But in the Christian diagnosis they are more pathological than that, for the self that the strong competitor was intended to be was a self in communion with God and the brothers and sisters. And this love is precluded by strong competitiveness. In short, the strong competitor wants to be a self, and this is something he should want; but he fails miserably in attempts to be a self because he does not attach himself to what is really great and seeks glory from what precludes real glory. The Christian psychologist reads serious competitiveness as a restlessness that indicates failure to reckon with God's love and to attach oneself to God's projects.

So on a Christian diagnosis, the first two causes of serious competitiveness are cultural indoctrination with the PBC and an attempt to fulfill the selfhood drive of the *imago dei* without God. The third is the agent's own choices. The serious competitor never fully understands how powerfully he is held in the thrall of the PBC, nor does he understand with full emotional awareness that his competitiveness is a wretched substitute for a relationship with God. He may, however, understand these things in a veiled way, and he is virtually always aware, to some degree, of the darker side of serious competitiveness. When, therefore, he surrenders himself without reservation to the attitudes of serious competitiveness, when he "invests" himself in competitions in the way characteristic of this pathology, he acts — or at least acquiesces — with freedom. He could resist his urge to be competitive — probably not with total success, it is true, but he could at least put up a struggle and achieve a certain mitigation of the ill. So when he doesn't do this, he cannot lay all the blame for his condition on his culture, his anxiety to fulfill the selfhood drive, or his already established compulsions. The more fully a person is aware of the evil of serious competitiveness, the more responsible he is for resisting it, and the more guilty if he does not do so.

Giving Competition Its Due

Does this mean that Christians must never have balloon stomps, or run marathons to win, or play softball at church picnics, or root for their football team, or try to make their own college the best in the world? Where there is competitive winning, there has to be losing; is it inconsistent with kingdom attitudes to want to win when that means somebody else has to lose? Can we separate serious competitiveness from the practice of competitions and our natural enjoyment of competitive play? Can we compete with a healthy attitude? As the title of this chapter suggests, I don't think all competition is sinful or pathological. I suggest that we distinguish between competitions (which are activities, more or less institutionalized), serious competitiveness (which is the chief virtue of the beak-and-claw philosophy of life), and playful competitiveness (an attitude — disposition — another virtue, in this case belonging to Christianity). To condemn all competition or even all competitiveness because serious competitiveness is a vice and a disease is like condemning all drinking because some people become alcoholics, or condemning formulaic prayers because some people repeat them vainly.

My wife, Elizabeth, and I used to play volleyball under the auspices of the local parks district. The competition — actually playing a *game* against another team — was essential to the fun. One could of course volley the ball back and forth outside the game, and the physical actions might resemble game-play, but it wasn't nearly as much fun. Playing the game did bring out a competitive spirit. But in most of us the competitiveness was not serious. Nobody's selfhood was at stake, and nobody got irritated about being on a losing team all evening. The losers had as much fun as the winners. We joked, played hard, and razzed the other team triumphantly when we made an impressive point or they fell for a clever strategy. Again, this competitiveness was saved from degenerating into something unhealthy and unfun by the attitude — in particular, the playfulness — of the participants.

I must admit, though, that serious competitors came into the group from time to time, and they tended to be the better players. This fact raises a doubt about playful competition, one that advocates of the PBC are likely to urge on us. It is that playful competitiveness is associated with mediocrity, and that excellence in such competitive enterprises as sports, music, and business cannot be pried loose from serious competitiveness. I answer that although serious competitiveness may be more of a temptation for people of greater competence, the two are not necessarily associated.

The film *Chariots of Fire* depicts two British runners who competed (though as it happens not against one another) in the 1924 Olympic Games. It is a spiritual commentary on sport, illustrating two sharply contrasting attitudes toward competition and winning. Eric Liddell was a Scottish evangelical who later became a missionary and died an early death as a prisoner of war in China. Harold Abrahams was an Englishman of Jewish Lithuanian parentage who lived a long and honored life as a prominent figure in British athletics. I want to suggest that Abrahams presents an example of serious competitiveness, while Liddell represents playful competitiveness.

It is not running that Abrahams loves, but winning. Running is a way of establishing himself as the best. To lose in a running competition means losing in the game of life; it means failing to make a place for himself as a person. Early in their friendship, Sybil, the woman he later marries, asks Harold whether he loves running, and he replies, "I'm more of an addict; it's more of a weapon."

"Against what?" she asks.

"Being Jewish, I suppose," he answers.

At one point Abrahams loses a race to Liddell and is brokenhearted. Sybil says, "It's a race you've lost; nobody's dead," and he responds, "I don't run to take beatings. I run to win; if I can't win I won't run." Whereupon Sybil tells him to grow up. Later one of Harold's friends and running buddies tries to explain to Sybil why Harold is temporarily excluding her from his life. "The world's against him, or so he believes. He can't see or hear anything beyond that, not even you. And now he's got a chance to prove himself. That's immortality. To me the whole thing's fun; I don't need that. To Harold, it's a matter of life and death."

Unlike Abrahams, who is compulsive about securing his identity and saving his "life" through his running, Liddell has his identity and his life in his relationship with God. As a result, his running — and whether or not he wins — always occupies a subordinate position in the order of his concerns.

Liddell is a very hard-driving competitor, without being what we have been calling a "serious competitor." (Abrahams, watching him run a quarter mile, remarks in dismay that he's never seen a runner with such will.) But Liddell consistently sees his speed as God's gift and his running as an act of glorifying God. When Liddell's sister challenges him that preparation for the Olympics is becoming too important to him, he replies, "He made me *fast*. And when I run, I feel his pleasure. . . . To win is to honor him." But in the logic of God, Liddell does not infer the contrapositive: that to lose is to dishonor God. God cannot be dishonored by someone who loves him.

As he boards the boat for France, where the games are to be held, Liddell learns to his dismay that the heats for his event will occur on Sunday. Being a strict sabbatarian, he must choose between obeying God and running in the Olympics. After a brief struggle, he makes up his mind, and despite enormous pressure from the authorities, he refuses to compromise his belief. Winning is a great pleasure for Liddell, but the point of it is not to install himself as "the greatest." Instead, the point is to actualize a beautiful potential that God has planted in him. The basic value is an encompassing obedience, of which actualizing his bodily potential is a part. His talent for running and winning is not a matter of life and death but a conspicuous grace among the many with which God has blessed him and by which God glorifies himself through him.

Abrahams' compulsiveness about being the greatest is a function of his low self-esteem, which is connected to his sense that he is ostracized for being Jewish. He feels abandoned to himself. He lacks that sense of belonging to something larger and more solid than himself that Liddell gets from his relationship with God, the need for which we have been calling the passion of the infinite. We can guess that if Abrahams had felt Jewish in another way — as a member of the people of Israel, a son of Abraham and thus of God — he would have had another perspective on competition.

A Sense of Humor

When Kierkegaard called Christianity the most humorous view of life in world history, he wasn't expressing his admiration for jokes about Saint Peter at the Pearly Gates. He meant that, just as when we find something humorous we have a certain "distance" on it, so the Christian has a distance on the ways of the world. Things that are very important to non-Christians — for example, the things that most competitions are about, as well as the issue of winning out over other people — are a "joke" to the Christian, who is in this world but not of it, her life being hid with Christ in God. Her sense of identity isn't bound up with successes and achievements and recognition, although she takes on life's activities with gusto. Because Christ has cut her loose from the world's way of reckoning, she can take a playful attitude toward all contests. The mature Christian has a clear emotional recognition that the desperate desire to be admired for being outstanding is really a perversion of the desire to be loved. So when she wins the admiration of others, it makes no deep impression on her, and when she fails to win such admiration, it also makes no deep impression. She laughs off wins and losses with equal ease. Her self is not at issue. She may compete, but her competitiveness is playful.

Playful competitiveness perceives the opponent as a fellow, not as an alien, and presupposes something like love. After all, the mature Christian finds her true self in her love for God and neighbor. The humor of the gospel teaches us to see a brother in our "opponent" and to count "wins" and "losses" equally for the sake of Christ, who alone is the source of our life. It liberates us from the spirituality of the jungle by removing from competition the issue of our survival. By ensuring that the stakes are never ultimate, the gospel lightens the competition and makes possible the playful mood proper to "sport." Of course, I am not saying that a Christian sense of humor comes automatically or easily; no, it is as difficult to achieve as being a Christian is. Sin and death have a way of clinging to us, and we should not be surprised if we sometimes overinvest in winning, and our competitions degenerate into a spirit of beak and claw.

But this ideal of humor and playfulness ought to guide our child-rearing, our Christian education, our practices in the church and elsewhere, and our own efforts at spiritual growth. What are some ways we can manage competitiveness so as to foster healthy competition and discourage the spirit of beak and claw? How can we nurture a kind of Christian sportsmanship that gets the priorities right by keeping the playfulness in the play? This is a large question, but I will make some brief suggestions.

Attacking Beak and Claw ·

Serious competitiveness is a dehumanized way of focusing on other people, which typically derives its energy from a distorted concern for self-esteem. So it requires a double-pronged attack: a person needs to find other "terms" in which to focus the world and needs to be given a different, more adequate locus of self-esteem.

Let's say you're a grade-school teacher, and in the middle of a spelling bee the spirit of beak and claw begins to raise its ugly head. A couple of the children have an inflated sense of self-importance over their superior performance, and the ones who do poorly are being made the object of mumbled derision. What can you do to help the children — winners and losers — reconceptualize their situation in healthier, more playful and loving terms?

How about telling a story called "When I Lost the Most Important Spelling Bee of My Life"? Your story puts the catastrophe of losing a spelling bee in a comic light. You get the children laughing at your folly, and that has two positive effects. For one thing, it begins to dawn on the losers that doing well in a spelling bee is not a matter of life and death.

Look, Ms. Burlap is making light of losing. Perhaps even *their* losing is something they could laugh at! And the winners may be deflated and humanized by their laughter at you. The teacher, whom we all respect, is like *them*, those aliens, the nerds and dodos! (Could it be they're human after all?) Your humor works healing on both winners and losers by changing the meaning of the competition for them. It helps detach the competition from issues of respect and self-respect. It's important that you accomplish this by making *yourself* the object of laughter rather than any of them. By becoming an object of their common laughter, you make yourself a mediator and reconciler, breaking down the dividing wall of hostility between them.

Soccer, says Wheaton coach Joe Bean, is especially prone to degenerate into "war," and so he stays on the lookout for ways to foster a humane concept of the game among his players. He tries to instill two fundamental ideas. First, soccer is a game, not a war; it is a platform, given by God, on which we can develop and display our talents to his glory, so winning is secondary to playing. And second, we play as a team, so the win or the defeat, as the case may be, belongs to all of us together. Coach Bean believes that keeping these principles in mind helps guard against the nasty conduct that is so likely to erupt when things get tough; Christians are judged, he says, on the basis of their spontaneous reactions, not their "philosophy" of life.

Before the third division championship game one fall, the Wheaton players hosted a banquet for the Brandeis team. The men were seated in an alternating pattern according to teams, so as to get personally acquainted with their competitors in a noncompeting context. The banquet was punctuated with humor, as when the Wheaties announced to Brandeis team member Jim McCully that as part of their hospitality effort they had named the playing field (Wheaton's McCully Field) after him. Sharing food and stories and laughter around the table put a human face on the other team. However ferocious these players may have looked the next day on the field, this event impressed on the heart what the Word says: that these individuals are so many image-bearers of God, whom he intends to be our brothers in the kingdom.

The other strategy for heading off unspiritual competitiveness is to provide a deeper basis and locus for self-esteem. If you can keep a sense of humor about all your competitions, you signal that winning is not a survival issue for you: your soul is anchored elsewhere. Had Harold Abrahams felt himself to be received and validated by the author of the universe and upheld by the communion of saints, as Eric Liddell did, he would not have had to invest the winning of races with pseudo-ultimacy. He would have been liberated to run for the sake of running well, and he would have been freed also to regard his competitors as fellows.

The Word of God's love, embodied in a community of love, is the final foundation of any human being's selfhood. Other bases are variously analogous to the love of God. Love from other human beings, when it comes close to being unconditional, is a shadow of the love of God and seems to be a necessary medium through which that love is received. Innocent creative acts like carving something beautiful out of wood or singing a song well are also a natural quarry from which to mine self-respect. On the other end of the spectrum, self-esteem erected on the foundation of fancy cars and lavish homes, power over others, and lists of accomplishments is so far from what true human nature demands that it creates spiritual monsters.

To instill in our children a sense of worth that will minimize the seductions of beak-and-claw competition for them, we will want to enable them to have some experiences that are as closely analogous as possible to the experience of God's grace. In general, we should give our children a strong sense of being loved and approved without tying that to their being "winners" in the "game" of life. So when Pete comes home and announces that he's the champion speller in the class, credit him for it warmly enough, but without a dramatic show of affection. Instead, lavish affection on him when no winning or losing is in sight.

Pete may be a champion speller, but when it comes to gym he consistently places last. Being often humiliated, he "hates" gym. He tends to find his sense of worth in connection with more intellectual activities, and avoids the athletic whenever possible. If you put a very high value on athletic prowess, you may have difficulty not feeling disappointed in your boy. You may even nag him and try to push him, even shame him, into greater accomplishments. By imposing on him such "conditions of worth," you train him in the spirituality of beak and claw. He won't fashion his claws out of athletic prowess, but he will look for some way to establish himself, since he won't feel established in grace. The right approach is to give him the sense that you empathize with his humiliations, that you are with him in his failures. Thus you reflect, in a distant way, the love of the Father of mercies, who comforts us in all our affliction.

CHAPTER NINE

Stamping Out Envy

I Win, You Lose

Clyde and Bonnie Vogelgehirn have in-law problems. Clyde's brother Bosco and his wife Ravinia find numerous ways to one-up them. Bosco flaunts his son's successes on the soccer field. (Clyde's son, by comparison, is all knees.) Or it's the fantastic meals they had vacationing on the West Coast — meals Clyde and Bonnie couldn't quite afford. But Bosco is not a jock-neck, belly-worshiping hedonist. His family are refined. They pride themselves on reading Frederick Buechner, and when Bonnie and Clyde visit Bosco and Ravinia's home, they are subjected to a tour of the basement gallery, where paintings by the eldest daughter hang. Endless lectures on art appreciation put Ginny's techniques and style in historical perspective. But Bosco and Ravinia aren't just aesthetes, either. Ravinia shows her moral depth by suggesting, in subtle tones, how much more intimate her relationship with Bosco is than Bonnie's is with Clyde. Being a couple of years older than Bonnie, she's kept a motherly eye on their marriage over the years. Indirectly but unmistakably, she urges approaches they might take, if they're wise, to bring their marriage a bit closer to the ideal.

By now I've probably turned you against Bosco and

Ravinia. I bet you think they're disgusting people, and you'd never have *them* for friends. And you're feeling pure pity for Clyde and Bonnie, who have the bad luck of being their relatives. But let me adjust that impression. Bosco and Ravinia are nice. They have a number of friends, or if that's too strong a word, at least fairly close acquaintances. Bosco is always ready to help Clyde with his tax return, and Clyde is glad for the help (though he often wishes he could get it somewhere else; assistance from Bosco means swallowing his pride). The one-upping I just described is more or less reserved for family members, so some of Bosco and Ravinia's acquaintances don't know this side of them. In the church they teach Sunday school, head up the Mission and Outreach Commission, and often open their home to the youth group. They *do* take their marriage seriously (if a little too clinically). They are a close couple with a good family life. They would give you the shirt off their back.

I'm not kidding. There was the time the fake Moonie took that shirt — in fact, several shirts. He appeared off the dark street one winter night just as the potluck in the church basement was winding down. Len looked so pathetic. It was painful for him to speak of what he'd been through, but reluctantly he told his story as the compassionate Christian potluckers drew him out. His escape, in the last few hours, from a group of Moonies in Indianapolis was a traumatic experience that left him rather helpless. He had no food or money, and only these clothes in this paper bag. He didn't know where to turn next.

Ravinia and Bosco took him home. They gave him a room and fed him at their table. In the next few days they found him several jobs, but nothing worked out. He said it was his birthday, so they invited their friends over and they all showered him with gifts and felt sorry for him and felt good about themselves. Bosco went out and bought him three shirts. But Len kept being so pathetic and shiftless that they didn't know what to do next. Eventually Ravinia called a Moonie de-programming agency in New York for advice. When she described Len to the woman on the phone, she found out that Len had a national reputation. The woman said, "Oh, he's no Moonie. He's just a guy who goes around to churches acting pathetic and telling his Moonie stories and getting a handout. He always tells people it's his birthday."

I tell this story just to set the record straight about whether Bosco and Ravinia are disgusting. But the fact that they are also self-giving, upright citizens, Christians, and morally serious makes their one-upping even more difficult for Clyde and Bonnie to digest. This gives it the sharper bite of truth: the Vogelgehirns really are overshadowed by their in-laws.

After an encounter with Bosco and Ravinia (say, a lasagna dinner), Clyde and Bonnie feel two things: they feel *small*, and they feel *violated*. The anger comes from a sense of being victimized. It's like being knifed with a smile. And they react by wanting to belittle Bosco and Ravinia. They're not so great, after all. Clyde suspects that Bosco didn't really care about Len when he took him in but just wanted to impress his fellow Christians at the potluck. Clyde likes telling himself this; it comforts him to cast Bosco as a hypocrite. He and Bonnie delight in comparing notes about Ravinia's airs of having deep psychological insight. Clyde's deliciously malicious imitation of Bosco's lectures on art history is right on target.

It wouldn't be so bad if they didn't let themselves get sucked into Bosco and Ravinia's game of comparing wonderfulness in the competition for self-worth. Why can't they just let Ravinia play her games but keep their distance, staying out of the competition themselves? Why not enjoy Bosco's lectures for what can be learned from them? But no, the suction is too great: down they go into the whirlpool, where they suffocate in their envy.

It's like it used to be on the playground, thinks Clyde, when some stupid kid would say, "My Daddy's smarter than your Daddy." And you'd feel as though you had to prove —

had to prove — that your Daddy was smarter. It was a matter of life and death. Or at least the stakes were tremendous humiliation — being deflated, brought down into the muck, with the other guy looking down on you, looking down from the invisible shoulders of his Phi Beta Kappa daddy, and laughing. You couldn't let that happen, so you did a lot of lying to yourself and mental gymnastics to cut the legs out from under the tall laugher.

Bosco and Ravinia don't come right out and say, "We're better than you," "We're smarter than you," "We're more important than you." They're not like the kids on the playground. If they did that, their one-upping would become too obvious to give them pleasure. (The joy disappears from this game when you admit that a game is being played.) Also, the one-upping would lose its suction: Bosco and Ravinia would look like stupid kids on the playground, and no adults would be drawn into the contest.

Bonnie and Clyde find themselves looking for chinks in the armor of Ravinia's righteousness, scouting for weaknesses in Bosco's intellect, inventing flaws, enjoying innuendo and gossip. When somebody else remarks about Bosco's braggadocio, Bonnie's heart finds satisfaction, though outside the family she seldom lets criticism escape her own lips, and even defends her relatives against the criticisms of others. Clyde and Bonnie find themselves fantasizing about the downfall of their in-laws, and they take a malicious joy in misfortunes that seem quite unrelated to their bragging. What a rapturous pleasure to get one up on the one-uppers! (Envy wants the downfall of the other, not just the correction of the injustice. It is, finally, not just a form of anger, but of sneaking hatred.) Clyde and Bonnie know that these feelings of pain and joy are no credit to them, and they would be embarrassed to be caught *showing* them. So they have to deceive themselves a bit. They have to put on a show, not only for others but also for themselves, that they don't really envy Bosco and Ravinia.

I don't want to suggest that Bonnie and Clyde have no

affection for Bosco and Ravinia. They see them frequently, enjoy dinners at each other's homes, exchange work, and help one another in many ways. And so, mixed with the feelings of anger, resentment, envy, and malice, there are, in a weak form, better feelings — of admiration, of gratitude, of shared joys. But their friendship is fatally compromised by the undercurrent of spiritual hostility; it is not friendship. They lack wholehearted goodwill for one another. The Christian assessment must be that the relationship is sick.

The Invidious Twins

Christian psychology has names for the emotions that are destroying the relationship between these couples, corrupting the souls of the individuals, and preventing the growth of love. They are envy and pride, the invidious twins. In some ways the twins are very different. Pride is pleasant, and envy is painful. Pride is a feeling of superiority, while envy is a sense of smallness and worthlessness. Pride brags and expands and actively seeks to build itself up, while envy belittles the other and contracts itself and passively wishes misfortune on the "superior" one. Pride is self-love, while envy is self-hatred.

Yet, despite these differences, they are spitting images of one another. They mesh together like precision gears. The proud person is nothing without someone inferior to himself from whom to get his sense of worth. And who fits this role better than one who involuntarily shows, by his envy, that he recognizes the proud person's superiority and hates it because he wants the very same thing the proud person cherishes — ascendancy? The envious one would not suffer this particular self-hatred if he did not join the proud person's game of making his personal worth depend on how well he is doing in the competition.

We can see how close envy and pride are by noting how little it takes to reverse the roles. What if Ginny's promising start as a painter peaks and declines when she is twenty-two? Her professors advise her to go into teaching, while Clyde's son Jeff emerges as a violinist of growing promise, and at age sixteen gets a full scholarship to Julliard. The sense of worth that Clyde gets from beating out Bosco in the smart-kids category is sweetened by a sense of revenge against him for all the quiet suffering he has caused Clyde and Bonnie over the years. Now it's Bosco and Ravinia who find themselves minimizing Jeff's accomplishment and half-wishing some tragedy would befall the other Vogelgehirns. And their envy is further embittered by the humiliation of this reversal in the pecking order. To *fall* from pre-eminence adds injury to the insult of mediocrity. Of course, it is typical of envy that all this is hardly acknowledged, and co-exists with fairly friendly intercourse.

Nagy can help us notice the "systemic" character of envy/pride. Just as trust belongs and is fostered in a social context where there's a reciprocity of trust and trustworthiness, so the invidious twins belong where an invidious spirit creates a reciprocity of envy and pride. These emotions feed on each other, and where one is absent the other tends to die out too. This is why envy is subject to the whirlpool effect — the proud person shows glee in being one-up, and the envious one responds with some belittling gesture or remark; the proud person responds by reasserting his superiority, perhaps with a subtle gesture of contempt, and the envious person must invent yet another, preferably more potent, belittling response. Thus by each invidious word or gesture the partners in the one-upping game suck each other deeper into the spirit of invidiousness. (People used to worry about the sinful influence of honky-tonks, but their effects might be considered positively salubrious by comparison with the atmosphere in some families and universities.) Some people suck us in by their invidious spirit, and others discourage our envy with a humble, honest, noncompetitive spirit that puts us at ease. The fact that the "system" promotes envy doesn't remove our individual responsibility for letting ourselves be sucked in. Indeed, the insight that envy is systemic places responsibility on individuals to do something *as* individuals to drive out the spirit of envy from the context.

So pride is always poised to become envy, and envy poised to become pride, with no more provocation than a reversal of circumstances. At bottom they are very similar vices, springing from the same structure of personality, the same view of the world, the same disease of the spirit. Where do they come from? What causes them? The Christian diagnosis says that envy and pride come from underrating ourselves, misperceiving others, and forgetting God.

Three Sources of This Illness

Underrating Ourselves

Who are we and what are we worth? The biblical story of God's dealings with us says that he made us for fellowship with him and with one another. This fellowship he calls "love," and he is the first lover, the one who came to us in humility, identifying with us in our suffering and our waywardness and lifting us, by his death, to life. The source of our worth is his love for us, his abiding involvement with us in this special way, our belonging to him and his kingdom. That Word is the Christian vision of who we are and what we are worth.

Envy and pride have a different vision, a different word; they tell a different story. They say that worth is something we have to win, not just in the sense that we have to earn it, but also in the competitive sense that for us to win, somebody else has to lose. We are fundamentally competitors for self-worth, and whatever worth we have comes from our superiority. We are valuable to the extent that there is some significant other person we are better than — more wealthy, more talented, more shrewd, more accomplished, more moral, more "Christian." But in adopting this pathetically poor substitute for true greatness, we deeply underrate ourselves. Christianity says that pride, as well as envy, is a form of low self-esteem! The way to cure them, then, is to learn to think better of ourselves. Our worth is to be found not in such things as being wealthy and having intelligent children — much less in being wealthier than somebody else or having more intelligent children than the neighbors — but in the fact that we are creatures of God and belong to him, that we are privileged to be associated with him.

Misperceiving Others

Corresponding to the special way that envious and prideful people underrate themselves is their flawed perception of each other. My psychologist friend Dorsey Grice once did an experiment in which he put eyeglasses on chickens. The glasses would cause a chicken to see a kernel of corn about one centimeter to the left of where it really was. So when the chicken pecked at the corn, it tended to miss. The point of the experiment was to find out whether chickens are smart enough to adjust to their new glasses. He found that they aren't.

Envy and pride are like those glasses. They cause us to see things askew. And we are like the dumb chickens who can't learn to see straight by compensating for the distortion. Their competitive philosophy of life gives the Vogelgehirns social astigmatism. When they look at each other, they see not brother and sister, not fellow children of God, but *living stools.* (It's important that they're living; nothing short of a living soul will serve as a riser for envy/pride.) If Ravinia can step up on Bonnie and Clyde, then she's above them and they are under her, holding her up, as it were. If Clyde can step up on Bosco, then Clyde is up because Bosco is down. In such a relationship the individuals see each other either as a *threat* (when the other tries to step up on his stool) or as an *opportunity* (when the other seems to be in a position to be stepped on). What a travesty of human relationships! What a false perception! The reality is that all of us are children of God. We don't need to step up on anything or anybody because God has *lifted* us up in Christ. We are brothers and sisters of each other, fellow travelers, fellow children of the one Lord.

Forgetting God

When I speak of "forgetting God," I'm talking about a subtle kind of forgetfulness. It's the kind that lets a Sunday school teacher who regularly teaches truths about God get personally out of touch with God. It's not a lack of theological knowledge but a lack of spiritual awareness. It is a lack of the immediate presence of God in one's life — a lack of the Holy Spirit. And whether a person lacks the Holy Spirit because he is an unbeliever, or lacks the Holy Spirit as a Christian who has fallen out of touch with God, it is this forgetfulness, I am saying, that causes us to sink into the mire of envy and pride.

God is our "life" in the sense that our communion with him is the foundation of a proper communion with our fellow humans. It is in the matrix of his love, his support, and the firmness of his guiding hand that our self-understanding and our perception of others remain true and healthy. Those who remain in touch with God will not envy others or be prideful. They will not see others as living stools, nor will they regard themselves as having their worth in winning. God is the great leveler and lifter up of human beings. He levels by lifting up, whereas we humans in envy level by cutting others down "to size." God humbles himself, to lift us up, while we humble others, to lift ourselves up. To be in touch with this God is to be both humbled and lifted up. ("He has put down the mighty from their thrones, and exalted those of low degree"; Luke 1:52). It is to be dissolved of one's envy and pride and given clear social vision.

Throughout this chapter I've been saying that there is something sick about pride and envy. People who are proud or envious are not doing well. They are not flourishing any more than are people whose blood pressure is too high. They may seem basically healthy, but they are not functioning as they were designed to. The symptom of dysfunction can get obvious in the case of envy; envy is a nasty feeling. But equally, if less obviously, the proud person feels anxious and vulnerable (restless, to use Augustine's word) because he senses the precariousness of placing the great weight of his worth as a person on so slight a foundation as his superiority; and he feels lonely, cut off, alienated, for he lacks friendship both with God and with his fellow humans. In the proud person these emotions may be intermittent, repressed, and/or hard to notice. But they are there, and they indicate that all is not well. To the Christian psychologist they are a confirmation that our true life is to be found in friendship with God and neighbor.

Stamping Out Envy

We have seen that envy and pride are sicknesses that kill us spiritually. And we've diagnosed such illness as coming from underrating ourselves, misperceiving others, and forgetting God. Now for the practical question: What can we do about our envy and pride? Our Christian diagnosis suggests some strategies, and we can pick up some hints from the secular psychologists. I suggest three psychotherapeutic strategies: acts of generosity, confession of sin, and meditation on the fatherhood of God.

Acts of Generosity

Bonnie and Clyde, concerned about the invidious undercurrents in their relationship with Bosco and Ravinia, hit upon the following Christian strategy: to undertake a program of "dying to self." They say to themselves, "Somebody has to stop this cycle of one-ups and put-downs. It is very tempting, when they're one-upping us, to want to put them down. But the more they do it, the more we do it, and the more we do it, the more they do it. If we sincerely try to break this cycle, God will help us. It will hurt when they put us down, but we must accept this suffering and, forgetting ourselves, give them full credit for their accomplishments. If we refuse to step up on them, maybe they'll feel less need to step up on us, and a little of the kingdom will begin to peek through."

So the next time Clyde and Bonnie visit Bosco and Ravinia, they make a conscious effort to give their in-laws the attention they desire, to give them full credit (being careful not to exaggerate and produce the effect of a caricature) for their accomplishments. Aware that there is something sinful about the one-upping self-display of their in-laws, they decide quite deliberately to take an attitude of God in Christ: to humble themselves under this sin and this humiliation for the sake of the sinners and for the sake of the kingdom. When Bosco launches into one of his long lectures on art history in praise of Ginny, Clyde and Bonnie don't fidget and grunt grudgingly and look for a chance to change the subject. Instead, they ask him respectfully to clarify this or that detail. They look for admirable qualities in Ginny's paintings and point them out themselves. When Ravinia comes out with her not-so-subtle suggestions for the improvement of Clyde's and Bonnie's marriage, they do not get angry and put her off. Instead, they look for what help can be found in Ravinia's comments (we can all stand a little improvement in this area), and they acknowledge Ravinia as the source of this help.

This strategy has two effects. First, crediting Bosco and Ravinia for their accomplishments paradoxically reduces their insistence on their accomplishments. Carl Rogers's therapy emphasizes that empathically sharing someone's "internal frame of reference" and treating her with "unconditional positive regard" tends to detach her from her "conditions of worth." If we assume that pride and envy are rooted in a distorted desire for worth, then perhaps we can explain why Clyde's strategy works: the respect that Clyde shows for Bosco begins to satisfy Bosco's desire for worth, though not in the invidious way that Bosco initially sought. Perhaps without Bosco's even realizing what has happened, Clyde's acts of generous humility change the game that is being played between them. And once this happens, Bosco naturally tends to start playing the new game of acknowledgment and reciprocal respect. The generosity of one or two individuals breaks the back of the invidious system.

Second, even apart from the changes that Clyde's and Bonnie's generous acts inject into the relationship system, their behavior may have a healthy effect on their own emotions. We sometimes think that a person must first undergo a change of heart, and then better behavior will follow. But bchavioral psychologists point out something that has always been a part of Christian wisdom: that a powerful way to change our attitudes is to change our behavior. So when Bonnie and Clyde start *behaving* generously and humbly toward Ravinia and Bosco, some of the spiritual fundamentals of envy/pride tend to drop away. Being better than others may seem less important to their self-esteem, and the ones to whom they direct their acts of generosity will begin to look less like stools and more like brothers and sisters.

Confession of Sin

I have called envy/pride a sickness, but it is more than that. It is a sin, and proper therapy must treat it as such. (It is standard in the Christian tradition to see sin as sickness, but the secular therapies tend to reduce sin to *mere* sickness.) To say that some act or condition is sinful is to say (1) that it is an affront to God and (2) that the person in whom it exists is not just a victim of it but is responsible for it and so needs to be forgiven. (We don't forgive people for mere diseases.) To confess your sin is to articulate — to God or to another human being — what offense you are responsible for and to express sorrow and a willingness to take steps to correct it. It is clear enough what affronts God about envy/pride. It degrades — in attitude, at least — a creature of his so dear to him that he had his son die for this creature.

We've seen too that envy/pride devalues the sinner's own proper glory and replaces it with something cheap and unworthy. We were created to love God and our fellows, but in envy/pride we forget God and abuse our neighbors.

Articulating sin in confession helps give you this vivid sense of what you have done, and of its import. So you should be as specific as you can. Do not just say, "I am an envious person; forgive me, Lord." Instead, say, "I have envied so-and-so (name her) for such and such (name it), and I have (in mind or speech or action) belittled her in the following ways (name them) or wished upon her the following harms (name them). I have staked my worth on such and such (name the terms of the competition) and have ignored your love. Forgive me and restore me to fellowship with you and my sister." True confession is always articulate, but articulation is particularly important with envy/pride, since self-deception is so characteristic of this sin. Articulating cuts through the self-deception, enabling you to take responsibility for the sin and to undertake strategies of correction.

Since envy is an offense not only against God but also against people, it is best to confess the sin also to the fellows you have offended: for Clyde to go to Bosco and articulate to *him* the attitudes he's been taking and his remorse for them. This act itself will promote reconciliation between Clyde and Bosco, and may even prompt Bosco to do some self-searching of his own. The humility of Clyde's confession will work to reduce the competitive struggle between them. But short of this ideal, the sin should at least be confessed to God or a third party — perhaps a minister or a friend. Only in the kind of recognition that confession fosters can you intentionally undertake such measures as the acts of generosity I described above.

Contemplation of the Fatherhood of God

Envy and pride are forms of distorted vision. We see ourselves as having worth because we are superior, and the other as a living stool. We see the world as an arena of competition for self-value. But the Christian notion that God is our Father, the common father of us all and equally the loving father of us all, provides us with another vision of ourselves and our neighbor and the world.

Like the elder son in the parable of the prodigal son (Luke 15), we need to get through our heads what our Father is like. Though the elder son lives in the bosom of his father's love, he seems to have got satisfaction from being the good boy while his younger brother was a rotter. And so he is proud. His pride soon turns to envy when his father pours out his love in lavish demonstration on the younger, "worthless" son. In the defensiveness of his pride, the older brother cannot see that his father's exuberance betokens not a preference for the younger son but only the joy of his return from sin: "My boy, you are always with me, and everything I have is yours."

A father's love is a great source of self-worth in his sons, and the elder son was so steeped in his father's love that he should have felt no envy when the younger son was royally welcomed on his ignominious return. But the equality of the father's love offends him: How can Dad love this tramp as much as he loves me? That this offends his pride shows its potential to cut through his pride and transform him. For if he can somehow contemplate the reality of his father's love, really see from his own heart this love which is equal for him and his brother, then he can also get free from the illness of envy/pride in his soul. If he can submit himself in humble recognition of the fact that he and his brother share equally in this love that gives them both their worth, he will also be reconciled to his brother.

Since envy/pride comes from ignoring God's love, it stands to reason that a cure for it will include paying attention to God's love. We need to be constantly working at this, reminding ourselves of it, in the context of the Christian community and the reading of Scripture, and setting this contemplation squarely against the invidious tendencies that are so resilient in the human breast. We need to keep before us images of God as Father alike of the rich and the poor, the talented and the untalented, the privileged and the underprivileged, the Christian and the non-Christian, the righteous and the unrighteous. We need to hear sermons in which the fatherhood of God is not only presented intellectually as a doctrine but made emotionally unavoidable as a reality. We need to develop an empathic way of reading Scripture such that it touches us with the reality of God's universal love. And above all we need saints — probably the most therapeutic "intervention" in the whole Christian repertoire — who show us by their living example what it is to have God for our Father, who thus cauterize our hearts against the corruption of envy and pride by the fire of their joy and hope.

Sin in Christian Psychology

In the first two chapters of Part Two, I have tried to impress on the reader the centrality of the concept of sin in Christian psychology. This concept overlaps in some ways with concepts of human dysfunction that we find in the secular psychotherapies, but it is also a distinctive concept of Christian psychology. My concentration on competition and the related emotions of envy and pride does not suggest that these are the only sins that Christian psychology will address. This book is a beginning exploration of some themes in Christian psychology, not an attempt to be systematic or exhaustive. Other sins to be addressed by Christian psychology are greed, lust, grudge-bearing, negligence of stewardship, idolatry, racism, cruelty, disregard for life, bitterness, anxiety, despair, and hatred of God. I have chosen competitiveness as an example, though I think an important one. We turn now to a distinctively Christian psychological intervention, and one that is directly related to sin as a psychological category — forgiveness.

CHAPTER TEN

Forgiveness as Therapy

In the Christian view of things, forgiveness is an enormously important source of healing. Indeed, one might say it is at the center of God's therapeutic program in Jesus Christ, who comes to us as mediator, reconciler, unifier, healer of our broken relationship with himself and with one another. Jesus mediates to us God's forgiveness, thus making possible and necessary our forgiveness of one another.

In this chapter I want to think with you about forgiveness as a way of overcoming anger, and I hope to show a difference between the Christian understanding of therapy in this connection and the understanding of therapy characteristic of what one author has called the "culture of narcissism." One might think that since anger is a rather painful and destructive emotion, and since forgiveness overcomes it, then forgiveness is really for the comfort, convenience, and health of the forgiver. Forgiveness becomes a way of taking care of yourself, and so might be marketed in somewhat the same way as low-cholesterol foods and exercise videos. Our reflections about anger and forgiveness will show that when this motive for forgiving has been made central, the forgiveness — and thus the therapy and the psychology — has a different logic from Christian forgiveness, therapy, and psychology.

Anger and Health

Anger degrades our life in many ways. It messes up our marriages, alienates us from our children and our parents, destroys friendships, depletes our energy reserves, and distracts us from getting on with the important things in life. It can cause anxiety, depression, guilt, and despair, and it can lead to loneliness and hatred of our life. Hostility expressed in some punitive or vengeful way can return to us with compound interest — in response to which we of course get angry again, and all the more angry, and may end up being honest-to-goodness enemies with the person at whom we were originally only angry. Besides all these "relational" and "psychological" problems, sustained anger causes (I am told) such bodily problems as heart disease, high blood pressure, and stomach ulcers. If Christianity empowers us to forgive, surely it is a very therapeutic view of life.

But anger is not pure detriment. The New Testament warns us against it, but it does not condemn anger without qualification, as it does hatred and envy, for example. Our Lord himself is depicted as sometimes intensely angry, as Jahweh was in the Old Testament. We are told, "Be angry but do not sin" (Eph. 4:26); the apostle Paul himself expresses anger a few times in his letters. It seems that anger can be justified, indeed, morally righteous — even required. Someone who never got angry, no matter what sort of injustice confronted him, might well be thought to lack an organ of moral perception. Someone who was never angered by offenses committed against himself might be suspected of lacking a certain self-respect. Christianity supplies special reasons for forgiving — reasons that a non-Christian will not have; but it also supplies reasons for being angry that a non-Christian may not have. For example, a nature lover will get angry when she sees people wantonly polluting the earth for short-term gains, but the Christian, because she has a personal relationship with the Author of nature, has an added reason for getting angry about this. To get a clearer idea of the therapeutic place of forgiveness in

Christianity, let us think a bit about anger. Our reflections should lead us to see *both* what is right about it *and* why ultimately it must be dissolved in forgiveness.

Diana and Maria are best friends from college,[1] and when Diana hears that Maria is coming to work in Chicago, she suggests they get an apartment together. Diana's present one is too small for two, so she agrees to look for a larger apartment and start fixing it up for Maria's arrival in about six weeks. Diana finds one (though the rent is higher than she'd anticipated) and sets to work with the paintbrush. She works happily, her mind set on the pleasures of friendship and life together. About a week and a half before Maria's appointed arrival, she phones Diana and says she's decided not to come to Chicago after all. She's met the most wonderful guy, and she doesn't want to jeopardize the relationship by moving away from his part of the country just now. She wishes Diana a happy time in her new apartment and luck in finding someone to share it. Diana is furious.

I think we can see (and feel) that there is something right — even healthy — about Diana's fury. Anger is a proper response to an injustice, to a blameworthy offense, and clearly Maria is guilty of such an offense. What if Diana didn't get angry but only felt disappointed? The explanation would probably be that she somehow does not notice how badly she has been offended. Maybe she doesn't know that agreements like Maria's are morally binding, or maybe her self-image is so poor that she thinks it's morally all right (though of course annoying to her) for others to back out on commitments to her. By getting good and angry at Maria and feeling it unmistakably, Diana shows that her powers of moral perception and her sense of her own dignity are in proper working order. Anger is a way of seeing offenses and offenders vividly, in all their offensiveness.

But of course there is a down side to Diana's anger. It is a

---

1. I owe this story to Albert Ellis, but I have varied it freely for my own purposes.

punitive or vindictive emotion. When Diana sees Maria's offensiveness in that vivid way, she wants to hurt her or see her hurt;
Maria looks like someone worthy of punishment, a bad person,
an enemy. This perception is discordant with friendship, for it is
a mark of friends that they wish one another well and look fondly
on one another. Diana may have mixed feelings about Maria.
She may not *only* be angry at her; she may also love her. In fact,
the intensity of her anger may be due in part to this love. But to
the extent that Diana is angry with Maria, she views her in a
way that is antagonistic to friendship. Her anger tends to blind
her to Maria's good qualities. It makes Diana want to forget or
discount the many good things that Maria has done. Anger is
ungenerous, unwilling to give the offender "credit." I think this
spiritual stinginess and the blindness to the offender's goodness
are what people have in mind when they say that sustained anger
causes a person's soul to shrink. At the same time that anger
makes our perception of offenses very clear, it tends to shorten
the reach of other perceptions that are even more important to
our mental and relational health. And we have already noted
that anger, if intense enough and harbored long enough, may
eventually diminish the body's health as well.

It seems that the Christian ideal of health, with respect
to anger, is to be the kind of person who can *get* angry when
this is called for but who is not dominated or possessed by
anger, or blinded by it. It is to be someone whose spirit is so
broad and generous that she can give up anger by calling into
play other dimensions of her personality, other commitments
and other concerns. In a Christian psychology, the most important way of giving up anger is by forgiving the offender.

What Is Forgiveness?

Forgiving the offender is not the only way to overcome anger.
If Diana's relinquishing of her anger is to count as forgiveness,
there are two main conditions it must meet. The first is that

Diana *neither exonerate Maria nor condone her offense.* The
second is that Diana give up her anger *for Maria's sake.*

Diana might overcome her anger at Maria by excusing
what she did. She might say to herself, "Maria grew up in a
family of moral knuckleheads, and since she had that kind of
upbringing I can hardly expect her to behave responsibly." Or she
might think, "Maria has always had a desperate need to be loved
and a dearth of boyfriends. So what can I expect of her when she
gets some attention from the opposite sex?" Such excuse-making
is quite different from forgiveness. It involves saying in effect
that Maria's really not to blame for her misdeed. When you
excuse a person of all wrongdoing, then there is no longer
anything to forgive, because forgiveness is directed at someone
who has culpably done something wrong. You will remember
that in Chapter Five we criticized Nagy's psychotherapy for
using exoneration in circumstances where forgiveness would be
called for in Christian psychotherapy. By explaining so much
deviant relating in terms of "destructive entitlement" and by
"crediting" the offender to the extent of excusing him of wrongdoing, Nagy takes away the blameworthiness that forgiveness
presupposes.

But excusing does not always rule out forgiving. Sometimes our excuses are only partial — mitigating considerations.
In this case, the excuse will leave room for forgiveness, while
making the crime somewhat less shocking than it seemed at
first and thus "easier to forgive." Diana might hold Maria
responsible for her promise-breaking, but she may also think
that Maria's offense is less awful in her case than it would be
with most other people because of her desperate need to be
loved. This way of understanding Maria's action leaves room
for Diana to forgive her because it does not remove *all* responsibility from Maria.

Condoning differs from both excusing and forgiving. Like
the forgiver, the condoner acknowledges the offender's responsibility for what she did. But if Diana condones Maria's action,
then she takes an improperly nonchalant attitude toward it. She

just "blows it off" or chooses to ignore it. Condoning involves knowing that the offender is responsible and blameworthy for what she did and yet not holding the offender accountable; it is a mixed response usually motivated by some fear. For example, workers may condone the unjust treatment they receive from a factory owner out of fear of losing their jobs. Or Diana may condone Maria's behavior because she is afraid that Maria will "dump" her as a friend if she gets angry. Condoning is a kind of double-mindedness in which one acknowledges a rather important matter (some moral offense against oneself), but then in a sense doesn't acknowledge it or doesn't take it with the seriousness it calls for.

Forgivers, by contrast, are persons of integrity who do not play mental games with themselves. They do not shy away from the moral seriousness of the offense, but they have morally and spiritually proper reasons for overcoming their anger. As a character trait, condonation is not a virtue and thus, from a Christian point of view, is not an aspect of mental health. But forgiveness is. We are instructed to "be perfect" as our heavenly Father is perfect (Matt. 5:48), and part of this perfection is found in our forgiving one another as God in Christ forgave us (Eph. 4:32–5:1). What are the spiritually proper reasons for overcoming anger?

I said that the second condition of forgiveness is that the forgiver overcomes the anger for the offender's sake. Another way to put this is to say that forgiveness is directed outward: it is a form of generosity. It is significant that the word *forgiveness* encloses the little word *give*. If somebody gives away three lawn-mowers with the sole motive of getting them out of his garage without the trouble of selling them, we don't call him generous, no matter how wonderful the mowers are and no matter how much they benefit their new owners. To show generosity is to act out of concern *for the recipient*. When Diana forgives Maria, she overcomes her anger by taking certain generous considerations to heart. These considerations are ones which themselves tend to dispel anger, because they are at odds with the alienating and punitive dimensions of anger that we noted in the last section. Let's look at four kinds of considerations: repentance, compassion, relationship, and complicity of the forgiver.

Repentance

Let's say that after a week Maria begins to feel remorse that she has let Diana down. She calls her up and says, "It was an awful thing I did to you, leaving you in the lurch like that. I'm very sorry, and I hope you'll forgive me." Now of course Diana may hold on to her anger and refuse to forgive. But if she has any love or generosity in her, Maria's repentance will deal a telling blow to her grudge. Why? Because anger cannot thrive without envisioning the offender as alien, as on the other side, as opposed to one's own cause. And now Maria comes along and says, in effect, "I'm on your side in this matter. I, like you, think that what I did was crummy and reprehensible. And I'm asking you to accept that I'm on your side in this matter." If Diana forgives her by acknowledging that Maria is indeed on her side, then the abandonment of her anger is in this sense *for Maria*. It is a gift to her; it has her in view. Diana is not getting rid of her anger simply because it's uncomfortable, upsetting, inefficient, or unhealthy to be angry, like the man with the cluttered garage who just wants to be rid of his lawnmowers. Instead, like the generous man who gives away lawnmowers because he wants the recipients to have something useful, Diana abandons her anger for Maria's sake and for the sake of their friendship.

Compassion

Repentance is probably the most powerful and characteristic reason for forgiving someone, but it is possible to forgive someone who does not repent or to forgive her before she repents. (Often a forgiving attitude can *precipitate* repentance.) Imagine that, when Diana starts thinking about Maria's poverty of suitors, her heart goes out to Maria. She does not abandon her belief that Maria has taken a significant moral misstep and that she is accountable for it, but she begins to see things from Maria's viewpoint. In empathic imagination she experiences Maria's anxiety about men, her present joy, and the urgency Maria feels about giving this romance a chance. In her anger Diana saw things very much from her own viewpoint, which was opposed to Maria's viewpoint. (Maria was the offender, and she was the victim; Maria was bad, she was good.) But now that Diana empathizes with Maria's situation and concerns, she finds it increasingly difficult to be angry — or at least to be *as* angry. Compassion tends to root out anger, just as anger tends to preclude compassion.

So if you feel as though you ought to forgive (say, because God commands it), but don't feel like forgiving, a first step you might take is to try seeing things from the offender's point of view. (This is not at all the same thing as excusing the offender — after all, when you take your own point of view, you do not thereby excuse all your wrongdoings.) Taking the offender's viewpoint may require *denying yourself* — an important concept in Christian psychology and psychotherapy — that is, denying your own immediate preferences and taking a course in opposition to them. But once you succeed in seeing things to some extent from the other's viewpoint, you will find that the process of forgiveness takes on a certain inertial progress of its own.

Relationship

Imagine that Diana does forgive Maria and that, upon hearing their story, Carla is shocked. "How could you forgive her? What a pain in the neck she is! What a lot of trouble she caused you! You *forgave* her? Why?" And Diana answers, "Because she's my friend."

On one interpretation of this answer, Diana is not forgiving Maria but condoning her action. A cynic might take Diana to be saying, "I'm afraid of losing my friend, and if I stay angry I risk losing her. So I'd better get over my anger." But this seems to make friends a kind of commodity to be retained at certain costs, and here the cost is one's integrity. But if we take Diana at her word and interpret friendship not as a commodity but as a genuine caring for another, we see that friendship can be a reason for forgiving; that is, we see an *internal* connection between friendship and overcoming anger. I've remarked more than once that anger alienates, puts emotional distance between the angry one and the object of her anger. It is in friction with love and friendship, with cherishing someone and wishing her well. The converse is also true: that cherishing someone is in friction with being angry at her and tends to overcome the anger. If love thus overcomes anger despite recognition of the offender's blameworthiness, then we have a case of forgiveness. On the noncynical interpretation of Diana's reason, she is saying that she has dropped her anger at Maria out of love for her. So this reason too shows forgiveness as oriented to the other.

Other close relationships are often mentioned as reasons for forgiving: "Because he is my father (son, brother, husband)"; "Because she is my mother (daughter, sister, wife)." These relationships can be mentioned because it is typical to cherish people who are in these relationships with oneself. Christianity offers us a vision of the earth's population in which this kind of reason for forgiving an offender can, in principle, be given for any offender under the sun. In Christ we are all God's adopted children (at least by his intention, and it is not for us to judge that some are not to be adopted), and so every offender is our brother or sister, and the love of God that is shed abroad in our hearts by the Holy Spirit is the spirit of forgiveness in Christians. Mental and relational health in this context, then, is extended, deepened, and certified by taking to heart the gospel of Jesus Christ and coming into the fellowship of the Holy Spirit.

Complicity of the Forgiver

A reason for forgiving that is rather different from repentance, compassion, and relationship is the consideration (a) that the offended one is also an offender, and (b) that the offended one has been forgiven.

(a) Full of anger at Maria, Diana may start thinking about *herself.* She may call to mind some times when she was less than fastidious about keeping her own commitments. As the similarity between herself and Maria sinks in, Diana's anger fades. Why? One might suspect a form of excuse: Maria's offense is something that other people do, and the more people there are who commit a certain crime, ·the less criminal it is. So Diana's finding similar crimes in her own past is a kind of excuse for Maria. I admit that people think this way, but a little reflection reveals this as submoral thinking — no ingredient of proper forgiveness. That many people go back on their promises does not make going back on one's promises less blameworthy. Why, then, does Diana's anger fade as she reckons with her own complicity in this kind of sin?

Anger is judgmental. In her anger, Diana sees herself as the righteous victim, sitting high above Maria in a sort of emotional judgment seat, glaring down at her in all her criminal wretchedness, waiting skeptically for Maria to defend herself. Contemplating her own sinfulness gets Diana off the judgment seat and allows her to see Maria as a fellow human being again. This humility opens the way to compassion, to seeing matters through Maria's eyes. It dispels the anger and re-establishes the sense of equality essential to friendship.

(b) It may come to pass that Diana, being a Christian, sets her mind on one of the things of the Spirit — namely, the fact that God has forgiven her. Unlike the unforgiving servant of the parable in Matthew (18:23-35) who, despite having been forgiven a great debt of his own, refuses to forgive a small sum that is owed to him, Diana contemplates this grace of God with *gratitude.* That is, she happily sees herself as a sinner who is eternally and inescapably indebted to God for unmerited favor. Happy in this one-down position vis-à-vis the true Judge, she is prepared by humility to accept her rough equality with other sinners like Maria. In this way the vision ingredient in

Christian gratitude also brings her down from the judgment seat of anger and sets her on the way to renewed affection for her wayward friend.

The four typical reasons for forgiveness that we have considered all point in the same direction: forgiveness, a typical and central expedient of Christian therapy, is oriented to the *other*, to the person forgiven. Its aim is reconciliation with him, fellowship with him, acceptance of him. As such, forgiveness is not just ridding oneself of anger with all its adverse consequences, but displacing anger with love. Even this last consideration, which involves Diana in reflecting about *herself*, is not a narcissistic kind of self-reflection. The aim of Christian forgiveness is not to rid the forgiver of an unpleasant and disruptive emotion but to strive toward the attitudes and relationships characteristic of God's kingdom. Forgiveness is therapy, and love is the health at which it aims.

Forgiveness Under the Influence of the "Therapeutic Mentality"

Throughout this chapter I have been arguing that Christian forgiveness is importantly and powerfully therapeutic. But I have tried to do so construing health in the distinctively Christian way that such a therapy aims at — in particular, health as love of the fellow human creature who, like oneself, is a forgiven sinner before God. Lewis Smedes's best-selling book *Forgive and Forget: Healing the Hurts We Don't Deserve*[2] contains many insights and much helpful advice about forgiveness, but it also distorts the concept — at least from the Christian point of view — in odd ways that seem traceable to the secular "therapeutic mentality" and an excessive focus on the wellbeing of the forgiver.

2. Smedes, *Forgive and Forget: Healing the Hurts We Don't Deserve* (San Francisco: Harper & Row, 1984).

One property that Smedes rather oddly attributes to forgiveness is that forgiveness cannot be granted for a hurt which the offended one has forgotten. Smedes tells of refusing to forgive a friend for a wrong the friend had committed against him, on the grounds that Smedes couldn't remember it: "If he had brought back old pain by bringing back my memory, I should have forgiven him. But as it was I could not really forgive him; I could only love him and by loving him heal the separation that he felt, though I did not."[3] Presumably Smedes could not forgive the friend because there was no hurt in himself for the forgiveness to heal. But this is not the Christian concept of forgiveness. If a friend convinces me that he wronged me, why should my inability to remember the injury and thus to feel the alienation be a reason for not forgiving him? Why can't I simply accept his account of the wrong as authoritative and pronounce him forgiven? Like Smedes, I have presented forgiveness as a way of overcoming anger and located its therapeutic power there. But it is a mistake to focus so strongly on the forgiver's freedom from anger that forgiveness cannot be granted where there is no actual anger. In asking forgiveness, Smedes's friend implies that Smedes has a right to be angry, or that it would be understandable if Smedes were angry. And if Smedes forgives him, he forswears that (possible) anger. Forgiveness as I have presented it is "oriented upon the offender." It essentially involves *his* well-being as well as my own; indeed, its point is our *relational* well-being. So if the offender needs forgiveness, it is perfectly fitting for me to forgive him even if I feel no anger. Smedes correctly sees that forgiveness is therapeutic but narrowly interprets therapy to mean the emotional relief of the individual — in this case the "forgiver," the offended.

Smedes shows us how he believes forgiveness is therapeutic when he says, "Perhaps more to the point . . . is our need to forgive *for our own sakes*. Every human soul has a right to

3. Ibid., p. 39.

be free from hate, and we claim our rightful inheritance when we forgive people who hurt us unfairly, even if their intentions were pure."[4] No doubt the forgiving spirit will increase a person's freedom from emotional pain, as well as from ulcers and hypertension. But it is hard to imagine Saint Paul exhorting his readers, "Forgive one another, for each of you has a right to be healed of your hate." It is typical of him to tell his readers to forgive one another because Christ has forgiven them and in doing so they will be like Him, or because it will increase harmony in the church, or because in forgiving one another we will become fit for the kingdom of God or ready for the judgment day. In other words, Paul does give a therapeutic rationale for forgiveness, but it isn't the narrow kind of emotional health that modern "psychological man"[5] aims at. Instead, it is well-being within the kingdom of God, and individually, it is the emotional attitude that fits one for that kingdom.

In the traditional Christian understanding it is unfitting to forgive somebody for a hurt that he is not to be blamed for. Imagine that Maria is prevented from keeping her promise to live with Diana by the illness of her aged mother. Her backing out is still a big disappointment and inconvenience to Diana, but Maria is not to blame, and so there is nothing for Diana to forgive. If Diana is nevertheless angry at Maria, then we say that her anger is irrational, and the "therapy" she needs is not to forgive Maria but to understand emotionally that Maria is not to blame.

Smedes recognizes a connection between blameworthiness and forgiveness. But because he makes forgiveness therapeutic in the narrowly modern way, he is led to interpret blameworthiness in ways that weaken the concept: "When Bob hung himself, he did not tell anybody what his motives were. Did he have to end his life? Is he to blame for the awesome

4. Ibid., pp. 12-13, his italics.
5. See Philip Rieff, *The Triumph of the Therapeutic* (New York: Harper & Row, 1966).

pain he left behind? Should his wife forgive him? I cannot tell. Only she can tell."[6] Why say, "Only she can tell"? What makes *her* a special authority on whether Bob is blameworthy? Maybe her status as wife made her unusually privy to his inmost thoughts. But it's possible that his therapist or his lawyer would have even more insight into his motives. One suspects that whether Bob is "blameworthy" is for Smedes an issue that finally is not about Bob's mental life but about his wife's, and that *this* is why she is an authority. It seems that the issue is not really Bob's blameworthiness but how strongly inclined his wife is to blame him — that is, how much she needs to be "freed from hate."

If Christian forgiveness applies only to someone who is blameworthy, it will make no sense to forgive God. Smedes acknowledges this: "You may react automatically: God cannot be blamed for anything, so he cannot be forgiven for anything."[7] But, says Smedes, our reaction is "automatic" (and presumably unreflective?), and his observation does not deter him from entitling one of the longer chapters in the book "Forgiving God."

> Would it bother God too much if we found our peace by forgiving him for the wrongs we suffer? What if we found a way to forgive him without blaming him? A special sort of forgiving for a special sort of relationship? Would he mind? Let us try; let us talk a little, reverently but honestly, about forgiving God.[8]

Smedes has indeed found "a special sort of forgiving," and not just in this chapter. His entire book is about something different from Christian forgiveness, something skewed away from Christian psychology and Christian therapy. This chapter, which may appear odd and even blasphemous on first sight,

6. Smedes, *Forgive and Forget*, p. 9.
7. Ibid., p. 83.
8. Ibid.

is not odd given the assumption, typical of "therapeutic man," that the ultimate purpose of forgiveness must be to find personal peace, to heal the forgiver of the hurts he doesn't deserve. It would be odd only if Smedes were expounding Christian forgiveness.

So we have before us two overlapping but incompatible concepts of forgiveness. Modern individualistic, therapeutic forgiveness can be directed toward God because it requires only that the forgiver *experience* God's acts as unfair. Since the whole emphasis is on how we feel and on figuring out how to make ourselves feel better, we can make "blameworthiness" a matter of how we feel about our "offender" and even forgive one party (God) who we know can't be blameworthy. Christian forgiveness, which is also therapeutic but in a quite different way, cannot be directed at God because it requires that the forgiven one be truly blameworthy, and because it is not driven by the sole concern of the forgiver's freedom from emotional hurt. I do not deny that someone can *think* he has forgiven God with Christian forgiveness, but this will stem from confusion, either about forgiveness or about God.

Conclusion

Let me summarize what we have learned from this discussion of forgiveness. We have seen that, in its own way, Christianity is very much in the business of psychotherapy, if by that we mean the restoration of souls to a state of health. But I emphasize "in its own way" because the health at which forgiveness aims is quite distinct from that of many of the therapies which have shaped our modern concepts of health and therapy. For one thing, forgiveness as therapy is uncompromising in its insistence that we not minimize or dismiss the responsibility of individuals for their actions. Forgiveness does not even apply to cases in which someone is not responsible for wrongdoing and thus not blameworthy. The importance of the offender's responsibility is also indicated by the fact that despite the pain and disruption caused by the morally judgmental emotion of anger, Christianity does not absolutely condemn it but proposes to overcome it with forgiveness. The Christian concept of psychological health is also distinctive in that it is uncompromisingly other-oriented: to be a healthy *self* is to love one's *neighbor*. This dimension of Christian psychology is evident in the fact that forgiveness is not just getting rid of one's painful, debilitating, or inconvenient anger but getting rid of it *through* considerations like the four that we examined — all of which orient the forgiver less upon himself and more upon the one he forgives. Health, in Christian terms, is finally the life of the kingdom, summarized in the double commandment: You shall love the Lord with all your heart, and your neighbor as yourself.

CHAPTER ELEVEN

Reconcilable Differences

If you are between thirty and fifty, you probably don't think about marriage the way your parents do. An article in *Redbook* put the difference this way:

> Not so long ago problems were regarded by both a wife and her mother (to whom she was most likely to go with a marital problem) as natural and normal. ("I had the same trouble with your father.") Unhappiness alone was rarely justification for leaving a marriage. ("He doesn't drink, he doesn't beat you, and he brings home his money. What else could you want?")
>
> Most modern women, on the other hand, regard happiness as the principal goal of marriage. If they cannot find happiness with a man, they regard divorce as a reasonable alternative.

Maggie Scarf describes a couple, Kathleen and Philip Gardiner, whose twenty-three-year-old marriage was in crisis as their adolescent children started leaving the parental nest. Philip began feeling that he too needed to leave home: "Philip's belief, in this middle era of his life, was that he had to leave the marriage in order to find himself — that 'self,' hidden deep within, which he experienced as having been imprisoned by the demands of the relationship to Kathleen."[1] We don't need to deny that deep factors in Philip's upbringing, as well as entrenched patterns of his relating to Kathleen, figured in his urge to leave. But in the early chapters of this book we have seen enough of how ideologies of fulfillment shape our sense of our selves and our needs to suspect that some therapeutic "word" was behind Philip's sense of his needs, his dissatisfaction with his life, and his identification of Kathleen as the source of his troubles. In particular, we seem to hear echoes of Carl Rogers and the human potential movement in the suggestion that the marriage is imprisoning him and impeding his self-realization. Consider how different Philip's diagnosis of his situation and his wishes for well-being would be if couched in the terms of contextual therapy — in terms, that is, of ontological relatedness, intergenerational responsibility, loyalty, and justice.

God seems to agree that the fulfillment of the partners is an important purpose of marriage. Looking down on Adam, who was surrounded by a wonderful array of plants and animals, God said, "It is not good that the man should be alone" (Gen. 2:18). So he made Eve to be Adam's partner. No matter how many beautiful birds and animals and flowers Adam had, his loneliness would not be filled up by anything less than someone who was bone of his bone, flesh of his flesh. *"Therefore* a man leaves his father and his mother and cleaves to his wife, and they become one flesh" (Gen. 2:24, my italics).

But this agreement between God and *Redbook* may not run deep. What is "happiness," "fulfillment," "realizing one's potential," "having a full life," "finding oneself"? God and *Redbook* agree that marriage is supposed to help us realize our potential, but this agreement won't amount to much unless they agree on what that potential is. In this chapter I hope to clarify what it means to seek and have a "full life" through

1. Scarf, *Intimate Partners: Patterns in Love and Marriage* (New York: Random House, 1987), p. 18.

marriage. To do this, I will present three ways of thinking about marriage: the self-realization model, the contract model, and the one-flesh model. I have been arguing throughout this book that how we think about something determines what it means to us, and that how we think about ourselves influences what kinds of selves we are. If this is right, then a couple's marital relationship itself may suffer damage or enjoy blessing according to which model operates in their thinking. It is a question of which of these three "words" nourishes the marriage.

The Self-Realization Model of Marriage

According to the first model, the ultimate point of marriage is to bring fulfillment to each of the partners individually. "Fulfillment" here means having interesting and exciting experiences, being loved and affirmed, having the freedom to "express" yourself and "grow" and be "creative." For example, divorcées often explain that their marriage wasn't "satisfying," wasn't "meeting their needs." They felt "stifled" in the relationship. In reflecting on reasons for divorce, marriage therapist Albert Ellis voices the self-realization model: "[The husband] may sense . . . that his wife hinders his and her growth and development by her tyrannical possessiveness. Or he may vaguely feel other qualities about his marriage, of which he is only semi-conscious, that actually constitute excellent reasons for his leaving it."[2]

On this view marriage is soil. Its purpose is to help you grow sleek and wonderful, and make you like yourself very much. If instead your marriage holds you back and makes you small and withered, pale and dull and grumpy, then it's time to shake the old, depleted soil off your roots and repot yourself.

2. As this book went to press, I looked in vain for the source of this quotation. However, those who are intrigued by Ellis's ideas about marriage may want to take a look at his *The Civilized Couple's Guide to Extramarital Adventure* (New York: Peter Wyden, 1972).

The repotting may shock your system a bit, but you can hope that in a while you will flower more than ever, and your deep green leaves will glisten. Of course, when the new soil, in its turn, runs out of nutrients, it will be time to start over yet again. In this perspective marriage becomes a gentle (and sometimes not-so-gentle) form of mutual exploitation. There is no room here for lifelong promises: if you enter into a marriage for "growth," it makes no sense to promise to love and cherish your partner in sickness and in health, forsaking all others, until death do you part. If he becomes an invalid, that can put a cramp in the pursuit of your human potential. Or she may just become a dull person, or lazy; and then maybe someone more exciting will come along.

A paradox sleeps in the bosom of the self-realization model. No love whose primary purpose is individual self-realization can be deeply self-realizing. At least this is a corollary of biblical psychology, which holds that people were created in the image of a God who is self-giving love and thus are intended to find their fullest flourishing and mental health in loving and being loved by him, and in loving and being loved by fellow human beings. Adam needed not just someone who could gratify him, amuse him, and be a seedbed for his "growth," but someone to whom he could cleave for better or for worse, someone to whom he could give himself and *thus* find himself. Adam needed someone *in common* with whom he could find his life. A special kind of fulfillment comes from loving and being loved, different from the kind you get from jogging or woodworking or playing the piano or writing books. It is not odd to jog for your own individual fulfillment, with the assumption that if it stops fulfilling you, you'll quit doing it. But if a couple think of their love for one another as a means to being individually fulfilled, they will not reap from it the kind of fulfillment they rightfully want from love.

It is self-thwarting to adopt fulfillment as the purpose of marriage. You must never quite admit to yourself that you're in this for its health benefits. If you don't keep telling yourself you're in love, you get only a defective form of fulfillment. For example, it won't do, on the day of your repotting, to look your new partner in the eye and say, "I pledge you my troth, that I will abide with you and honor you and cherish you and be faithful to you as long as I am growing and feeling good about myself." This very way of thinking about the relationship puts a distance between you and your "partner" that undermines your "love" and thus the benefits you're supposed to be deriving from love. A little self-deception is needed, which explains why people are often squeamish about frankly advocating the self-realization model.

The Contract Model of Marriage

So the Christian wedding service, with an eye for *real* human fulfillment, introduces an element of commitment that by-passes the self-realization motive. It accomplishes this by having the couple vow mutual faithfulness in something like these words: "I promise before God and these witnesses to be your loving and faithful spouse, in plenty and in want, in joy and in sorrow, in sickness and in health, as long as we both live." The service serves notice: If actualizing your individual potential is your highest goal, we suggest you look for another way. In marriage you throw in your lot *with this person.* If she frustrates your growth, limits your social contacts, impedes your career, or stifles your creativity, you're still committed. Improvements in these areas will need to be worked out within the parameters of your commitment to her.

Contracts serve to make relationships predictable, to enable one party to trust the other and so to get on with whatever business the contract bears on. A builder contracts with a lumber company to supply 2×4's in a certain quantity at a certain price for a certain period of time. This serves to ensure the builder that she'll have the 2×4's she needs, and to ensure the lumber company that it will have the market it needs. If the market price of 2×4's goes up to $2.50 and the contract calls for them to be supplied at $2.25, the contract enables the builder to count on 2×4's at $2.25 and requires the supplier to forgo opportunities to sell them at a higher profit.

Marriage differs from a business contract in the very odd fact that what is contracted for is *love!* You can supply 2×4's at $2.25 grudgingly, simply because you agreed to do so, and that will count just fine as keeping your contract. But if you supply love grudgingly, then you haven't supplied it, and you haven't kept the contract! So the promises of marriage are not just promises to behave in a certain way, but promises to have goodwill and to *work* on having it in case it doesn't always come spontaneously. (I guarantee that goodwill toward your spouse won't always come spontaneously.)

But, odd as it may be to make a contract for love, that is what the wedding ceremony does. When it's taken seriously, this produces a dimension of commitment. In front of the congregation the couple take a solemn vow to love one another. Some of the conditions most threatening to the bond are enumerated: for richer, for poorer, in sickness and in health, forsaking all others, and so on. Thus the bond is lifted out of the dimension of whim and passing fancy and personal satisfaction and established above the vicissitudes of life, in the ethical transcendence of a promise. If being yoked together seems stifling at times and the couple wavers about sticking together through thick and thin, then God and these witnesses can come to the couple and say, "Look, Kathleen; look, Philip — *you promised.*"

These days people are less fatalistic about marriage, less willing to accept it unquestioningly as a "given" within the bounds of which they must conduct their lives. A sign of this change is that many couples now write their own wedding vows, sometimes from scratch, sometimes by modifying traditional vows. Some of this simply personalizes the ceremony; some of it is harmless sentimentality. But what often gets left out of "customized" vows is the promise "to love one another until death do us part."

This is a symptom of ambivalence. A couple may want to go through the wedding service, all right. They aren't content just to shack up with individual fulfillment in mind. They sense that there is something unfulfilling about being so casual. They are looking for the deeper bond, but still they aren't quite ready to promise. They know the dangers of commitment; they're realistic and cautious about the prospects. He may be thinking, "Frankly, if she became chronically ill, the relationship wouldn't be satisfying any more, and I would pull out." She may be thinking, "If living with him meant, at some point, giving up the level of comfort to which I've become accustomed, I would leave." And so, being realists, they quietly delete the harder promises in the ceremony. They keep talking about love, but it's a love without ethical grip. It's a love based on "vibes," "chemistry," "attraction."

The One-Flesh Model of Marriage

"But," you will say, "your tone is all wrong. A wedding is a joyful occasion, full of promise, but you paint something daunting, full of losses and sacrifices and threats and obligations, even if these are, like brussels sprouts and dental appointments, 'good for you.' Sure, there's a serious dimension to wedding vows, but you make it sound like an army induction oath. Didn't God say, 'It is not good that the man should be alone'?"

And a nobler reason than morally flabby, narcissistic self-indulgence is often given for deleting the promises. Aren't promises out of place in a love relationship? Isn't a contract the wrong kind of glue for binding two people in a relationship of love? Shouldn't that be a spontaneous, natural, *living* thing — something not reducible to a pair of signatures on the dotted line?

Couples today are critical of the strongly ethics-based marriages that seem to have been the norm a few decades ago, especially in Christian circles. There was a strong sense of marital "duties" and a strong ethic of sexual fidelity. Each was there when the other was needed. They persevered together through thick and thin, for richer and for poorer, in sickness and in health. It was fulfilling enough to them to contribute their part to the stable and stabilizing social arrangement of marriage, to raise a brood of healthy children, to remain fairly cheerful and friendly toward one another, and thus to fulfill their duty to God and man. But were Mr. and Mrs. Barnes in love? Did they delight in one another's company? Were they real companions to one another? A sense of marital obligation (reflected in the promises of the wedding ceremony) doesn't necessarily make for that deeper, joyful harmony.

The desire to avoid this "externalism" in marriage reinforces the attraction many younger couples feel toward the ideology of self-realization. The way to protect love, romance, "genuineness," and spontaneity, they reason, is by doing away altogether with the "legalities" of marriage. This, however, is not the only road to take; Christianity, with its "one flesh" model, has all along had a deeper understanding of marriage.

In the Christian view, it is wrong to think of marriage either as merely a forum for individual self-realization or as merely a covenant to stick it out dutifully to the end. As the objections we have just heard point out, a "thin" contract view would make the marriage relationship just as "external" as the private self-realization view does. The one-flesh model makes place for a kind of self-realization, and accomplishes this through use of a contract, but it has much more going for it. Let's take a look at it.

It may seem odd to say so, but the ethical toughness of the Christian wedding ceremony, with its exaction of promises and its enumeration of the difficulties the couple's commitment will be expected to survive, is *therapeutic*. It is not a grim hurdle erected by the "moral law"; it is there in the interest of human flourishing. In view are the children the couple may have, and their children and children's children in turn, and the fabric of society, but this ethical rigor is also in the interest of the lovebirds' own flourishing. It is a wise and healthy inoculation against the unwholesome and destructive —though all-too-natural — narcissistic view of today's self-absorbed "I" that the "love" should serve my own individual ends, that I can bail out when I want, keep my options open. The contract is an aid in the service of Christian death to self — the therapeutic death that leads to *life*. According to a Christian psychology, we are made not to center our lives on ourselves but to center them on others in "outgoing" love. Marriage is a wonderful opportunity for this, and the vows are a corrective of the natural/sinful tendency that would thwart this healthy development. Christianity says that we are certainly to satisfy our own needs, but that our true need is to get out of this cramping and destructive focus on our individual needs and to find our true selves in our service to others. (Even to the "natural" man, I believe, there are few things uglier than a person who is totally focused on herself, who demands in her every gesture that our attention be trained on her, who is needy and greedy for attention.)

The apostle Paul tells us that Christ loves his church not as a group of people external to himself with whom he has entered into an agreement (say, as a crew to do his work) but as his own body. And, similarly, God intends that a husband shall love his wife as an extension of himself, and that a wife shall love her husband as an extension of herself. We do not usually have to promise to look out for our own interests in the daily affairs of life. We are naturally enough disposed to do so anyway. In the same way, in Christian marriage the promise to love one another until death parts us ideally becomes superfluous as the bonding between the man and the woman grows and deepens. The promise is in the service of this bonding.

The illustration that most readily comes to mind when we speak of being "one flesh" is the relationship of parent and child. Genetically, we are more literally of one flesh with our children than we are with our spouse, and this physical identification with our children is something we feel powerfully. When my child is sick, I am "sickened"; when he is threatened,

I am threatened to the depths of my being; when my child is insulted and humiliated on the playground, I am insulted and humiliated. And, similarly, my child's joy is my own: when my kid hits a homer, it's even better than hitting one myself.

We all have a vestige of the one-flesh concept of marriage, even if our thinking has been secularized by psychobabble and other influences. This comes out when a couple we have known for a while gets a divorce. Unless they have been very obviously alienated from one another, we perceive them as bonded, and so when they divorce, each of them looks like a sundered, incomplete individual. We say, "Hi, Kathleen. How's — ?" We catch ourselves, and we have the impression that the divorce means not just that Philip is no longer a "part" of Kathleen's life but that this isn't quite Kathleen, either. A "member" of her has been amputated. The personality inheritance of an era in their history takes on an aura of death.

To be one flesh with another person, in Paul's spiritual sense, is to see that person, quite naturally and without effort, as an extension of oneself. We rarely see this in marriages. It is far more common to see mutual tolerators and coping cohabitors and — moving toward the less humane — competitors, adversaries, enemies. But every now and then we do see a couple who seem to have become one flesh.

A Scene from Married Life: Three Versions

To get a clearer view of these three conceptions of marriage, let's take an episode common to the lives of many couples and see how it would look in each kind of marriage. The partners have different desires regarding a vacation trip. Bob's idea of the perfect vacation is three weeks in Toronto: one week attending a philosophy seminar, one week doing research at the Pontifical Institute, and one week visiting intellectual friends. Elizabeth has a different idea: a week and a half spent in Toronto shopping, visiting art galleries, and drinking coffee in the sidewalk cafés, and a week and a half at the lake, lying on the beach.

Self-Realization

Because of the demands of their jobs, Bob and Elizabeth don't see much of each other during the normal course of their lives, and so they are hoping that this vacation might be an opportunity to "renew acquaintance." As it becomes clear that they have different notions of what kind of vacation would be fulfilling, they begin to see that if they take their vacation *together,* one or the other will be "stifled." They are sorry to recognize this, but at least their preferences overlap for a week and a half in Toronto, so that during that time they can be "together" — which is to say, in the same city! During the day she goes to the galleries while he is at the seminar or doing research, and at night they sleep together. During the other week and a half they go their separate ways: she leaves for the beach while he remains in Toronto. At the end of the three weeks, they meet and drive home together.

Contract

Bob and Elizabeth are committed to taking their vacation together — not just to sleeping in the same hotel room after all-day separation. Their different interests pose a problem, but they are willing to "compromise," to give and take, to "sacrifice" for one another and for the marriage. Bob doesn't feel that he will be "stifled" if his vacation lacks full intellectual stimulation, and Elizabeth doesn't resent too much a loss of self-fulfillment in spending less time than she would like in the art galleries and cafés and at the beach. Over the years they have learned to resign somewhat their private preferences, thinking first of the marriage and its duties. So they compromise. Elizabeth attends the seminar, knitting on the sideline. Saturdays are spent at the beach, with Elizabeth's face toward the sun and Bob's in some dusty tome under the umbrella. They do some café-hopping: Bob converses with his intellectual friends while Elizabeth mostly watches the weirdos on the street, undistracted by the talk of politics and theology that drifts past her. On Tuesdays, when admission is free, they go to the galleries, where Bob brouses dutifully, gritting his teeth only a little, his soul listing gently toward the hope of closing time.

One Flesh

Like the Bob and Elizabeth of the contract version, this couple are bent on taking their vacation together, and they connect this commitment with remembering their vows. But their notion of "together" is richer. Being together doesn't just mean spending time in the same physical vicinity. Ideally it means *sharing* activities that are characteristic of each of them in their *individualities*. (Contrary to what the self-realizer might say about Christian marriage, the one-flesh model does not weaken the individuality of the partners.) It means getting significantly into each other's lives. It means embedding their bond in the larger common bond of the kingdom of God, and thinking of the diversity of their activities as under the impetus and limiting of Christ's will. Bob's efforts at being together with Elizabeth involve trying to see her not just as an individual with some needs to be met but as a child of God who in a *very* special way is an extension of himself. So if she likes galleries and cafés, he seriously tries to "get into" going to galleries and cafés. He seeks to learn art history from Elizabeth, and he uses the time they spend in cafés to reminisce about their European vacation of five years ago. He does this for her sake, but the more she becomes an extension of himself, the more he does it for *their* sake. Similarly, in Elizabeth's efforts at being "together" with him she is not just trying to resign herself to his love of intellectual pursuits and altruistically give him room to engage in them. She wants to engage his world a bit, to see things from his perspective, to see and hear with *common* eyes and ears, to share his interests, joys, and concerns. She tries to get to know Bob's friends, and to enter, as she can, into their discussions.

Marital Self-Realization

Becoming one flesh doesn't happen on the wedding day (or night), nor is the process very likely ever to be complete. It is a *calling* of Christian couples, a destination toward which they ever travel. Even in the best marriages it remains a challenge and a goal that requires creative efforts. How can those of us who are on the way foster our growth as couples, a growth that makes the promises superfluous because it achieves their intention so perfectly? Let me end with a few comments on a Christian psychology of marriage based on Ephesians 5:21.

Paul says, "Be subject to one another out of reverence for Christ." Subjection to one another can take many forms: learning from one another, honoring the other's desires even when they conflict with your individual preferences, working alongside the other in an apprentice capacity, yielding place to your partner in social settings. But in all cases this subjection bonds the couple together only if it is a spiritual subjection, an *honoring* of the other in his or her individuality, with time spent, attention given, and efforts made to understand and enjoy. It is an exercise of humility in which one sets oneself aside for the moment and becomes absorbed in the activities, interests, and abilities of one's spouse.

For a fully mature bond, this subjection must be mutual — to one another, as Paul says. Thus you learn together and your capacities and activities intermesh so as to make a co-unity, a single working, playing, thinking, feeling unit which in the deepest sense is a *couple* — that is, two persons who have been coupled by this growing common history. Repeated acts of humility to one another have a powerful bonding effect over the years.

Paul says this subjection to one another is to be "out of reverence for Christ." The subjection of wife to husband or of husband to wife is not to be absolute. Absolute subjection is only to Christ; subjection to one another is always a relative thing, qualified by the integrity of both members of the couple in his and her absolute subjection to Christ. One is not to enter into the other's life in any way that is inconsistent with Christ's will. So Ravinia and Bosco Vogelgehirn can never qualify as realizing the one-flesh ideal of Christianity as long as their goal is to one-up Bonnie and Clyde — no matter how perfectly they are united in this goal. The communion of one flesh is nested in the communion of the church whose head is Jesus; the friendship of husband and wife is "qualified" by the friendship that each has with God. And this means that the new marriage self that emerges over the years as one member submits to the other out of reverence for Christ will be a self that "belongs" in the church. Its activities and concerns will be shaped and styled by their larger context, which is the kingdom of Christ. Since the "self" that is formed around a common envy and an invidious pride tends to destroy the church, disrupting the communion of saints, it is in the larger picture a pitiful and sickly thing. If such a couple are one flesh, the flesh in question is diseased, according to the diagnosis of a Christian psychology.

In the psychology of Ivan Nagy that we looked at in Chapter Five, we discovered an emphasis quite congruent with Christian psychology: his idea that we are "ontologically related" to some others, and that our psychological well-being thus depends on our being rightly related to them. In this respect Nagy's psychology is vastly superior to the individualist psychologies of Rogers and Ellis and Jung. But we noted that Nagy makes the primary context of ontological relatedness the intergenerational family, and that Christians must reject this idea and affirm that the primary ontological relationship is to God himself. Other intimate relationships, such as those with our spouses, our parents, and our children, must be set in the larger context of our place in God's kingdom. It will be distinctive of Christian psychotherapy that our mental health is grounded ultimately in our friendship with God and our membership in his church. The marital therapist, for example, will work to promote oneness of flesh in couples that he counsels, but he will not lose sight of the fact that each counselee's ultimate identity is that of child of God, and it is that relationship which must ultimately be set right.

Even in secular marriages we sometimes see the powerful bonding effect of a couple's having some common goal that is beyond the narrow context of the marriage — a political cause, a project of art, a business. Christians have such a "common cause" — the greatest and most perfect that can ever be — built into their marriages. As the Christian Reformed form for the solemnization of marriage says, "The purpose of marriage is the propagation of the human race, the furtherance of the kingdom of God, and the enrichment of the lives of those entering this estate." The focus of this chapter has been "the enrichment of the lives" of husband and wife. According to a Christian psychology, that enrichment will be completely healthy only if the marriage communion is nested in the communion of those seeking God's kingdom.

The Bible's vivid metaphor for the marriage bond, that the two become "one flesh," ought to be the guiding idea for our thinking about marriage. Our selves can be significantly brought to realization in and through this intimate human bond. The vows are in the service of this "self-realization" and are really a promise to pursue the "one flesh" goal with all seriousness and concentration. Ideally, the marriage reaches a state of maturity in which *the promises are no longer binding,* not because what is promised ceases to be incumbent on the couple but because their union is so complete — their marriage self is so fully realized — that the promises, as bindings, fall down loose around them.

CHAPTER TWELVE

Children: Who Needs Them?

A Distraction from the Business of Life?

You only have to be an adult to know how annoying children can be. They cause a lot of noise pollution, make inconvenient demands and sticky doorknobs, break into adult conversations with irrelevancies, and require an inordinate amount of attention and care for their upkeep. At a barbecue once the small children were laughing noisily, crying when hurt, darting here and there, and generally making a hilarious nuisance of themselves among the adults who were trying to talk. A friend who was then single said to me with disgust, "Boy, am I glad I don't have any children." Most of us would be less frank, I suppose, and wouldn't put the matter so categorically. But I think Ted speaks for us all at certain moments. No wonder, then, that in this age of scientific birth control and easy abortions, some couples who are serious about their careers and getting the most out of life decide against having children.

It seems that children in first-century Palestine were not very different from our own. At least the disciples seem to have thought it disruptive to Jesus' ministry to have parents bringing their little children to him so that he might touch and bless them. I can imagine Peter and Andrew thinking to themselves, "It's hard enough for Jesus to teach and be understood without having children around. And who are children, anyway, that Jesus should be required to spend his precious time with them? We're trying to get a message out, a message that the children can't understand. (We can hardly understand it ourselves.)" So the disciples spoke rather harshly to those parents and told them to get the children out of Jesus' way. But Jesus was angry with the disciples (once again, they seem to have missed something about the kingdom of God), and he told them not to hinder the children's coming. And he took them in his arms and touched and blessed them. And then he commended the children as our teachers in two ways: he said that we have to be *like* children if we are to be fit for the kingdom of God, and that *receiving* children in his name is an especially appropriate way to receive God. I wonder whether mulling over these claims might give us some insights into issues of maturity and mental health. What can children teach us about being human, about being fully functioning persons, and about what we can do to grow toward that ideal?

Ideas about childhood and children are of course central in much psychological thinking in this century. Psychoanalysis stresses the importance of childhood experiences in shaping our adult character. Transactional analysis (TA) challenges us to give our Child its due: our Child (free or adapted), our Parent (critical or nurturing), and our Adult are three ego states that need to be mutually balanced to make a properly functioning personality. We have seen that Carl Rogers idealizes infancy with its absence of conditions of worth; he believes that the infant hearkens unerringly and without inhibition to the organismic valuing process. In the recent literature on codependency, the codependent is often pictured as a person who has become too much of an adult or a parent and has got out of touch with the "child" that dwells within him or her. We will interact with some of these ideas in this chapter, especially the idea of codependency, but our main agenda is to see what the biblical concept of the child might contribute to a Christian psychology.

Having children signals a change in your life from

which you will never wholly recover. Initially it's a change from being footloose to being able to go out only rarely (and then only with the hassles of finding a decent babysitter), and of having your "free" time at home reduced to that evasive hiatus between the moment you get the last child cajoled, pajamaed, storied, peed, tucked in, kissed, watered, and prayed with, and the time, forty-five minutes later, when you flop exhausted on your bed and sink into that similitude of death from which you will not rise until the wails from the crib commence at about 2 A.M. Yes, if you've been used to spur-of-the-moment outings for pizza, visits with friends, and trips to the hardware store, there's no doubt that having children announces a stunning change in your life.

To one degree or another, this change is both inevitable and obvious to everybody. But another kind of change that children can bring on is not inevitable and not so obvious. It is a kind of spiritual growth that, if it occurs (and it doesn't always occur), is a blessed by-product of parenthood, a debt of deepened humanity that parents owe to God for the privilege of being given children to rear.

Jesus dares to commend to us the lilies of the field and the birds of the air as spiritual teachers. They are there, for those who have eyes to see, as reminders of truths that often evade us. Like the lilies and the birds, children do not force their lessons on us; witness the fact that so many of us fail to learn from them. And yet they are not like books of wisdom that sit silently on the shelf waiting — maybe for years and then finally in vain — to be opened. Nor are they like lilies that present themselves only during one season of the year and then perhaps only if we go out for a walk, or like the birds in our trees whose songs we so easily ignore. With children in your house, you have books that climb down off the shelves, jump into your lap, and demand to be read every day, every hour, and every minute. It is like having lilies and birds that sit at your table and interrogate you year-round about your soul.

The avoidance of children, so greatly facilitated by birth control, abortion, and day-care centers, is not the unmixed blessing that some take it to be. Indeed, as a basic outlook and policy, it is a curse wrapped in the false cloak of freedom. Some couples, after falling into spiritual laxity, have run back to the bosom of the church after having children. Children have the power to transform us in a variety of ways. They enhance our sense of vulnerability, and so they may incline us toward greater dependence on God. Knowing that in our children our stake in the well-being of this planet extends beyond the years of our own life may provoke a greater sense of responsibility about the environment. And of course, child rearing is an excellent school for learning virtues like patience and self-control. But right now I want to dwell on just four of the many ways that children's presence among us can be a force for deepening our spirituality, establishing our mental health, transforming our vision, and fitting us for God's kingdom. Children can remind us of our kinship with every human being, calling us to acts of self-sacrifice, self-denial, and self-emptying such as are essential to our development as persons; they can put us in touch with the child that is in each of us; they can call us back from cynicism to a childlike demand for perfection; and they can impress upon us a healthy intergenerational consciousness and catalyze our relationship to the eternal.

Of course I am not saying that any of these moves toward psychological health comes automatically with having children or is impossible for people without children. Obviously, children can be abused, not only as children but also as teachers; and those who are open to being taught can learn humanity from other people's children, or even (though it is difficult, I think) in the absence of children.

Children as a Reminder of Our Ontological Relatedness

One reason we flee the company of children is the pursuit of achievement — getting important things done, building careers and businesses, writing books, and gaining powers social and intellectual. If you let children become a serious part of your life, they inevitably slow you down, and quite a few parents these days slight their children because they aren't willing to slacken their pace. But Christians know that the pursuit of "goals" and "results" is at best of secondary importance and at worst the formula for losing what is most precious in life. You may in fact gain the world — or at least an impressive little chunk of it — but in terms of a Christian psychology, the cost may be loss of your self, your soul, your "psyche," your "mental health." This is true not just for what we normally think of as "worldly" pursuits but also for some "spiritual" ones. The apostle Paul, thinking of church-related powers and achievements, even some enormously heroic ones, warns against their potential emptiness:

> If I speak in the tongues . . . of angels, but have not love, I am a noisy gong or a clanging cymbal. And if I have prophetic powers, and understand all mysteries and all knowedge, and if I have all faith, so as to remove mountains, but have not love, I am nothing. If I give away all I have, and if I deliver my body to be burned, but have not love, I gain nothing. (1 Cor. 13:1-3)

If spiritual emptiness and loss of self are possible for the most eloquent evangelists and preachers of the gospel, and for Christian prophets and miracle workers and martyrs, how much more for people who give themselves without reservation to money making, intellectual brilliance, medical and political careers, fame, and influence? And being a *Christian* business person or politician is no guarantee against the danger. As Paul makes abundantly clear, even if these activities are pursued in a Christian context and for Christian goals, the danger remains. We seem to have here a principle of Christian psychology: that "love" of a certain sort is needed to integrate the self, to give a person the kind of identity that alone makes for full functioning. A person who lacks this love is "nothing," or "gains nothing" despite all his achievements.

Living with a three-year-old makes it harder for a parent to fall into thinking of life as the pursuit of one or another achievement. I don't deny that some parents value their children for their achievements and even think of their children as their own achievements. (I've seen some pretty crazy things at Little League baseball games; and SAT scores, both high and low, bring out the worst in many parents.) But there is something about the vulnerability of a young child and her identification with her parent that makes it seem unnatural and perverse to value her as an achievement or for her achievements. Most natural is for the daddy to cherish the child and desire her well-being not for the sake of any goal beyond her, but simply for her own sake. And when he looks into her eyes, centers down into her presence, and converses with her, his own achievement mentality fades into the background, a better self emerges, and life is focused in something more like God's perspective. In the presence of this child, in the contemplation of her, in which he sees this other person as intrinsically precious, the parent momentarily becomes "something" — somebody, a substantial, genuine self — the opposite of the inflated "nothing" to which the apostle refers.

Frederick Buechner makes this point about the Christian concept of selfhood when he says, speaking of his mother,

> She never developed the giving, loving side of what she might have been as a human being, and, needless to say, that was where the real suffering came — the two failed marriages after the death of my father, the fact that among all the friends she had over the course of her life, she never as far as I know had one whom she would in any sense have

sacrificed herself for and by doing so might perhaps have begun to find her best and truest self.[1]

Self-sacrifice and being a person disposed to sacrifice oneself are not regarded as healthy in most of our modern psychologies, and a resistance to sacrificing oneself is not thought of as a plausible diagnosis of psychological dysfunction. But here Buechner, speaking out of a Christian view of persons, holds up this "love" — which I am suggesting we can learn through having children — as a condition of true selfhood. And he explains some of his mother's deepest psychological problems by her lack of this loving disposition. Some pages later he sheds further light on the matter:

> We were just about to have a pleasant dinner together when a friend of mine telephoned to say that his family had been in an awful accident and to ask if I would come wait with him at the airport where he was to catch a plane to where the accident had happened. My mother was furious. She said I was a fool to think of ruining our evening together for such a ridiculous reason as that, and for a moment I was horrified to find myself thinking that maybe she was right. Then the next moment I saw more clearly than I ever had before that it is on just such outwardly trivial decisions as this — should I go or should I stay — that human souls are saved or lost. I also saw for what was maybe the first time in my life that we are called to love our neighbors not just for our neighbors' sake but for our own sake, and that when John wrote, "He who does not love remains in death" (1 John 3:14), he was stating a fact of nature as incontrovertible as gravity.[2]

Most demands that our children make on us to put their interests before our own are less dramatic than that of Buechner's friend. But they are no less important, and they

---

1. Buechner, *Telling Secrets* (San Francisco: HarperCollins, 1991), p. 15.
2. Ibid., p. 49.

are a lot more frequent. And I am saying that in the "outwardly trivial decisions" we make in response to the opportunities that our children offer us for self-transcendence, a significant part of our adult development in humanity is achieved or lost.

We are sometimes told that Christian love is not a matter of liking people; after all, we are called upon to love "neighbors" with whom we have no natural ties of affection, and even enemies. And so we get a picture of Christian love as a kind of gritting our teeth and doing our cold duty toward people who mean nothing, or less than nothing, to us. We are supposed to love without having our hearts in it, and if we care too much about people, some may even suspect that our love is not genuinely Christian. But this picture is false to the New Testament. Jesus is said to have had compassion on a mixed crowd (Mark 6:34) and on a leper whom he presumably did not know (Mark 1:41). His demeanor toward people in general was one of affection, not that of a man doing his cold duty. And the apostle Paul tells us to be "tenderhearted" to one another (Eph. 4:32).

Few are the places in life where being tenderhearted is as naturally powerful in us as in our role as parents. The psalmist, wanting to describe God's compassion for his people, chooses the familial image: "As a father pities his children . . ." (103:13). In the New Testament no writing is more tender than the First Letter of John, infused as it is with the affection this old man feels for his disciples. Nor is it accidental that he repeatedly calls them "my children." It is as though John's family life has given him a way of "seeing," an emotional matrix through which to perceive his friends. We take a natural joy in the well-being of our children and feel a natural sorrow in their troubles. Here, if anywhere in life, we feel that organic connection with other human beings in which we suffer when they suffer and rejoice when they rejoice (1 Cor. 12:26). The Christian's relation to his children is an educational advantage for coming to see his ontological connections to others who are not biologically related to him, but are still ontologically related to him in their common relation to God.

These facts suggest a spiritual exercise. Let's say that you come into contact with a morally disreputable person, a selfish, callous, and deceitful person — you who are a parent. He is not a person toward whom you are naturally disposed to be "tenderhearted," but in Christ you are called to love him. The exercise is this. Contemplate him — that is, look at him, listen to him, or just think about him — with your child's help. Thinking of your own child, remember that this man was once a child, one who desired above all else acceptance, security, the warmth of affection. Look at him now, but picture him as the age of your own little one. (Is this anything like "receiving" a child in Jesus' command in Mark 10:15?) In doing so, you will see through the calluses to that central core of personality around which so much thorny growth has accumulated. You will see beyond the cruelty and ruthless ambition to the essential human passion of which it is so ugly a perversion — the passion for acceptance and love, for an identity of his own. You will feel a certain tenderheartedness — of your human kinship with even this person — when you remember where this man has come from: from a childhood which was in essential ways like the one in which your little boy is now sojourning.

It seems to me that this perception of connectedness to other human beings and the sense that they are like children will be central to any Christian psychology. A chief aim of Christian psychotherapy will be to foster an awareness of connection to others — in friendship, parenthood, filiality — so that the individual lives beyond the confines of his own psyche, as it were, ready to sacrifice his own interests, achievements, self-cultivation, and prominence for the sake of the other. For in such "loss of self" — in such love — is to be found, according to Christian teaching, the truest selfhood.

Getting in Touch with Your Inner Child

In this book I haven't addressed the shortest-term fads in psychology and psychobabble. I have tried, instead, to examine some psychologies that have lasted a while or seem to have the promise of doing so, because these are the ones most likely to make stimulating discussion partners in our efforts to articulate a Christian psychology for our day. Besides, the flashy fads tend to be little more than hyped variations on the themes of the major reigning psychologies. But I do want to mention *codependence*, which is very much a buzzword at the time of writing this book. It is a mark of a buzzword that it buzzes more than expresses any definite idea, and I definitely get the idea that *codependence* sometimes functions as a catchall for whatever it is that ails you. For example, A. W. Schaef has defined codependence as "a *disease* that has many forms and expressions and that grows out of a disease process that . . . I call the *addictive process*. The addictive process is an unhealthy and abnormal disease process, whose assumptions, beliefs, behaviors, and lack of spirituality lead to a process of nonliving that is progressively death-oriented."[3] But originally the word had a more determinate sense. It is part of an effort to understand why alcoholics and other compulsives become the way they are and tend to stay that way.

The codependent is a person who needs to be needed and so behaves in ways that tend to keep the needy needy. The codependent tends to lack a strong, independent self and to feel better about herself if she is "helping" somebody who is also weak and confused. If the needy one is an alcoholic, the codependent may shield him from the painful consequences of his alcoholism — lie to his friends when he's drunk, do what she can to keep him from being booked on drunk driving charges, hide his bottles, take responsibility for his drunkenness, speak

---

3. Schaef, *Co-dependence: Misunderstood — Mistreated* (Minneapolis: Harper/Winston, 1986), p. 21.

for him when he can't (and maybe when he can) speak for himself, and generally "take care" of him, thus ensuring that he stays an alcoholic and remains dependent on her. (The word *codependence* makes sense: the codependent *also* depends on the alcohol.) If the needy one is anorexic, the codependent one will nag her to eat, weigh her, plead with her, watch her eating with an eagle eye, and let her know that his world will come to an end if she doesn't eat. And of course all this attention and pressure is just what anorexia thrives on. Codependents also function as "helpers" or "enablers" to gamblers, depressives, and other people who are not doing very well. Codependency is sometimes evident in teachers, who take so much satisfaction in being needed by their students that they encourage fawning discipleship and discourage independent thinking. Although codependents get satisfaction from "caring" for misfits, they are, all things considered, miserable: they don't understand themselves or their dependents, their "help" is really part of the problem, and they meet mostly with abuse and ingratitude. They typically feel guilty, depressed, and angry.

The patterns of codependency can be construed as a sort of misguided and misapplied parenting: the codependent plays the parent to his dependent, even if his dependent is his spouse or his parent. And some parents do exhibit something resembling codependency in the desperate satisfaction they get from controlling their children's lives and living vicariously and parasitically through them. They want to keep their children dependent, and have a terrible time letting them go.

Some therapists for whom codependency is a leading diagnostic concept make it a primary goal of therapy that the client stop being a "parent" and become a "child" again — that he discover or get in touch with "the child within." Indeed, reminiscent of Carl Rogers's thought, the child within is sometimes identified with the true self: the child becomes a model of maturity and mental health for the adult. These therapists suggest that codependent people need to become self-indulgent, concerned about their *own* well-being, in touch with their own

needs, spontaneous, and self-accepting like little children —
that they need to stop diverting and distorting their own needs
through the byway of "caretaking."

Codependency is no doubt an unhealthy pattern of attitudes and interaction, but the philosophy of life that often goes
with this diagnosis is, I'm afraid, usually the narcissistic put-
yourself-first one that we discovered in Rogers and Ellis. In one
self-help book, the codependent is told repeatedly to take care
of himself, put himself first, and give himself what he needs.
Ultimately this is supposed to enable the client to love others
more maturely, and maybe it can where something like vestigial Christianity is still shaping the self-understanding. But
the positive teaching seems to be an individualist philosophy
of live and let live: "Self-care is an attitude of mutual respect.
It means learning to live our lives responsibly. It means allowing others to live their lives as they choose, as long as they
don't interfere with our decisions to live as we choose."[4] Little
effort is made to teach *proper* self-sacrifice, communal mutuality, proper caring, and helpfulness — to teach positively what
it is to be a self so integrated that it can be genuinely for others.
Melody Beattie models the healthy attitude by placing the
following words at the beginning of the book: "This book is
dedicated to me." This does remind us of children: they're
forever saying things like, "Look at me!" "Me first!" and "Can
I have one?" But I doubt that this is what Jesus had in mind
when he said that we must become like little children before
we are fit for the kingdom of God. What did he mean? In what
sense is the child a paradigm of mental health in Christian
psychology? Does Christianity also affirm something like "the
child within" each of us that needs to be nurtured?

One day Jesus and his disciples walked to Capernaum. At
the end of the journey he asked what they had been discussing
on the road. They were embarrassed to say, but it came out that

---

4. Beattie, *Codependent No More* (San Francisco: Harper/Hazelden,
1987), p. 105.

they'd been discussing who among them was the greatest — a childish thing to do. In response, Jesus said to them, "If any one would be first, he must be last of all and servant of all." Next he took a child in his arms and said to them, "Whoever receives one such child in my name receives me; and whoever receives me, receives not me but him who sent me" (Mark 9:35, 37).

The issue to which Jesus makes the child speak is that of self-importance and the obstacle which that creates to having the proper and healthy attachment to Jesus. We have seen again and again in these pages that a Christian psychology is a relational one in which you become an articulated, self-delineated, and autonomous individual self by giving yourself to others — first to God and second to the neighbor. And Jesus is pointing out in this passage that if you are concerned with being important in a certain way — in particular, *more* powerful, *more* privileged, *more* prominent than some others — you won't be able to give yourself to God. Accordingly, the concern with this kind of importance stunts your growth, prevents you from being all you can be, keeps you from being psychologically healthy. The significance of the child in the biblical story is that he is out of the running in the contest for importance. This is perfectly obvious to the disciples, who in the next chapter of Mark's Gospel turn away the parents who bring their children to Jesus for touching and blessing (10:13-16). The child, as one who has no claim to importance himself, provides the perfect test of emotional maturity, one the disciples fail: see if you can receive *him* in Jesus' name.

The codependent might "receive" the child and do so without concern for social status (exactly), and yet it is clear that codependent "receiving" is far from what Jesus has in mind as fitting disciples for the kingdom. For the typical codependent[5] is "using" the person he helps rather than

---

5. I don't deny that there may be a more purely behavioral form of codependency in which the motivational structure of the "need to be needed" that I am taking to be typical of codependency is less pronounced.

loving her for her own sake. This is evident in the codependent's inability to let the child go when the proper time comes, even when it is patently obvious that the child needs to go. From the Christian point of view, this is the most saliently pathological thing about codependency: the codependent is not self-possessed enough to be able to love, to give himself to God and neighbor. His "love" turns into something clinging, parasitic, and mutually destructive because he is concerned — for the most part unconsciously, no doubt — to satisfy his own unmet needs.

Let us return to our question: In what sense is the child a paradigm of mental health in Christian psychology? The answer seems to be that it is chiefly in her humble condition, in her being out of the competition for social status, in her having no claim to comparative greatness. We must not take Jesus to be speaking of the child's own *attitudes* toward competition. A little experience with children indicates that they are as competitive, within their own sphere, as their adult counterparts — and more frankly so: they have less false humility. But Jesus is not referring to children's humility in an attitudinal sense. He is referring to their public status. They have no objective claim to greatness because they have no achievements to point to, no social roles that give them importance, as adults do. So when Jesus says we must become as little children if we are to be mature, he is really calling us to be *adult* children — or, more fully, adult children of God. We are to assimilate into our attitudes, in a way not characteristic of children (see 1 Cor. 13:11-13; Heb. 5:11-14), the recognition that before God, and before all our neighbors as God's children, we have no claim to superiority or special status. When our character embodies that truth, then we can love God with all our heart and our neighbors as ourselves; then we are fit for the kingdom in which such relationships are actualized. We can help others with a self-forgetfulness quite the opposite of the self-concern typical of the codependent.

In a Christian psychology we are children, and the child in us is to be brought out as we mature in the faith, but the child is conceived quite differently than in the "child within" literature. Here we have a child that needs discipline and reproof, a child that is brought out by love, all right, but is certainly not just a spontaneous upwelling of something that is naturally in us and only calling to be released. To be a child of God is to love God with something like the wholehearted trust and devotion with which a little child "loves" his human parents. But the analogy is far from perfect: Here is a child that needs not just to be liberated or allowed to express itself but to be formed by a kind of suffering and discipline to which no reasonable adult would subject a real child. If we are to become adult children of God, the birth of the child in us is a rebirth that requires first a kind of death — the death of the immature, self-important, self-concerned "adult."

What approach might a Christian psychotherapy take toward the desperate, clinging, hungry, controlling self-sacrificers called codependents? I must warn the reader again that I am no clinician, and that my answer to such questions remains tentative and speculative. With that warning I offer the following thoughts.

The Christian diagnosis of codependency will differ from that typical in the literature. On the level of behavior, what is most salient to us is not that the codependent fails to take care of herself, but that she takes care of her dependent so poorly that her behavior ends up being mutually destructive rather than helpful. Thus therapy will aim to teach her more genuinely helpful behaviors and to do so in a cognitive context that emphasizes the relationship and being helpful rather than the codependent's "needs." We can imagine, for example, a kind of behavior therapy in which the client is affirmed for her concern to help and then trained in healthier patterns of interaction with her "dependent" — patterns aimed at giving him the kind of freedom he needs to kick his dependency. It is true that the codependent's own real needs will be better met once she becomes truly helpful, truly mutual, truly respectful of the other's freedom and responsibility; but the client can easily be given a false conception of maturity if the therapist stresses, as most of the codependency literature does, the client's looking out for her own needs. (Obviously, if she is neglecting her basic needs, it would be good to encourage some attention to this.) On the level of motivation, the Christian diagnosis will likely be that the codependent helps out of a pathological need to be needed rather than out of genuine concern for the one she "helps." To use Kohut's language, she has a narcissistic behavior or personality disorder, a weak or fragmented self. A Christian psychoanalytic exploration and reconstruction of the self might also be prescribed, a process in which the client's narcissistic needs are met through the transference. Transmuting internalization would help to insure that the client's self becomes autonomous rather than remaining simply parasitic on the therapist as self object. Inducing the client to credit family members would bring about further delineation of the self, and would do so in a context which would make clear that the self is defined in community with other selves, even alcoholic ones. After all, in crediting others for their contributions, the client concretely articulates for herself that she is not responsible for *all* the good that gets done! All of this would be pursued in some connection with specific but judicious articulation, often in prayer, of the Christian Word about God and his kingdom.

Such a course of therapy might be thought of as partially actualizing the child within, the true self, the adult child of God that sleeps as potential in the heart of every human being.

The Passion of the Infinite

When our youngest daughter was about two, Elizabeth had to go to Ontario for a few days to be with her ailing father, leaving me alone with the children. During her mother's absence, Maria never cried for her, and I'm not sure that she even asked about her. But when someone would come through the front door, Maria would look eagerly and then, when it was not Elizabeth, she would get gloomy. And after a couple of days of that she became distant, didn't talk much, and seemed generally depressed. On a couple of evenings she vomited for no apparent reason. When Elizabeth came home, Maria's spirit returned. She became vivacious, started chattering, and did not vomit again.

Christian psychology is Augustinian in affirming that our hearts are "restless" until they "rest" in God. We were made to "praise" God, to honor and trust him, to find our joy in him, to admire his beauty and holiness and power, and to serve him. Unless we live in his presence, we will not function as we were designed to do; we will be subject to anxiety, depression, a sense of emptiness, and poor relationships with our fellow human beings. We are all children, then, children who tolerate poorly being outside the presence of our heavenly Parent. In Chapter Seven I noted that Heinz Kohut inadvertently provides a way of understanding Augustine's point. For he sees in the young child a demand for a "perfect idealized self object" — that is, a parent who is perfectly good and perfectly powerful. In Kohut's view, however, this demand is "infantile," meaning that it's a demand that must be given up if we are to become mature. People who hold onto this demand into adulthood are those who have not become properly resigned to the fact that there *is no* perfect idealized self object. But as Augustinian psychologists we know that God is this perfect self object; by loving him and being loved by him, we become selves. We know that the restless yearning to find him is not a sign of immaturity but a light shining through the defenses that our cynicism and worldly resignation have built up. It is a cry, from our psychic child, for God and his kingdom. So Kohut gives us another angle on Jesus' saying, "Whoever does not receive the kingdom of God like a child shall not enter it" (Mark 10:15). This "infantile" passion of the infinite is not something to be transcended, outgrown, or put aside as we mature, but a human potential to be realized in our relationship with God. In Christian psychology it is one of the most distinctive marks of our humanity. To stifle or deny it by getting "down to earth" and realizing that all self objects are imperfect is to sell ourselves short and do ourselves basic psychological damage.

Issues of Immortality

Several years ago we took our annual Christmas trip to Wichita to visit my parents. My 78-year-old father renewed his acquaintance with my one-year-old daughter. The human distance between these two close relatives was striking: the fresh, soft-skinned young one, plump as a transparent grape, just starting out in life; and my father, the raisin, with so many years behind him — "many years" by a certain myopic human way of reckoning things, that is. In a short time, as the history of the world goes, my little daughter will herself be an old woman, bouncing a beaming baby upon her knee. "A generation goes, and a generation comes, but the earth remains for ever" (Eccles. 1:4).

With the thinning of the ozone layer and the destruction of the rain forests we are less certain than the Preacher that the earth will remain "forever." But that the generations pass away — of that there is no doubt. And the coming of the new generation, those little bunk dwellers and Hot Wheels riders who soon will take our place as the "productive members of society," reminds us of our own passing, and also of theirs. In reminding us, they also make the fact more poignant by the beauty of their enthusiasm, their heedless zeal for life, their astonishing aptitude for wisdom and folly, their sheer lovability. To love children is to love life, not like an egoist who cringes in the face of his own annihilation, but like a connoisseur who appreciates the treasure for its intrinsic worth. And so, finally, children can help us learn a right appreciation for the gospel of Jesus Christ, the message of redemption and eternal life.

Without that message, the beauty of children would, by impelling us into cosmic frustration, compel another conclusion: "All things are full of weariness; a man cannot utter it; the eye is not satisfied with seeing, nor the ear filled with hearing. . . . I have seen everything that is done under the sun; and behold, all is vanity and a striving after wind" (Eccles. 1:8, 14). Of course, this conclusion does not really force itself upon us, at least not with the force of perception. Most of the time our psyches protect us, by a natural defense mechanism, from beholding this truth too freshly, from feeling the despair. And so, in the absence of the gospel, we live in a kind of befuddlement in which we are chronically out of touch with our deepest needs.

Clinging to Christ we are not forced, in beholding the unutterable value of life, to conclude that all is vanity, and that creation — at least from our point of view — is a colossal bad joke; or, on the other hand, to live a half-life in which we stifle an important part of ourselves. In Christ the delectable goodness of human life, so vividly exampled in our children, becomes something in which we can take joy without reservation.

CHAPTER THIRTEEN

Welcome to the Kingdom

A few years ago my family and I went to Belgium for an academic sabbatical. We were warned that the Flemish are private and hard to know; we would probably not be invited into anyone's home during our stay. So we resolved to be as friendly as we could from our side, but we braced ourselves for a lonely year in a foreign land.

As it turned out, we were warmly welcomed by a number of families and had several meals in Belgian homes. But one family — Marc and Reinhilde Eneman and their five children — welcomed us in especially remarkable ways. They invited us on day-long outings to see Belgian sights: the royal gardens, a reconstructed historical village, the Ascension Day parade in Bruges. We were asked to Marc's birthday party, at which we met another couple with whom we became friendly, thus extending our circle of Flemish acquaintances. The Enemans packed the twelve of us into their Volvo station wagon and took us on outings of interest to the children. Once a month Marc would deliver heavier grocery items to our door, since we didn't have a car. Soon after we met them, Marc and Reinhilde had said, "Please let us know if there is anything we can do to help you get settled here." And it became abundantly clear that the offer was serious, despite Marc's demanding medical practice and Reinhilde's hectic schedule with a new baby and four other young children.

Hospitality in the Bible

Surprisingly often, Scripture speaks of hospitality. The psalmist envisions God as a generous host at table:

> Thou preparest a table before me
>   in the presence of my enemies;
> thou anointest my head with oil,
>   my cup overflows.

And the psalmist depicts himself as a permanent guest in God's home:

> Surely goodness and mercy shall follow me
>   all the days of my life;
> and I shall dwell in the house of the Lord
>   for ever. (23:5-6)

In the opening verses of John's Gospel, the Lord is depicted initially not as the host but as one *looking* for a welcome, hoping to be received with hospitality. For the most part he is shut out. He knocks at the door of what is really his own home and is turned away: "The true light that enlightens every man was coming into the world. . . . He came to his own home, and his own people received him not" (1:9, 11). But not everyone left him standing at the door, and to those who did welcome him, the humble Guest became the lordly, abundant Host:

> But to all who received him, who believed in his name, he gave power to become children of God. . . . And the Word became flesh and dwelt among us, full of grace and truth. . . . And from his fulness have we all received, grace upon grace. (1:12, 14, 16)

This reversal or mixing of the guest/host roles is found repeatedly in Jesus' ministry. He is the wandering preacher of the coming kingdom, without even a place to lay his head, who depends on the hospitality of the householders he meets along the way. But wherever he is taken in, he somehow becomes the host.

Simon the Pharisee invites Jesus for dinner (though his hospitality leaves something to be desired), but before long Jesus is filling with forgiveness the cup of a sinful woman who comes in, and pouring a bitterer but still-needed drink into Simon's cup (Luke 7:36-50). Mary and Martha have Jesus over, but it turns out that Martha, the compulsive hostess, has the wrong attitude, and Mary, who is willing to sit at Jesus' feet as his guest, is approved (Luke 10:38-42). Zacchaeus entertains Jesus for dinner, but Jesus invites himself, and his very willingness to be Zacchaeus's guest is a grace by which Zacchaeus is welcomed into the kingdom (Luke 19:1-10). On the road to Emmaus, two disciples invite the unrecognized risen Lord to spend the evening with them, but somehow the guest becomes the host: "When he was at table with them, he took the bread and blessed, and broke it, and gave it to them." And in this hostly gesture they recognized him (Luke 24:13-35).

In his letter to the Ephesians, Paul speaks primarily to us Gentiles, us outsiders who were "separated from Christ, alienated from the commonwealth of Israel, and strangers to the covenants of promise" (2:4). And he says,

> God . . . [has] raised us up with him, and made us sit with him in the heavenly places in Christ Jesus, that in the coming ages he might show the immeasurable riches of his grace in kindness toward us in Christ Jesus. . . . And he came and preached peace to you who were far off and peace to those who were near; for through him we both have access in one Spirit to the Father. So then you are no longer strangers and sojourners, but you are fellow citizens with the saints and members of the household of God. (Eph. 2:6-7, 17-19)

We've been taken into God's living space, adopted as members of his family, and by this act of God's hospitality a peace and unity have been established between us and all others who belong to him.

What Is Hospitality?

I have tried to convince you, in earlier chapters of this book, that Christianity has a psychology, a view of what human beings are and what makes them tick and what they are like when they are are maladjusted and what they are like when they are fully functioning. And I've suggested that a Christian psychology is an especially relational one because of the Christian notion of the kingdom of God. With a view to teasing out what Christianity has to say about self and other, we have looked at the relationships of competitors, extended family, offenders and their offended, spouses, and parents and children. In the chapters that remain, we'll look more closely at friends, the God relationship, and church membership. But I think it is significant that in a Christian psychology not only our relationships with others who are close to us but also our relationships with strangers are important to healthy functioning.

What are some marks of hospitality? Hospitality is welcoming into your home territory people who don't belong there — people to whom the territory doesn't belong. We're hospitable when we frequently and gladly invite others into our home. But the others have to be outsiders. When we let our own small children live with us in our home, no one praises our hospitality. After all, it's their home too. We can be generous toward our small children, but not hospitable. Once our children are grown, however, we can be hospitable to them because they have become outsiders in a certain sense.

To be hospitable you must have some territory, at least of a temporary sort. It doesn't have to be much. You can show hospitality in your hotel room. The homeless person who shares his exhaust grate with another is being hospitable, even though our society's laws don't recognize that that grate is his. Whatever territory we preside over, in the Christian perspective it belongs to us only temporarily anyway. We are sojourners on earth and better or worse *stewards* of the territory we occupy. The difference between the homeless person on his grate and the suburbanite with a deed to his "property" is finally a matter of degree. And yet it is our nature to belong somewhere, to need some space that we call our own and distinguish from other people's spaces. It is this space that we open up in hospitality.

Hospitality means providing outsiders with the benefits of one's home territory. A hospitable person shares with outsiders the food and comforts of his home, or perhaps his car, his friends, the beautiful sights of his country. It is a form of generosity, and the more generously he shares these benefits with his guests, the more hospitable he is. In thus freely giving, the hospitable person treats his guests more or less like "members of the family." Someone who runs a bed and breakfast welcomes strangers in and lavishes care on them, and so her sign can advertise "old-time hospitality." She may indeed have a hospitable style and make her guests feel "at home," but she is called hospitable by courtesy; she isn't treating her guests like members of the family because she is selling the benefits of her home.

A difference between generosity and hospitality follows from the fact that hospitality takes *guests*. If I hand a thousand dollars to a homeless person on the street, I may be generous, but to be hospitable I have to take him home. The hospitable person *fellowships* with his beneficiary in a way unnecessary for generosity.

I mentioned that when we are hospitable we treat our guests to some extent as though they were members of the family. It may not matter to the keeper of the bed and breakfast if her "guests" disappear into the morning mist, leaving no other trace than their check, and remain strangers to her forever; but something in true hospitality resists this prospect.

Behind the true host's welcoming behavior, he is warm to the prospect of his guests' becoming something more than strangers — at least friends and, in the extreme case, perhaps even literally members of the family. It was clear that the Enemans were open to — indeed, bent on — our becoming their friends. And we did.

A family that takes in foster children is showing unusual hospitality, which becomes even greater if the family is open to adopting the children permanently. But now a paradox occurs, for at its extreme hospitality's success makes hospitality impossible. If the family does adopt its foster children, then its hospitality self-destructs, since adoption breaks down the distinction between the insiders, whose home territory is shared, and the outsiders, who are invited in. Maybe the goal of all Christian hospitality is to self-destruct into the perfect familial fellowship of the kingdom of God, where the distinction between insiders and outsiders, between those who belong and those who don't, is broken down, and all become insiders — brothers and sisters, fellow citizens with the saints and members of the household of God.

Hospitality is also the greater depending on how strange the stranger is. The Enemans' hospitality was great because we were not only outsiders to their household, like many who lived on their street or worshiped in their parish church. We were stranger than that: we spoke with a funny accent, didn't understand Belgian politics, ate peanut butter and popcorn, and weren't Catholics. Similarly, it is an act of profound hospitality to adopt a child, but it is an act of superhuman hospitality to adopt a retarded or handicapped or disfigured child — one that is truly a "stranger."

Strangers in the Eyes of Hospitality

How do strangers look? You may think this an odd question, and reply, "There is no *way* that strangers look; they have as many appearances as there are kinds of strangers. To see how they look, go to an international airport and wander around for a couple of hours. They may be wearing a turban or a skullcap, have a shaved head with a little ponytail at the back, or green and purple striped hair, rings in their noses or a little red dot on their foreheads; they may look like 350 pounds of jello in a 300-pound bowl, or like those skinny models you see staring out hungry and sexless from the pages of fashion magazines; they may be so gorgeous you can hardly believe they're human, or shiny blue-black like a new bowling ball, or tall and pale with wisps of cool white steam for hair; they may be dirty and old and slow and smell of urine, or riding in a wheelchair pushed by their mother, or lamely limping along, or leaping lively; they may look like atheists or abortionists or homosexuals or New Yorkers."

Thanks for the poetry, but that isn't quite what I had in mind. I was thinking of the way that strangers *in general* look to one or another *kind of eyes.* And the eyes I have in mind are those of the heart. How do strangers look to the eyes of hospitality? Well, the first thing to say is that to the eyes of deep hospitality, the strangeness of strangers is muted by a vision of their common humanity. To hospitality they do look and sound and smell different from oneself in the obvious ways; but they don't look strange in the sense of weird. There's something fundamentally nonalien about them. They look like people with whom one might get along, people who might fit in if you had them over to dinner. Of course, it could be difficult: there might be a language problem, or *they* might not be able to see any common humanity in *you.* They might be spooked by your culture, or outraged that somebody of your station should dare approach them with an invitation. But until they prove otherwise (and perhaps even after they do), they have the look of potential friends. If the hospitality is Christian, this befriendable look is begotten of the belief that for all their obvious strangeness, these are finally not strangers but fellow recipients of God's fatherly concern, fellow sinful travelers on (or off) the way to God's kingdom.

Not everyone has such eyes, or such a heart. Take Molly Mample, for example. To her, strangers look evil, spooky, dangerous, weird, and threatening. They don't look like proper human beings. They have the look, not of potential friends, but of people who would harm her if she let them get too close. In fact, just about the only people who do look like human beings to Molly are clean, well-educated, well-dressed, smooth-shaven, polite white people who don't speak with a foreign accent. If push came to shove, she would admit that these others *are* human (she does believe this). But to her heart they don't *look* so human. They look like outsiders, like people who belong in the outer darkness.

When I was young, over the years my family had a number of dogs and cats, and I was very fond of some of them, but it never occurred to any of us that these animals should be welcomed into our home. The cats lived under the house; the dogs stayed in the back yard and had a doghouse for shelter. These animals were above the chickens and turkeys, which were eaten and not petted. We played with the dogs in the yard, but they weren't part of the family. My eyes, unlike those of many, do not see potential friends in dogs; they look on dogs a little the way the eyes of Molly Mample look on the strange humanity in the international airport. Of course I don't fear most dogs, as Molly fears men in turbans; but dogs don't come across to me like beings one would invite into one's home. They just don't have that look. My heart isn't big enough for hospitality to dogs.

It would no more occur to Molly to share the benefits of her territory with those "weirdos" in the international airport than it would occur to a Klansman to invite a black family to the church picnic. Some would call her hospitable because she entertains friends and family and selected others for dinner; she prides herself on setting a splendid table, and also on the quality of her guests. But a Christian, with God for her standard of hospitality, will make no mistake about it. Unlike Jesus' guests, Molly's guests are only people very much like herself and her family. So small is her heart, and so little in touch with God's, that only these chosen few look like real human beings to her. From a Christian point of view, Molly is relationally "dysfunctional."

A friend of mine has quipped that hospitality is the knack for making people feel at home when you wish they were. The saying is funny partly because feeling that your guests are a bother is precisely the contrary of true hospitality. Connected with seeing the stranger as a potential friend is *hospitality's joy*. The generous person also takes joy in sharing his substance with others, but generosity contains no requirement that he enjoy being *with* his beneficiaries. With our friends we gladly share not only what we have but also our own presence. Because the hospitable person sees outsiders as fellows and potential friends, he takes something like this joy in hosting them. In the early stages of hospitality, the relationship is more friendliness than friendship proper, but friendship is the destination toward which hospitality tends, and so the joys are akin. If you take pleasure in lending out your summer lake home to your friends, but without joining them there, your pleasure is that of generosity but not of hospitality proper. The hospitable person takes joy in the presence of his guests, in acts of providing them, "hands on," with the benefits of his territory.

In one of his parables Jesus speaks of a passionately frustrated host. The table is set and the invited guests are to be brought in to dinner, but the servant returns guestless, saying that for various reasons they cannot come. But so intent is this man on being a host that he tells the servant, "Go out quickly to the streets and lanes of the city, and bring in the poor and maimed and blind and lame." He is ready, and must have guests on whom to lavish the feast. When the servant has gathered the unfortunate of the town and there is still room at table, the host says, "Go out to the highways and hedges, and compel people to come in, that my house may be filled" (Luke 14:15-24). Like this prodigal host, God wants a full complement of guests, that his joy, like his house, may be full. If we are his children, formed in his likeness by his Spirit which dwells in us — that is, if we are fully functioning human beings — we will see potential guests, befriendable ones, in the varied faces of many strangers.

Motives for Hospitality

I've already mentioned that a profit motive isn't compatible with true hospitality, and that the genuinely hospitable person is open to a deeper relationship with his guest, one in which the guest becomes less an outsider. Thus we might examine our motivation by asking ourselves this question: Why do we invite outsiders in to share the benefits of our home territory?

Some of the answers are not very flattering. We may like the glory that comes from throwing lavish parties with important outsiders as guests. Or we may like to show off our houses; we get invidious pleasure from a sense of superiority. (So we don't invite only fancy people; sometimes we get a kick out of inviting people just below our station in life, because they are *really* impressed.) What often passes for hospitality is not the real thing; it should spring from a spirit of humble generosity, but it sprouts instead from a spirit of pride.

I have in mind people whose "hospitality" is driven by a concern to make an impression. They want a guest to have a good time, but not so much for the guest's sake as for their own sake, because they want the guest to leave with a certain impression. They are less concerned with the mutual enjoyment of one another's company than with a certain effect that the interaction is calculated to have on the guest. The metaphor of making an impression is worth thinking about. One makes an impression *on somebody* and *with something*, and one makes an impression *of something*. The guest is the one on *whom* the impression is made, and the impression is made

with one's home territory; but what is the impression *of?* It is
of oneself. It is as though each of us has a stamp — made of
metal or plastic — with our picture or name on it. It has hard
edges, so that if we press it firmly into someone's flesh, it
leaves an impression. And we go about trying to press it against
people hard enough and long enough to make our mark. The
more impressive we are, the more people there are with our
stamp on them. I like to see and think about such people
because in looking at them I see my own importance, as though
my name were written on them, or a little portrait of me were
imprinted on their foreheads. Of course there's no literal "impression" that we leave on people's flesh, yet we can see it in
their eyes, can hear it in their comments. Unmistakable little
reflections of our glory in their eyes and voices. They admire
us, or envy us, or consider us to be as important as themselves.
And if our "hospitality" is driven by the concern to make an
impression, then our home territory and its benefits become
a lever by which we apply the pressure of our image upon
them.

Guests as Hosts

I must admit that the intense welcome we got from the
Enemans set the wheels turning in my ungracious head: Why
are they doing this? What do they stand to gain? At one point
I thought, "I bet they want to learn English, and they think
they can use us Americans to practice on." Then it occurred
to me that since professors are more respected in Europe than
in the States, maybe this was a misguided effort at social
climbing. Then a really implausible thought occurred to me:
Maybe Marc wants to discuss philosophy! All these guesses
were refuted by experience as time went by.

Gradually the truth emerged. Marc and Reinhilde were
active in a renewal movement in the Catholic Church called
the Focolare Movement. A central idea of the movement is

Christian unity. The Focolari are fond of the words of Jesus' prayer in John 17: "The glory which thou hast given me I have given to them, that they may be one even as we are one, I in them and thou in me, so that the world may know that thou hast sent me and hast loved them even as thou hast loved me" (vv. 22-23). Their hospitality was born of a belief that strangers are to be treated as brothers and sisters in Christ — since in Christ that's what they are! But it was more than a belief; it was a proposition that had altered their vision. This vision of humanity as one in Christ, of humanity breaking bread together, partying at banquets whose real host is the invisible Lord, working side by side for the coming kingdom — this vision and the love of the Lord who is depicted in it were the source of the Enemans' hospitality.

Something like that reversal of the roles of guest and host that we see in the ministry of Jesus holds for all Christian hospitality. Starting as outsiders, we are all guests in the heavenly places in Christ Jesus, guests taken in from the streets and hedges and byways and now sitting at God's banquet table, strangers welcomed in a foreign land, orphans through sin taken into God's home and nurtured as adopted daughters and sons. And this is always through God's human agents on earth. It is they, these human beings offering their food, their time, their homes, their cars, their friends — it is these by whom God welcomes us into his kingdom. But the natural sequence, when all goes well, is that the welcomed become welcomers, the guests become hosts, the strangers become adopted sons and daughters welcoming new strangers in, ambassadors of reconciliation, purveyors of peace, ones who open their home territories to the outsiders, with a view that he and she should become our friends. Perhaps this is one of the things the apostle Paul meant when he said, "Be imitators of God, as beloved children" (Eph. 5:1).

Hospitality as Therapy

Clearly, Christian hospitality is therapeutic. Many of our emotional distresses, our depressions and anxieties, our unhappiness and aimlessness, originate in a sense of not belonging, of being "strange" and being outsiders. In Christian hospitality the strangers are taken not into some temporary society that may leave them in the lurch as unexpectedly·as it welcomed them, but into an eternal community with roots deeper than any that exist merely on earth. The outstretched arm of welcome is God's, and it is a welcome into the church, the fellowship of his children. The strangers are adopted into an eternal family, a branch of which they can find just about anywhere they may go on earth. Even those who "cope" and "function" and would never be thought to need therapy may be sick at heart and lost, and thus in need of *this* therapy. Therapists cannot even pretend to offer us anything so deep and satisfying unless they happen to be Christians and thus can offer us the family of God. At most they may offer us a long-term therapy group — hardly fit soil for the depth-thirsty roots of the human soul. Church members who practice the unpretentious hospitality implied by the Christian message and exampled in the ministry of Jesus do therapy in a way that no mere therapist can do it.

Hospitality is therapeutic not only for the guest, but for the host as well. By Christian standards of mental health it is sick to do everything for profit and nothing for love, to gorge one's ego by impressing people while letting the poor of spirit go hungry away. Such a life centered on the fat ego is a perfect formula for anxiety and teeters at the edge of despair's abyss. Much healthier is the ego grown slim through giving to others and through enjoying them for what they are. The true host goes out of herself in giving her guests the benefits of her territory and in enjoying her guests for God's sake.

CHAPTER FOURTEEN

Friends with God

Two Kinds of Loneliness

It's your eighth day at college, far from home. You're getting used to herd showers and a mattress that varies randomly between two and three inches in thickness over *its* length, which happens to be just two inches less than yours. You're improving at small talk with strangers, and some faces in the dorm and classrooms have acquired a faintly familiar look. The foreignness of it all, and the prospect of the friends and physics you'll come to know in the next four years, ripple anxious joy through your being as you amble across campus, checking out the girls in their late-summer attire and catching snippets of conversation, all of which seems so self-assured — obviously these are upperclassmen, people in the know about profs and parties and places to be, people at *home* here. In the evening, you're in the library trying to take your first American Lit. assignment seriously, when the weight of the strangeness of this place embraces you like the air in Gary, Indiana.

This sense of being out of touch with a part of yourself can be called homesickness, because it is a sickly feeling resulting from a failure to fit where you are. To be homesick is to feel separated from where you belong, from familiar surroundings, people you love, people you belong to. They — the "family" — are there at home, out of reach. You are here, living in a far country. Homesickness tells us something about human nature: we need to be embedded, set, planted in a familiar context. Even the most independent of us needs to be at home in an extended sense: he needs a familiar social and physical context in which to be himself, because such contexts make up an important part of our selves. No doubt, some people are more prone to homesickness than others, and perhaps it's a mark of immaturity if you get homesick on a month-long trip to Europe. But we all have our limits.

Homesickness is disagreeable, but it is often a sign of health because it comes from having roots. You know in your gut who you are, and this place, these people, ain't it. You feel your roots, and however painful the separation from that home soil, still, you are solidly planted in it, in spirit if not in body. (Think of Israel in Babylon, or refugees from Palestine or Ethiopia or Southeast Asia or Cuba.) Until you can put down some roots in the place in which you presently find yourself, those deeper roots will be a source of pain. But your identity is not really threatened by the strangeness of this place; indeed, your homesickness is a sense of your identity.

Another kind of loneliness is deeper and nastier, even if it is often not felt as loneliness. It's deep and nasty because it does touch your identity as a person. It's not just a pain in the soul but a sickness, an emptiness — a basic, and not merely circumstantial, deficiency in your life. It is not the proper hunger of a man whose meal awaits him at home; it is famine. It speaks not of soil to which you basically belong but are away from for the moment. It speaks instead of rootlessness, of being lost in the cosmos. One of Jesus' images for hell is that of being thrown into the outer darkness (Matt. 8:12; 22:13). The image suggests utter disorientation, complete loss of any sense of belonging. Imagine being pushed out the door of a cabin in the remote Alaskan wilderness on a starless night. Inside all is cozy, warm, familiar. Outside is endless darkness, the unknown and unknowable, except for the lighted windows of the cabin, telling you where you are. Then the shutters are closed and fastened tight, and your disorientation is complete. This is the paralyzing loneliness that may be felt by an orphan who has been shunted from one institution or foster home to another. Even what he calls home — the address of his latest foster parents or the locale he may write down on forms that require his place of origin — is not really *home*. He literally has nothing to go back to. He is cut off from fellowship, in the outer darkness, and so he feels not "homesick" but lonely nevertheless (though he may not identify the feeling as loneliness). And this loneliness is despair, an absence of self, a sense of being ungrounded and so in a sense nonexistent.

Christians hold that to be fully functioning and whole, we have to be planted happily in God (Psalm 1). God has put eternity into our hearts; he is the soil in which we must be rooted to receive the nutrients our spirits require, to flourish, and to bear the fruit properly characteristic of our kind. God is our home, our true family, the rock on which we must build the houses of our lives. Without him, we are all like orphans with no place to call home, floating disoriented in the outer darkness of this passing world. We need good human friends and a warm family context too, but if this is our only "home," then Christian psychology tells us that, whether we recognize it or not, we are in despair; we lack a self.

And at certain moments, if we're honest, we become *conscious* that we need a mooring in the eternal. We may be like the college freshman who doesn't realize until the eighth day that his identity is tied to that place, those people, that he calls home. At some point in our lives, when time and experience have prepared our spiritual noses, our need of divine fellowship strikes us as unmistakably as that air in Gary. People who do not have God for a friend are not just unfortunate in having missed a very good friend. They have missed out on the Friend of all friends, the essential Friend, the necessary condition of deeper life and fuller health, the one friend without whom all else is empty and a striving after wind.

We will better understand friendship with God if we think first about what human friendship is like.

What Is Friendship?

Cindy works as a makeup consultant in a large department store. Thousands of people walk by her counter each day, and she talks at some length to seventy-five or eighty of them. She lives in a pulsing sea of human noise, warmth, and movement. It seems that if anyone has company, Cindy has it aplenty! Then why is she so lonely? Why does her self seem so thin? The reason is that not one of these people is her friend.

We weren't created to live as isolated individuals — even isolated individuals floating in a sea of humanity. A powerful person, disliked and feared on all sides, may think he has a good life (he may proudly reckon his success in terms of money, sex, and power). But if he has no one to turn to, no one who shares his goals, no one to whom he can bare his heart, no one who loves him and no one to love, then his self is thin, whether or not he admits it.

In their book entitled *Habits of the Heart*, Robert Bellah and his colleagues suggest that people go to therapists because they lack friends. If these people had real friendships they would be less likely to have the "psychological" problems that impel them to therapists in the first place. Contemporary American life, with its mobility and its utilitarian view of relationships, discourages real friendships and causes a sense of isolation that leads to anxiety and depression. In this context the therapist functions as a substitute friend. You turn to the therapist because she will give you (albeit for a fee) her undivided empathetic attention and provide a context in which you can feel comfortable sharing your inmost thoughts and feelings. And if you are friendless, these are "services" you could not get from any of your acquaintances (nor would you want to). The first point to make about friendship, then, is that it is needed for a fully satisfying and emotionally healthy life.

The mention of sharing intimate thoughts and feelings reminds us that friends stay in touch. They have access to one another, are "open" to one another. They welcome one another into their homes, their offices, their schedules. They give one another their time. If they are separated by distance, they write letters and call one another on the phone. They travel to visit each other.

I'm not saying that if you don't visit someone, it shows that the two of you definitely aren't friends; friendship has other indications, and some obstacles to visiting are insurmountable. But still, friends want to see one another, to talk and spend time together, so if you don't do what it takes to stay in touch, this may be a sign that the friendship is dying. Often it can be revitalized by getting back in touch. An incident may remind us of a distant friend, and we may think, "I want to keep this friendship alive." A while back, out of the blue, I got a letter from Jack Bixby, a friend I hadn't seen for seventeen years and had lost track of. I was delighted to hear from him, and I felt a strong urge to see Jack again. In the summer of '89 my family and I visited him and his family in Vermont, and it was as though a part of me got put back into place — an older layer that had nearly been lost. Friendships have to be fed.

An important kind of contact that feeds friendships is doing things together. It's common knowledge that marriages tend to disintegrate if the spouses don't spend enough time together, and this is true of other kinds of friendship as well. The common activity may be aimless, like drinking coffee or playing cards around the wood stove at the feed store. But stronger food for friendship is found in goal-directed activities — jointly pursuing a hobby, a business venture, an artistic or intellectual pursuit, or some moral or political cause. In the best cases, friends share a vision of what life is about and pursue this vision in common activities.

Friends not only do things with one another; they do

things *for* one another. If Stan is drywalling his basement, Charley finds time to go over on a Saturday morning and give him a hand, even if he really doesn't "have" time. I've already mentioned listening, the sort of thing that tends to get shunted off to the professionals these days. Friends also listen to one another, sometimes quite deliberately, in effect saying, "You need somebody to listen to you, and here I am. Maybe I won't have much advice to give; maybe I'm not competent to give advice. But I can certainly lend a sympathetic ear." And Carl Rogers has reminded us that talking to a good listener is sometimes therapeutic in itself. The difference between the friend and the therapist is that the friend charges no fee! The fee quite purposely dispels the illusion of friendship that is created by the therapeutic intimacy. It guarantees that, despite the fact that the client shares her deepest thoughts and problems with the therapist, the two of them are not actually friends; the client is buying a service. (So much for *unconditional* positive regard.)

Throughout this book I've expressed a cautious appreciation for professional psychotherapy, and in contrasting the therapist-client relationship with friendship, I don't mean to detract from therapy's importance. Given the realities of our social life, therapy may be as close as some people will get to friendship, and we should not censure them for taking this opportunity for help and comfort. Further, some people suffer from psychological dysfunctions so deep that ordinary friendship may not be enough. In some therapeutic modes, the imitation of friendship is an indispensable aspect of the therapeutic process. As for the fee, therapists, like everybody else, need an income, and the fee may also head off unhealthy dependency on the therapist.

Still, the fee marks a clear boundary between therapy and friendship: the friend freely gives of his time and energy. He acts for the joy of contributing to his friend's well-being, or of working side-by-side with his friend, or of deepening the friendship. Making the contribution as a gift has an effect opposite that of the fee: instead of re-establishing the distance between the erstwhile "intimates," the free contribution binds the two more closely together. By giving free gifts to one another, friends invest themselves in one another and in the friendship, strengthening the tie that binds. It's a little like the relationship you have to some thing into which you put a lot of yourself — say, a sweater you've knitted, or a woodworking project on which you've lavished hours of tender care, or a farm you're improving. When you stand back and look at the farm or the sweater, perhaps it isn't very different from any other farm or sweater, yet it has a special look of *belonging* to you because you are invested in it in this special way. Friendships are our attachments to one another, and they come from investing ourselves in one another. They always cost something. The fee, on the other hand, cancels whatever time and effort the therapist's "friendship" may have "cost" her, symbolically revoking the investment.

Friends depend on one another. The deeper a friendship is, the more attached we become to one another, the more entangled our lives become, the more we will feel lost if our friend dies, or betrayed if she backs out on us. In the Christian view of things, dependency, though often emotionally painful, is a glorious fact of life: we all depend absolutely on God (whether or not we admit it), and members of the church are supposed to bear one another's burdens. We are to depend on one another's function in the church in the way that legs depend on eyes and eyes depend on hands. If you don't think legs depend on eyes, try walking around blindfolded; if you don't think eyes depend on hands, try reading a book with your hands tied behind your back. Maturity, according to a Christian psychology, involves learning to acknowledge and accept our dependency on others and to take responsibility for their dependency on us.

The more individualistic therapists, like Rogers and Ellis, are suspicious of dependency and tend to think that the more mature we are, the more self-sufficient we become. But this distorts our thinking about relationships and may undermine our spiritual and mental health. Christian psychology will distinguish carefully between healthy kinds of dependency that express emotionally our nature as dependent beings, and unhealthy kinds of dependency that are a distortion of our nature and God's intentions for us. Clearly, somebody who depends on alcohol to make himself feel cheerful and self-confident is not functioning well. Drugs, food, shopping, and sexual thrills are not among the things we were created to depend on for being cheerful. Likewise, there is something dysfunctional about a 35-year-old woman who depends on her mother to tell her when to go to bed and how to spend her money. But it is not improper for spouses to depend on one another for love and sexual gratification, or for the special expertise that one or the other possesses in some needed area of household maintenance. Nor is there anything wrong with depending on God. Dependency on God for one's sense of well-being is not the dysfunctional use of a crutch, as some psychologists of a Freudian or existentialist stripe would have us believe, though there are no doubt dysfunctional counterfeits of faith, and it will be a task of Christian psychology to catalog and understand these counterfeits. Nor is it wrong for friends to depend on one another for that sense of completeness that each of us can have only by loving and knowing ourselves to be loved. It is part of friendship that friends acknowledge their need for one another. They do not resist this dependency; they affirm it and glory in it. This leads us to our next characteristic of friendship.

Friendship is not just doing things with or for one another (it is not just "behavior"); it is also a matter of attitude. Let's say that Charley helped Stan with the drywalling out of a sense that he *owed* Stan this favor because Stan had helped him a couple of months back with his firewood. Charley has a strong sense of reciprocal justice, and he felt he must pay back what he owed. He didn't *want* to help Stan out, and the only sense of satisfaction he got was that of having done what he should. Now, if Stan finds out about Charley's attitude, he will have reason to feel disappointed, perhaps even betrayed as a friend. For such a dutiful attitude is one we more typically take toward people who are not our friends. Acts of friendship are not motivated most characteristically by respect for principles — even principles of justice or the welfare of humanity; they are motivated by concern for the well-being of the friend *in particular* and by a desire to spend time with this friend. A spirituality that makes friendship central to personal well-being will be shocked by the Jungian tendency to associate "individuation" with emotional detachment from others and to turn positive relationships into occasions for getting in touch with oneself.

This is just one example of the many attitudes that make up friendship. Besides this, friends rejoice in one another's good fortune and grieve over one another's misfortune or moral failure. They do not take the attitude that the Stoic philosopher Epictetus commends. He says that if someone is grieving the loss of a son who has gone away, "As far as conversation goes . . . do not disdain to accommodate yourself to him and, if need be, to groan with him. Take heed, however, not to groan inwardly, too" (*Enchiridion* XVI). Albert Ellis would probably be shy to come right out with this kind of advice, which sounds too much like an attack on friendship. It *is* an attack on friendship and on the Christian understanding of relational health, but it is actually quite consistent with Ellis's general view of relationships. Another attitude characteristic of friendship is a special kind of gratitude in which the friends dwell gladly in their dependency on and indebtedness to one another. Again, I can expect a good friend to miss me when I'm absent and to wish to see me again, to experience a special delight upon rejoining me after an absence. Friendship isn't just behaving in certain ways; it is a *spiritual*, or inward, relationship.

Friendship with God

The idea of friendship with God may seem strange. Since friendship is reciprocal, friends need to be roughly equals, and it seems an affront to God to consider ourselves his equals. It's more natural to speak of our loving God and of his loving us, because "love" suggests less equality: it is perfectly natural to say that a mother loves her two-year-old, and it makes some sense to say that the infant loves her mother (at least she's very attached to her mother), but it makes no sense to say they are friends. But friendship doesn't require complete equality, and the superior one in the relationship may elect to humble herself sufficiently to make friendship possible. If the daughter is eight or ten years old, and the mother is willing to accept reciprocity in terms that are possible for the girl, there can be a kind of friendship between them. Indeed, something like this condescension is at work when the Lord calls his disciples his friends: "You are my friends if you do what I command you. No longer do I call you servants, for the servant does not know what his master is doing; but I have called you friends, for all that I have heard from my Father I have made known to you" (John 15:14-15). In calling the disciples his friends, Jesus does not obliterate the difference between his role and theirs. It is, after all, an unusual form of friendship in which one friend commands and the others obey! Yet Jesus minimizes the difference between himself and his disciples: since he has shared the knowledge of God's will with them, they are his friends rather than his servants.

The story of our salvation is a story of God's becoming our equal, of his humbling himself and becoming one of us, incarnate in human flesh. God remains God, and we remain his creatures; we must never lose our impression of this distance between us. But that is not the whole story: it is a mark of Christian thought not only that Christ descends to us but also that we are raised up with him: "But God, who is rich in mercy . . . made us alive together with Christ . . . and raised us up with him, and made us sit with him in the heavenly places in Christ Jesus" (Eph. 2:4-6). It is almost an image of domestic hospitality, as though Christ has obtained for us an invitation, and now we are welcomed into God's household and sit with him and Christ around their hearth, like friends in happy conversation. We are divinized, as our Eastern Orthodox siblings might say. The apostle Paul prays that his readers may "know the love of Christ which surpasses knowledge, that you may be filled with all the fulness of God." (This verse, Eph. 3:19, is strikingly parallel to Col. 1:19, where Paul says *of Christ* that "in him all the fulness of God was pleased to dwell.")

At the beginning of this chapter I suggested that friendship with God is a form of health. That it is a human need to be friends with God is not an obvious insight. There are many people, even ones reputed to be experts in "mental health," who consider friendship with God an unhealthy crutch — if not a sign of mental illness, then at least a matter of arrested development. This of course begs the question about God and about our nature, because if, as Christians hold, God created us for fellowship with him, then fellowship with him *must* be natural, mature, and healthy rather than unnatural, infantile, and pathological. How can we tell which of these views is correct? The insight that maturity and health are to be found in friendship with God is not something that can be easily read off human nature simply by observing a lot of people to see whether they function better if they are friends of God than if not. The questions that must be addressed are "What is health?" and "What does 'functioning better' *mean?*" And how one answers these questions will depend on what one believes about God and human nature. We saw in earlier chapters that each therapist has a somewhat different notion of human nature and a corresponding conception of what it is to be functioning properly, and that in some cases these are rather strongly at odds with the Christian conceptions of human nature and mental health.

Furthermore, the insight that we become complete only in God is not just theoretical; it is one for which a person needs to be readied by certain experiences and the development of personality; it is a deep insight. It wasn't until the eighth day that our college freshman felt, in his homesickness, the full weight of his connections with "home." Something had to simmer in his soul and interact with his experience of separation. In a similar way, it may take decades of trying to flourish godlessly to bring a person to the realization that apart from God he is lost. (I commend Leo Tolstoy's *A Confession* as a gripping narrative of such a development.)

I said that friends hunger for contact with each other, and that contact maintains friendship. The same goes for our friendship with God. The analog of calling up your human friend or going to visit her is prayer, which is our chief way of pursuing contact with God. As Christians we practice the presence of God, and by that we mean that we talk to God (not always audibly, of course) and listen to him. We tell him how much we appreciate him, how much we're enjoying the life he's giving us, how glad we are that he has accepted us into his adoptive family, the church. We tell him our troubles and confess our failures to live as we ought. We listen for his voice in the Scriptures, in the actions of his saints, in the words of his other children, and in the events of our lives. So we are in a more or less constant conversation with God. This must be what the apostle has in mind when he asks us to pray without ceasing (1 Thess. 5:17). Obviously the Christian is not at every moment vocally or subvocally talking to God; but if she is mature (and this kind of maturity is rare), she is more or less constantly disposed to talk to God and attuned to God's voice. She is, while waking, almost constantly in the mood proper to prayer.

Staying in contact with a friend is seldom entirely natural. If she doesn't live right next door or work in the same office, it may take effort to cultivate the friendship, and there will be periods of lapse. For most of us the same is true of our friendship with God. We are easily distracted by the business of the daily routine, the attractions of entertainment (for example, TV), and the demands of work and family; and we "forget" to stay in contact with God, and our friendship with him deteriorates or never gets fully under way. Most of us are somewhere on the path to the ideal of regular communion — plodding along, straying again and again and, with the reminders that God sprinkles here and there, finding our way back.

God's friends do things for him. If a friend of ours is being maligned, we stick up for him: we say something in his defense or at least raise a protest. This isn't always easy; sometimes we risk being maligned, or worse, ourselves. My father-in-law, James Vanderkooy, was once among some people who were using the name of Christ in a rough and irreverent way. He didn't just cringe quietly, as most of us do, but said, "Listen, it's my Lord whose name you're using in that way." Friends of God undertake representative ventures on his behalf, acting like God's hands and feet in the world. My friend Bob Essert has organized and guided our congregation's involvement with a Christian school and community in Haiti. He flies down periodically to oversee the drilling of a well or the building of a wing on the school. Countless such stories can be told of ordinary Christians acting on God's behalf, acting out their friendship with God. But we must remember that friendship with God, like friendship with other people, is not just a matter of behaving in certain ways. It is an inward, spiritual matter of the emotions — of joy, peace, hope, gratitude, and contrition.

When we do things for God, it not only helps God and his little ones; it cements our friendship with him. Ben Franklin used the following strategy to endear himself to a fellow legislator in the Pennsylvania General Assembly who had shown opposition to him:

> I did not . . . aim at gaining his favour by paying any servile respect to him but, after some time, took this other method. Having heard that he had in his library a certain very scarce and curious book I wrote a note to him expressing my desire of perusing that book and requesting he would do me the favour of lending it to me for a few days. He sent it immediately and I return'd it in about a week, expressing strongly my sense of the favour. When we next met in the House he spoke to me (which he had never done before), and with

great civility; and he ever after manifested a readiness to serve me on all occasions, so that we became great friends and our friendship continued to his death. This is another instance of the truth of an old maxim I had learned, which says, "He that has once done you a kindness will be more ready to do you another than he whom you yourself have obliged."[1]

So if you wish to become a better friend of God — to cherish him more, to deepen your attachment to him and make your attitude toward him more positive, to depend on him more fully, to become more willing to act on his behalf and more grateful to him for his benefits — then, following Ben Franklin's advice, you should take your opportunities to do him favors. Some Christians preach that because God is sovereign we can do nothing for him and should be pure "receivers" of his grace. Of course it is true that he is sovereign and that without him we can do nothing. Yet it is part of his grace to us that he allows us to act on his behalf; he commissions us as his ambassadors (2 Cor. 5:20), his servants, his co-workers (1 Cor. 3:9). And this is truly grace, because acting on his behalf deepens that attachment which is life and health to our souls.

Christian Virtues as Forms of Friendship with God

I want now to show you that the Christian virtues — or at least some of the central ones — are forms of friendship with God.

Sometimes people say, "I don't believe in Christ or God, but I do believe in Christian love." The idea seems to be that Christian beliefs are one aspect of Christianity, but that separable from this is a set of "Christian principles" by which people can regulate their lives. The "life" part is Christian ethics, and

1. Quoted by David G. Myers in *Social Psychology*, 2d ed. (New York: McGraw-Hill, 1987), p. 56.

it includes such things as helping people in disasters, seeking peaceful solutions to conflict, and respecting the natural environment as though it were the handiwork of a loving God. Such behavior and attitudes do not require belief in God and the work of the Holy Spirit. But if Christian ethics is having the Christian virtues ("fruit of the Holy Spirit"), and the Christian virtues are forms of friendship with God, then it would seem harder to separate Christian ethics and Christian faith. One can hardly be friends with God if one doesn't believe in him or if one accepts no teachings about what he is like; one can hardly be in fellowship with the Holy Spirit if one doesn't believe in Jesus Christ, whose representative the Spirit is.

Other people tie Christian ethics strongly to Christian doctrine, but they talk as though the Christian virtues form the character by being a kind of "philosophy of life," a set of beliefs like those of Stoicism or Platonism or Darwinism. These people tend to be "rationalists" who get a little edgy in the presence of "charismatic" Christians. When it comes right down to it, they can't make much sense of the idea of "a personal relationship with Jesus Christ." But if the Christian virtues are forms of friendship with God, the Christian life can't be just a matter of internalizing Christian theology so that it shapes one's character. The Christian virtues are aspects of a relationship with a living person. I want to illustrate this point by looking briefly at three Christian virtues — hope, peace, and patience — to see how they are forms of friendship with God.

"Hope that is seen is not hope," says the apostle Paul (Rom. 8:24). And today we speak of hoping for something only when we are not certain that our hope will be fulfilled. We say, "I'm not certain the campaign's going to succeed, but I sure hope it will." But New Testament hope, though directed toward things that are "not seen," does admit of certainty: the author of Hebrews speaks of "the full assurance of hope" (6:11) and says, "Faith is the *assurance* of things hoped for . . ." (11:1). Where does the certainty of things unseen come from? "May the God of hope fill you with all joy and peace in believing, so that by the power of the Holy Spirit you may abound in hope," says Paul (Rom. 15:13). When Christians look forward with confidence to the kingdom of God, to God's subjecting everything to himself in Christ, we do so only in communion with God himself. The present Holy Spirit is the "seal" of our hope, the assurance that our hope is not vain. The Holy Spirit's present involvement with us is a guarantee of the outcome that God has promised and for which we hope. But of course this dwelling in the presence of God, or communion with God, from which the Christian's assurance derives, is a part of that happy relationship that I have been calling "friendship with God."

The peace of Christ that rules in the Christian's heart (Col. 3:15) is not just a lack of anxiety. Albert Ellis can reduce anxiety in his clients by teaching them not to give a flying fig about anything or anybody's opinion about them and not to ascribe any characteristics to themselves. By contrast, Christian peace requires belief in God and a relationship with God because it is primarily a peace "with God." It is an armistice whose emotional tone of joyful, grateful quiet is lent it by the living memory of the war now past. It is a peace such that peace with my fellow humans and the attitude I have toward myself in this peace are inseparable from my attitude toward the living and present God. This peace passes understanding in the same way and for the same reason that the forgiveness of sins passes our understanding: it is a gift beyond price and therefore beyond comprehension. In the mature Christian, the peace with others and the activities of peacemaking are products of perceiving oneself and the rest of the world in terms of the peace that God has wrought between himself and the world in Jesus Christ. This last peace is of course not a state of our minds, but an objective state of affairs — the consequence of Christ's having "broken down the dividing wall of hostility, by abolishing in his flesh the law of commandments and ordinances, that he might create in himself one new man in place of the two, so making peace, and might reconcile us both to God in one body through the cross, thereby bringing the hostility to an end" (Eph. 2:14-16). The attitude toward God that we call "peace" is an appropriation of this "fact" about the world: a new vision of God and self, guiding and embodied in one's interactions with God. A "personal relationship" with the forgiver quiets anxiety in a way that a mere belief in the forgiveness of sins (even *his* forgiveness of *these* sins) does not. Thus we can see that Christian "ethics" (which is also just plain old Christian psychological maturity) is not divorceable either from Christian doctrine (knowledge of the "facts") or from friendship with God.

Like human friends, God's friends not only do things *for* him; they also do things *with* him. In fact, among the spiritually mature, the distinction between doing with and doing for breaks down in the case of friendship with God. For everything that we do for God is done with his aid and in his fellowship. It is God who is at work in us, God the encourager, the motivator, the source of all our strength, who does "in" us what we do for him. This is the fellowship of the Holy Spirit manifest in the work of Christians. And this fact is perhaps especially evident when the work that we do for God requires patience. For we can be patient in him — that is, in the knowledge of his presence, in the encouragement of working hand-in-hand with the eternal one, the one with whom "one day is as a thousand years, and a thousand years as one day" (2 Pet. 3:8). Because our work is his work, we can rejoice in the present moment, though it is but an early stage in a difficult process that we may not live to see completed. The spiritual Christian has a very different attitude from the get-results-quick-and-get-out mentality of so many of our contemporaries. Each day is a fulfillment in itself, independent of visible results, to those who in Christian patience see their work as the work that God is doing.

Conclusion

Friendship with God is the satisfaction of the loneliness I spoke of at the beginning of this chapter. No matter how robust a person may seem, no matter how "well-adjusted" to his environment, no matter how successful in life, if he is not a friend of his Savior and Maker and Lord, he cannot be a fully formed and fully functioning human being. This is the Christian view, which holds that human nature is a nature created for and finding its completion in happy fellowship with God.

In this chapter I have spoken most of the time as though Christians are in constant fellowship with God, never feeling distant, never feeling that God is hiding or angry or perhaps even not there. Of course this is not so. Christians experience periods of "dryness" and varying degrees of alienation from God, similar to the ups and downs that we see in purely human friendships. All that I have said should be taken as descriptive of the Christian at her optimum. It is an ideal picture. But what of the person who, despite being a Christian, feels that loneliness for God of which I spoke at the beginning of this chapter? Of the two sorts of loneliness that I distinguished, what the Christian experiences when he or she feels that God is absent must be regarded as homesickness rather than homelessness, even though at times this loneliness may *feel* like despair. If there is any maturity in the Christian's life, there will be an underlying sense (perhaps quite unconscious) of rootedness in God that reflects the truth of God's eternal faithfulness, even though God may at times seem distant or absent or full of anger. And so the feeling is not a sense of homelessness but a yearning for one's true home, which is the bosom of God. It will be one of the tasks of Christian psychotherapy to bring about attitudinal changes corresponding to the fact that God is there and that he loves us, to bring out and facilitate the sense of rootedness in God that, we must assume, the Holy Spirit has worked and is working in the sufferer.

CHAPTER FIFTEEN

Belonging to the Church

Belonging: The Very Idea

People speak of "belonging to the church." This isn't a biblical phrase, but it's worth thinking about, because it has depth and some ambiguities worth tracing out. The central biblical way to say you belong to the church is "I am a *member* of the church." But when early Christians said that, the phrase rang differently than it does today. It sounded like saying, "I'm a church thigh" or "I'm a church nose" or "I'm a church bottomside." That's what a member is, originally: a body part. And the body in question is of course Christ's. So to say I am a church thigh is to say I am Christ's thigh. And that's what makes "belonging" a pretty good substitute for the biblical expression. Nothing belongs to a person more perfectly than his own body parts, and a church member is one who belongs in that way to Christ.

Notice the several ways we use the word *belong*. When we say, "The chair is beautiful, but it doesn't belong in this room," we're saying it doesn't fit: something about the style or color doesn't go well with the room. When our family moved from the mid-south to the north of the United States several years ago, Elizabeth and I had a strong sense that we belonged up here, and that we had never quite belonged down there. If someone says, "I belonged to the Baptist church for a while, but gradually I came to feel that I just didn't belong," the notion of fitting is present in the second *belong:* she didn't fit in (socially, perhaps) with the Baptists. Their style wasn't hers; their liturgy, their way of speaking of Christ, the way the gospel shapes their ethics. (*Belong* comes from the Middle English *belongen,* from *be + longen,* meaning "to be suitable.") On the other hand, if someone simply says, "I belonged to the Baptist church for a while," all he means is that he was signed up — he had done what it takes to get on the roll — and he had participated in some of its functions. It's this we have in mind when we say that we belong to the Cedar Valley Lunch and Service Club.

In still another usage, *belong* denotes ownership: That watch belongs to me. And something like ownership, yet unlike it too, is expressed when a father says, pointing to his son, "That little boy belongs to me." What does it mean, then, to say that we belong to Christ? In the New Testament, Paul tells us that the believer is "a slave of Christ" (1 Cor. 7:22). How are we to understand this assertion? When we belong to Christ, we are his slaves, it is true, subject to his will, but not in the normal way of slavery, which, sad to say, is more like a watch being owned. We are atypical slaves — slaves whose master died for us, slaves who are also his friends, adopted sisters and brothers, organs of a body of which he himself is the chief organ, the head. If Christ owns us, it is as I own my wrist, and not as I own my watch.

For many people in our secular culture, even church members, belonging to the church is pretty much on all fours with belonging to the Cedar Valley Lunch and Service Club. The church is one more voluntary association — you "join" it if you want to, and you can drop it when you want to, just like the CVLSC. Becoming a "member" is a rather casual affair. The difference, in their minds, is that the CVLSC is weaker on aesthetics and has a simpler ideology. In the church there's more hocus-pocus and more effort to indoctrinate members through sermons, scripture readings, and Sunday school. Thus some people prefer the CVLSC to the church: it's less weird and less invasive and does just about as many good works — though admittedly the CVLSC doesn't begin to measure up in the music department.

This is just the kind of misunderstanding that those ever-present sermons, readings, and Sunday school lessons aim to prevent. Their point is to shape and correct the members' perception of themselves and the world, to cause the congregation to take the Word of God to heart in such a way that they become "suited" to the church. They enable people to belong to the church in the full and spiritual sense of fitting into — having a proper place in — Christ's body. People who belong to the church in this sense see with their hearts the difference between belonging to the church and belonging to such organizations as the CVLSC. What then do they see?

The Church Is Jesus Christ

First, they see that belonging to the church means belonging to Christ. To the eyes of the world the church is a voluntary association: "After all, you don't *have* to belong, do you?" say the secular lips. But it does not seem so to those who spiritually belong to the church. To drop the church isn't like dropping your "membership" in the Book of the Month Club; it's more like cutting off your head. It's less like quitting your company and more like getting a divorce, tearing yourself from another with whom you are one flesh — except that in this case it's the Lord of creation you're divorcing. We don't just "belong to an organization"; we have become "a dwelling place of God in the Spirit" (Eph. 2:22).

You'll remember that according to the contextual therapist Ivan Nagy we are not just free-floating individuals, looking out for Number One and making our way as profitably and pleasantly as we can among the persons with whom we have to do. Instead, we are "ontologically related" to some of those people, especially to our parents and our children, but also to our grandparents and grandchildren. Our well-being as well as theirs depends on how well our give-and-take with them respects this "ontology" by following the rules of intergenerational justice. To be ontologically related to someone is to belong necessarily to him or her; these are relationships we can't escape, and to deny them is to deny an important part of ourselves. Because these blood relations depend on marriage, relations between spouses are also "ontological," and this is what makes divorce so devastating to all who are touched by it.

One thing that Sunday school lessons are supposed to be writing on our hearts is that we are all ontologically related to Jesus Christ. Just as, like it or not, Mom *is* your mother, so Jesus Christ *is* your Lord, whether or not you acknowledge him as such. If you belong to the church, you believe your relationship to Jesus is not a matter about which you have any choice, and so there's no such thing as casually opting out, "dropping" your membership. To belong to the church is to acknowledge and live out the fact that you belong to Christ, that you have always belonged to him, and that all human beings belong to him: he is the one Lord of all, the sovereign, the one in whom we were created.

Even when we "join" the church, this act is only superficially voluntary. "You did not choose me," says the Lord, "but I chose you and appointed you that you should go and bear fruit and that your fruit should abide" (John 15:16). "Blessed be the God and Father of our Lord Jesus Christ," hymns the apostle Paul, "who has blessed us in Christ with every spiritual blessing in the heavenly places, even as he chose us in him before the foundation of the world, that we should be holy and blameless before him" (Eph. 1:3-4).

In September through November of 1989, East Germany experienced what came to be called the October Revolution, in which the forty-year-old communist government fell with remarkably little violence. The church, especially the Nikolai Church of Leipzig, played an important role in encouraging and keeping nonviolent the increasingly large demonstrations that followed its Monday evening prayer services for peace. The church's involvement sometimes took courage. On October 9 it appeared that things might get very bloody, as the people were becoming bolder in the wake of Mikhail Gorbachev's recent visit and leader Erich Honecker had given written orders for a "Chinese solution" — shooting up the crowd. The Lutheran bishop warned of a bloodbath, and doctors cleared hospital rooms to accommodate the wounded, but the leaders at the Nikolai Church decided not to cancel the prayer service for that evening. After the service the demonstrators numbered 50,000; by the end of the evening there were 150,000 in the crowd. Because Egon Krenz, a Politburo member in charge of security, countermanded Honecker's order for violence in a striking act of insubordination, the demonstration remained peaceful and became the turning point in the October Revolution. Some weeks later, demonstrators hung a banner across a Leipzig street: WIR DANKEN DIR, KIRCHE (We thank you, Church).

We can well imagine how this touching tribute to the church's courage and gentleness might have been understood by secular citizens of Leipzig, who were saying to themselves, in effect, "Those church people have a philosophy of love and peace. They haven't always lived this philosophy, but this time they did so with remarkable courage and to stunning effect. Let's give the Christians a hand!" This is the word of an outsider (even if some on church rolls might share it); it is not quite the view of a person who spiritually belongs to the church. To the church member, saying "We thank you, church" is the equivalent of saying, "We thank you, Jesus Christ," and this is something no one can say unless he or she belongs to the church. When Christians see the church acting in character, they see Jesus acting in his present earthly body. People who do not believe that Jesus is alive and is the Lord — people who do not possess the Holy Spirit — can't see this. From the secular point of view, to say that Jesus was active for peace in Leipzig is either craziness, or superstition, or wildly figurative speech. Such is the great gulf between the Christian and the secular understandings of the church.

The Church Is Catholic

Something else you see if you spiritually belong to the church is that belonging to it means being catholic — it means belonging to the whole church, belonging to all others who belong to Christ. Being a church member is not the same as belonging to a denomination, or a congregation, or a theological persuasion. If the church is the body of Christ, there can't be more than one church, because there's only one Christ. Anyone clinging to him must cling to the others who are clinging to him. "In Christ there is no east or west," no Presbyterians or Eastern Orthodox, no Baptists, Mormons, Seventh Day Adventists, Episcopalians, or Roman Catholics — just the various limbs and organs of Christ's one body. Hermits and holy rollers, blacks and whites, adults and children, Jews and Gentiles, monks and married, charismatics and stiffs, high and low, standers, sitters, and kneelers, dunkers, dippers, and sprinklers, brethren and sistren — all are "members one of another" (Rom. 12:5) insofar as they are in Christ. Speaking of the former disunity of Jews and Gentiles, the apostle Paul says,

> For he is our peace, who has made us both one, and has broken down the dividing wall of hostility, by abolishing in his flesh the law of commandments and ordinances, that he might create in himself one new man in place of the two, so making peace, and might reconcile us both to God in one body through the cross, thereby bringing the hostility to an end. (Eph. 2:14-16)

The church — that is, Jesus Christ — is the great unifier of humankind.

How does this belonging to one another work out in practice? What does it mean in the day-to-day, often frictional interactions of Christians? In this connection Paul speaks of "agree[ing] with one another" (2 Cor. 13:11) and being of "one mind" (Phil. 1:27) and "thinking the same thing toward each other" (Rom. 12:16, my translation; see also 1 Cor. 1:10; Rom. 15:5-6; Phil. 4:2). This can't mean that Christians have no differences of opinion. It doesn't mean that we have to agree on every point of theology, or every evangelistic style or liturgical detail, before we are being faithful to Christ and expressing spiritually our belonging to one another. What does it mean, then? What kind of agreement is needed for Christian unity? In what way do we have to think alike if we are to live out our oneness in Christ?

It means that we have to be of one mind in this basic vision of who we are: that we belong to Jesus and to one another because of Jesus. There isn't much creed in this, but there is a little: if someone believes that Jesus is not the only and eternal son of God but just a teacher of peace and gentleness, then he or she doesn't belong spiritually to the church. (But since a Christian "hopes all things" [1 Cor. 13:7], in hope we can see even unbelievers as prospective members of ourselves.) When we see the other church member, the one with whom we perhaps disagree over a point of doctrine or strategy, or the one whose style of Christianity so differs from our own, or even the "sinner" who disgusts us, we see a member of ourselves. It is like an arm regarding the toe of its own body — different though it may be, and disgusted though the arm may be at that gnarled nail and the corns growing on the toe. Despite the pain the ingrown nail often causes the rest of the body, still the arm recognizes in that toe something that *belongs* to it, by virtue of being a member of the same body with it. So it is with the peace and unity of the church. The essential thought is this: *We are members of Christ and thus of one another.* If we "agree" on that, then we can disagree on much else, and yet do so in peace. But agreeing in this case doesn't just mean willingness to say the right words; it means really *seeing* the other as a member of oneself.

The unity that Plato wanted in his republic was something like the spiritual unity of the church. To bring it about, he proposed to do away with monogamous marriage and to declare everyone in a given age group (say, between the ages of twenty and forty) as "married" to everyone of the opposite sex in that group. The children of these unions would then be taken away from their mothers at birth and reared in communal nurseries. The mothers would not recognize their own children but would regard all the babies as theirs, and the fathers would take an equally fatherly attitude toward all members of the younger generation. Similarly, the men and women in the forty-to-sixty age group would regard all members of the newest generation as their grandchildren, and each age group would regard members of the next older generation with filial reverence and solicitude.

This arrangement, said Plato, would bring about unity in the city-state by causing each citizen to say "mine" of every other citizen — "my daughter," "my son," "my father," "my grandmother" — that is, by giving everybody a sense of belonging to everybody else. Plato thought that if he could create the illusion of the state as a large extended family, he would reduce quarreling, lawsuits, and factions among the citizens, increase the concern of all the adults for the city's children, create a greater willingness to share goods, and foster loyalty to fellow citizens in times of danger. His device for creating political bonding trades on the natural bonding that exists in the family, in which each family member sees the others as in one way or another ontologically one's own.

When Jesus prays that the disciples may be one, he is not praying for administrative or institutional unity, nor is he praying that they should agree on all points of theology and practice. Rather, he prays that "they may all be one; even as thou, Father, art in me, and I in thee, that they also may be in us, so that the world may believe that thou hast sent me" (John 17:21). The main unity of the church is that it has one Lord — that is, one God who says "my people" of the church, and one God of whom the members of the church collectively and individually say "our [my] God." By virtue of saying "mine" of the same Lord, they also say "mine" of each other. Jesus' "in" is spiritual, a matter of attitudes. It is not something that can be captured by church administration, though it may sometimes be *fostered* by institutional arrangements. Church unity is a matter of spiritual growth. As Paul tells us, "Christ Jesus himself [is] the cornerstone, in whom the whole structure is joined together and grows into a holy temple in the Lord" (Eph. 2:20-21). This formation of hearts, and not conformity of theory or practice, is the agreement on which the peace of the church is constructed, the resilient yet solid foundation of love.

The Church Is Foreign to the World

Another thing people are supposed to learn in Sunday school is that belonging to the church means not belonging to the world. Christians dwell in a spiritual ghetto surrounded on all sides by a reality that is not the kingdom of God. They venture out of their ghetto into other parts of the city to work, to represent the ghetto in the larger city and to infuse it with something of the culture of the ghetto. But they know the boundaries; they do not confuse the church with the world. What is the *world* in this biblical sense of the word? It is not the same as creation; Christians feel no alienation from the creation. The "world" is not the natural world that God made and provided to humankind as a dwelling place. It is instead that human culture in which Jesus Christ is not acknowledged and honored as Lord. The difference between the church and the world is not just an "ethical" difference. It is not that the church is good and the world is bad. There is ethical goodness in the world just as there is wickedness in the church. The difference is that the world is lost because it is without Jesus Christ, and the church is saved because it is the body of Christ.

Christ predicts that the world (those who are outside him) will "hate" us (but not that we will hate the world). And it is just this foreignness of the church that causes the world to hate us:

> "The world has hated them because they are not of the world, even as I am not of the world." (John 17:14)

> "If the world hates you, know that it has hated me before it hated you. If you were of the world, the world would love its own; but because you are not of the world, but I chose you out of the world, therefore the world hates you." (John 15:18-19)

> "And you will be hated by all for my name's sake." (Matt. 10:22)

The Nikolai Church was in good favor with the East Germans after the 1989 revolution. Democracy was a goal the Christian ghetto could heartily share with the "world" of secular Leipzig. But what if the church insists on its language, insists that its contribution to peace is the work of Jesus Christ? The world may humor the church members as good-natured crazies or move into a denial mode in which it conveniently ignores what the church is really saying. But the church may also find that because of its insistence on the centrality of Jesus Christ, the gratitude of Leipzig's secular citizens begins to fade. Their worldview is being called into question; they are being told that they do not worship the true God. They catch the church's implicit claim that Jesus Christ is asking secular Leipzig to submit to him. They feel that an alien view of things is encroaching, and that discomfort and alienation which Jesus calls "hate" begins to form in their hearts. It is different from the animosity that the communist leaders must have felt toward the church for aiding and abetting their detractors, but it is just as real, and it is that special kind of animosity of which Jesus says, "They hated me without a cause" (John 15:25). Some from Leipzig may be converted to Christ; that is, they may begin to see the world as the Christians do, and thus overcome the offense. But if the church is not arousing some "hatred" of this special kind, chances are very good that it isn't expressing clearly enough the truth that it belongs to Jesus.

The Church as Therapeutic Community

Encounter groups (also called sensitivity training) blossomed in the 1960s and have maintained a certain following to the present day. An encounter group is composed of a leader and a dozen or so people, usually strangers to one another but members of roughly the same social class. Individuals pay a fee to an organizing agency, often a resort, to meet together over a weekend or for a period of several days. The rules for the meetings invert normal social protocol. Group members are expected to share their problems and disappointments quite freely with these strangers, and to support one another emotionally with "positive feedback" but also to express freely their anger and disapproval of one another. Members are encouraged to touch one another's bodies. For example, they may be blindfolded and then instructed to get to know one another through the sense of touch. Or someone who has told of his grief or disappointment may be physically held up while other members of the group stroke him and speak soothingly to him. Or he may be hugged by two or three people seated near him. In the "trust-fall" one blindfolded member trustingly falls into the arms of others in the group, who of course always catch him. The leader makes sure that each member shares something important about himself with the group while the rest listen attentively and give "feedback." In this way each member gets to be the center of attention for a while, and each also gets many opportunities to give of himself in the support of others.

After hours and hours of such give-and-take, each member develops an attachment to the group. The others, who only a few hours or a few days earlier were total strangers, have come to seem extremely significant to you. Your sense of acceptance by the others is emotionally heightened by the fact that you have made yourself vulnerable to them and perhaps also have been strongly criticized by some of them. It is a little like the warm feeling you have in being reconciled with your lover after a fight: the emotional nakedness that the fight has occasioned intensifies the feelings of "love." You also have a feeling of commitment to the others (notice I say only "a feeling"); you have, after all, invested a large part of a weekend in giving them feedback and supporting them. Besides providing this powerful sense of belonging to an intimate community, the encounter-group experience is also attractive because it provides a thrill — the thrill of danger, of breaking such taboos as touching strangers, lashing out in anger, saying how you "really feel," figuratively taking off your clothes (as well as literally, in some cases). And finally, many feel that in the encounter experience they have discovered ultimate reality, the key to the universe, the meaning of being itself, reconciliation with the fundamental principle of reality — what one might, in an earlier, mythological age, have called "God."

It is not hard to see how encounter groups might seem to meet an unsatisfied psychological need in many people. According to Christian psychology, we are made for communion with God and with our human brothers and sisters. So if a person has no real community, no friends, no one who will listen as he talks about himself, if his life is empty of significant purpose, secularized and devoid of the experience of God, a dull routine that leaves him out of touch with others and his self and his Maker, then an encounter weekend may seem like the high point and the turning point of his life. This may strike him as "real" life, an island of solid ground in a sea of mere appearing, an oasis of light amid the shadows of unreality. In the euphoria of the encounter experience and immediately thereafter, many participants testify that it has deeply changed them for the better. However, the more sober proponents of encounter admit that it does not change people's character or behavior very much. Its value is mostly in the "here and now" of the experience itself: the momentary *feelings* of thrill and community are what it's all about.

We can see the encounter experience as an illusory satisfaction of the deep psychological needs that are satisfied by spiritually belonging to the church. Humans need to belong to a community in which they can both really give and really take: a community in which they have the importance symbolized in the encounter group by each participant being made the center of attention and being allowed to tell about himself or herself; but also one in which they bear the burdens of others, symbolized in the encounter group by giving oneself over to providing feedback and support for others. We need a community in which we can voice our complaints and confess our sins and in general exist partially disrobed of defenses in the security of knowing that we are accepted just as we are. And we are not made for mere human community but for something deeper and more solid, something eternal; to flourish is to be in touch with the ultimate source of our being.

The differences between an encounter group and the church point up the difference between illusory satisfaction of these needs and a real one. The encounter group gives an intense experience of community, but as a real community it is both pathetic and comical. The group members take no responsibility for one another beyond the confines of the encounter. When it is over, these strangers go their separate ways; the "supportiveness" and "caring" were really an illusion. It is like the theater: the actors play their parts, but outside the performance nothing that went on in the play has any continuity or consequences. Encounter is a futile attempt to deny that we human beings have a history, that there is inescapable continuity between our past, our present, and our future. The encounter group is literally another world, a fantasy. By contrast, the church is a permanent community situated in the world. Its members have continuing, real responsibility for one another. Its story is not an isolated, momentary flash of heat and light but a continuous historical solidity of two thousand years. Its "supportiveness" and "caring" are not a few hugs and words of affirmation, but the risk of freedom and limb and life, the blood of martyrs, the establishment of schools and hospitals, the evangelization of continents. Belonging to the church may seldom produce the intense *feelings* of community that one gets from an encounter weekend, but in exchange for the mildness of excitement one gets reality.

A reason often given for the popularity of encounter experiences is the mobility of the American middle class. We often don't stay put long enough to establish real friendships, and so we feel disconnected. Encounter provides an intense, if only momentary, experience of connection. These vivid, artificial experiences would hold little attraction for us, and might even appear disgusting, comical, desperate, and infantile, if we had a deeper and more realistic sense of belonging to a community. And this is something the church provides. In the sixteen years that Elizabeth and I have been married, we have lived four years in Kentucky, one in Minnesota, another two in Kentucky, three in Illinois, one in Belgium, another in Illinois, one in Pennsylvania, and now we are back in Illinois again. At this rate, we are perhaps even more mobile than the average middle-class American. Yet in all of the places we've been, we have felt very little alienation or disconnection, and the reason has largely been that we are members of a worldwide community. This community has varied in denominational form: Presbyterian, Christian Reformed, Roman Catholic, Episcopal, independent evangelical, and Church of the Brethren. Of course, the individual members are strangers to us when we first arrive in a new place, but they are not strangers in the way fellow members of an encounter group are and remain strangers to one another. These are sisters and brothers, members of ourselves because we are all members of the body of Jesus.

The church can be truly therapeutic, in the sense of meeting our deepest needs for community, because it is more than an occasion for therapy, more than an institution for the meeting of human needs. It is indeed a hospital for sinners and the dying, but it is not just an instrument for the promotion of human welfare. It is a reality into which we have been called by the living God, whose purposes are not entirely clear to us and may certainly extend beyond the fulfillment of our needs. Thus the attitude with which one properly belongs to the church is quite different from that with which one goes into therapy or becomes a "member" of an encounter group. Unlike the encounter-group member, the church member sees herself as under the authority of God, whose grace to her typically takes the form of a commission: Go and do this *work*. This too is grace and, paradoxically, even therapy (occupational therapy!), for it takes the Christian's eyes off her own psychological navel and fixes them on God and the world he is busy saving.

The Individual Member

We have focused on belonging to the Christian community, claiming that belonging to the church is basic for human flourishing. Such a claim runs counter to the views of the three "individualist" therapists of Part One. For them the individual is not properly embedded in a community; indeed, the community is more a threat to her well-being than an ally of it. For Rogers, most of our emotional problems stem from the "conditions of worth" that have been imposed on us by our families, our friends, our culture, and such organizations as the church. To become fully functioning is to get liberated from the strictures of established communities so as to get in touch with *oneself*, a self-contained, self-regulating, self-feeling, self-enjoying organism. On Ellis's view, personal maturity comes from learning to live "rationally," and this means knowing how to manage one's thoughts and concerns so as to minimize anxiety, anger, and other disturbing emotions. The fact that many of our disturbing emotions stem from our attachments to other people suggests to Ellis that to be rational we must regard others as disconnected from ourselves. The client must learn that it is no concern of hers what others think of her, and she must carefully distinguish her problems from those of others, so as not to be bearing other people's burdens. The Jungian individual is a complex, expanding, deepening, increasingly self-exploring, self-focused, and self-aware citizen of the human universe, the transtemporal community of the ages. The more one has integrated the diverse sides of one's own nature, the more fully functioning one is. This nature does have a social or quasi-social side: the "collective unconscious." But it turns out that the collective unconscious, the community of the ages, is all in one's (larger) psyche. There is no actual, living community to which one must relate properly to be fully functioning, and the church especially, as a historical community with "external" dogmas and rituals, is an enemy of differentiation. For all these therapists, "individuation" — the overcoming of dependency and social embeddedness — is a major goal of therapy.

Among the therapists we've considered, it is Ivan Nagy who most decisively makes good human functioning depend on the individual's relationship with an actual, existing community of other persons — in his case, the intergenerational family. Even with his emphasis on community, however, Nagy recognizes the importance of individuation: there are unhealthy as well as healthy forms of dependency, and so autonomy remains an ideal of personal functioning. The healthy family produces sons and daughters who can leave home and establish their own families; it produces individuals who can resist enslavement by unjust patterns of social interaction. But Nagy differs from the individualistic therapists in holding that autonomy is achieved not by *weakening* the individual's communal ties but by improving them — making them more "just."

What is it to be a well-individuated member of the body of Christ? A possible abuse of Paul's great metaphor is that the individual might be lost in the "system" — emotionally merged or "enmeshed," as the family therapists would say — with the rest of the body. This would of course be a mistake, since part of the point of Paul's metaphor is to emphasize the differentiation of the members. The bad sort of dependency — the opposite of individuation — shows up in anxiety: the improperly dependent person is anxious that the others will abandon her, that she will not please them, or that her contribution will be less important than somebody else's. It shows up in helpers needing the helped so much that they are anxious about losing them and try to keep them "dependent." In form the Christian approach to individuation in the body of Christ is like Nagy's approach to individuation in the family: one achieves individuation not through cutting oneself off from those on whom one is improperly dependent but through having right relationships within the family of God.

The well-individuated Christian can accept criticism and receive disapproval with equanimity, because he is in Christ's service, not the service of his own aggrandizement, and also because he is in Christ's forgiveness. Conversely, one who spiritually belongs to Christ can accept praise without enslavement to the praiser, because he knows that insofar as he is praiseworthy, the praise is really due to Christ — or, if due to him in some measure, is due for his merely doing what he ought. The well-differentiated Christian looks for her own ministry, her own niche, her own area of contribution, seeking to utilize her own gifts. She does not covet or envy the talents and ministries of others; instead, she regards them as allotments by Christ, whom alone she desires to serve. She is not enslaved by anxiety about whether her contribution is as important as the contributions of others. Whatever she accomplishes is co-accomplished with the others who contribute according to *their* gifts. She is not given to boasting and self-aggrandizement. She does not need to be the center of attention; she is not obsessed with her own "needs" but is free to notice the needs of others. The well-individuated church member views the other members of his community not just as people with roles in *his* life but as people with roles within the church, as fellow servants of Christ. And in humility the well-differentiated member doesn't mind depending on others, working together. Christian individuation means being aware that these others are Christ's as you are, seeing past their weaknesses and sins and "seeing Christ" in them — that is, seeing them as ones who belong to him. When your spirit and behavior are so attuned, then you "belong" to Christ not only in the sense of being owned by him but also in the sense of fitting into his kingdom, fitting *him*. Since there is always betrayal and guilt, belonging to him involves confession, repentance, and restoration.

My labor of writing this book is a kind of Christian work. How might I write it as a well-individuated church member? The writing is something I do largely alone, and some personal glory might attach to it. But if I do it spiritually as a member of the church, I see the work as an offering for the kingdom of God, as contributing a little something, a dab of mortar to the temple (or, more realistically, maybe to one of the outhouses) of the kingdom. When viewed this way, the accomplishment is not subject to the larger emptiness of doing it for money, fun, fame, or advancement of some kind. I see it as supplemented and enabled by the work of countless other Christians. Even if I do much of the work in the solitude of my office sitting in front of my Macintosh, still I am doing it in the "communion of the saints," in the company of the countless Christians whose faithful thought and lives have fed me spiritual food, and also in the company of those who will use the book. To be individuated as one who belongs to the church is to regard the book and the hours of writing it as a personal offering to Christ, a token of gratitude for life and welcome into his kingdom.

Conclusion

CHAPTER SIXTEEN

Christianity as Psychotherapy

The Task

In an interview with a couple she calls Tom and Laura Brett, Maggie Scarf asked Tom what attracted him to Laura, and he said that in addition to being pretty, smart, and funny, she was a challenge.

> "A challenge because of her sincerity, I suppose, and her honesty, too. It's all there," he added, with a small shrug, "in her language."
> "Her language?" I gazed at him quizzically. He, however, was exchanging a knowing, fond look with his wife.
> "Church language," he explained, running a quick hand through his curly brown hair. "Listening to Laura talk to her friends, you hear certain terms come up again and again. Things like 'letting yourself be vulnerable' and 'investing yourself in a decision.'"[1]

Given Tom's assertion that it was *church* language which was the clue to Laura's ethics, we might have expected Tom to say that she used terms like *sin, repentance, redemption, forgive-*

1. Scarf, *Intimate Partners: Patterns in Love and Marriage* (New York: Random House, 1987), p. 29.

ness, spiritual rebirth, the body of Christ, the kingdom of God, faith, hope, and *love.* But to Tom "church language" consists of what some of us fondly call psychobabble, the language of popular psychology.

Laura's church experience is not unusual. Congregations have latched onto the language of the psychotherapies with enthusiasm. In many churches the language of popular psychology has swamped the traditional Christian language about persons, their nature, the diagnosis of their condition, what they should become, and how they may achieve their destiny. Why the hunger for psychology in the church today? Well, it speaks quite directly to people's hearts. It speaks of things we all want — a fully human life, happiness, improvement in our relationships with one another, an end to anxiety, depression, a sense of inferiority, incompetence, and failure; it speaks of a sort of "integration" of our lives that we all vaguely yearn for and seldom really experience. Despite having just enough mystery to give it "mystique," psychology has some rather immediate and sometimes easy recipes for getting ourselves straightened out. Besides this, it satisfies a curiosity about ourselves; we like to know what makes us (and our neighbors) tick, and psychology offers answers. It gives us a wanted sense of control. By comparison with this language, the traditional preaching and liturgy (the ancient "Word of God") can seem remote from our lives, consisting of abstruse doctrines that, even if true, are not "true for us." So in recent decades it has seemed to many a pastor and priest that the way to breathe life into these dry bones, these "empty" words, is to read them as anticipations of Jung, or Rogers, or Kohut, or Ellis. In this way we can make them speak our language, the language of our hearts, the language of our needs. After all, Christianity has always aimed to make whole persons of us, and these psychologies promise to do that and offer practical and plausible methods. Surely the agenda of these psychologies must be the same as the Christian one?

I agree with this construction insofar as it claims that

the New Testament and the most vital parts of the Christian tradition do contain a psychology that has sometimes been lost to view. However, I disagree with efforts to read the tradition as simply an awkward way of saying what the leading secular psychologists of our day are saying. One of the claims of a biblical psychology, one I have been stressing in this book, is that psyches are word-shaped. Moses and Jesus agree with the modern dictum that you are what you eat, but would point out that human beings, in distinction from the rest of the animals, are verbivores. When the evil one tempts Jesus to use his power as the Son of God to make himself some bread in the wilderness, Jesus quotes Deuteronomy 8:3: "Man shall not live by bread alone, but by every word that proceeds from the mouth of God" (Matt. 4:4). The personal transformation that the apostle Paul calls salvation is brought about by a person's getting a certain word on his lips and in his heart (Rom. 10:10). The word of the cross, he says, is the power of God (1 Cor. 1:18). In the midst of a passage describing some of the personality traits and behaviors distinctive of Christians, he says, "Let the word of Christ dwell in you richly" (Col. 3:16).

That psyches are word-shaped is not only a truth of Christian psychology. It is a clue about how to read any psychology. And it tells us that psychologies are to some extent self-confirming: if people live in the terms of a psychology, then what it says about them will tend to be confirmed by their motives, their defenses, their personality traits, and their behavior, because the psychology is making them psychologically what they are. It also follows that as psychologies differ in their "logic," so the personalities they shape will be different. The help that the ancient Word of God offers us is not the same as the help that the secular psychologies are offering. Throughout this book we have seen that, at numerous and fundamental points, these psychologies vary starkly from Christian psychology, and if we let them, they will form us in ways that are inconsistent with our Christian calling to maturity. Christian psychology is distinct, and if we are to nurture Christians rather than Nagyans, Jungians, and Rogerians, we must be true to the *Christian* word about persons. Indeed, an implication of my argument in this book is that an important task of Christian preaching and counseling in our time is to clarify the differences between various popular psychotherapies and the psychology implicit in the Christian tradition. In our time, the Christian counselor or pastor may very well have two jobs: she must not only facilitate mental and relational health according to Christian standards and methods, but must also be ready to deprogram people who have been formed in improper ways by the secular psychologies.

The pastors who have turned to psychology are right in thinking that an important way to make the Word of God speak to people's hearts is through psychology. By "psychology" here I mean a word about what kind of beings persons are, what it is to function fully as a person, how people go wrong as persons, and what can be done to improve our personal well-being. Throughout this book I've assumed that the Christian tradition has definite things to say about these issues, and distinct related practices. Christianity does have a psychology, even if its parallels to the psychologies of the twentieth century have remained somewhat implicit. In Part One I traded on this implicit psychology by bringing it to bear critically on a number of those modern systems. Here we found that entering into a dialogue with Rogers, Ellis, Nagy, Kohut, and Jung brought out certain features of a Christian psychology that might otherwise have remained hidden from our view. The dialogue also helped us identify the pitfalls into which these psychologies might lead a pastor or Christian counselor. In Part Two I brought out features of a Christian psychology in another way by trying to think in explicitly Christian terms about healthy relationships — with competitors, family members, friends, strangers, God, and fellow members of the church. Here I made occasional mention of secular psychology, thus continuing the dialogue of Part One. The difference between the two parts is that in Part One the secular psychologies have the floor most of the time, with Christianity responding at certain points, and in Part Two Christianity has the floor for the most part, with an occasional contrasting or informing word from some secular psychology. My approach has been inductive. Nowhere in this dialogue have I presented an explicit outline or overview of a Christian psychology. I hope that this book will help prepare us for this task of synthesis, which is important for the vitality and integrity of the church in our present situation.

In this final chapter I want to gather together some strands of Christian psychology that the foregoing chapters have uncovered and indicate some places where work needs to be done to extend and deepen Christian psychology. It goes without saying that whatever success I achieve here is only a beginning and an outline. The details of Christian psychology remain to be worked out — largely by Christian therapists and other practitioners, in concert with more theologically or philosophically trained persons like me.

To Be Self-Realized Is to Be a Double Lover

Many of the secular psychologies identify some basic "need" or "drive" that sets the most fundamental agenda for a human life. Freud, for example, says that we are driven by a need for sexual fulfillment that we cannot properly satisfy in direct ways, given the social conditions that are also basic to human life. The fundamental task, then, is to find ways of satisfying our instinctual needs that are socially acceptable, to develop a character that has nonneurotic or only minimally neurotic ways of dealing with our biological drives. Rogers's idea of an organismic valuing process is analogous: the human organism has natural tendencies composed of certain expressive "needs" which it is the basic task of life to satisfy, against certain (mostly social) obstacles. In Nagy's psychology, loyalty to our parents and our children and the need for a balanced ledger of merits and debits hold a similar place. Kohut's idea is that we are driven, most basically, by "narcissistic libido," the need to become an autonomous, directed, self-approving "self." Jung holds that we are drawn to synthesize our finite and infinite aspects (that is, the conscious ego and the Self), and that we reach our potential only when this synthesis is achieved. In each psychology, the basic need sets the life task. It determines which virtues characterize the mature, well-developed person, and it is also a key link in explanations of pathology and a clue to leverages on those pathologies and interventions for correcting them.

Christian psychology can be read as having the same pattern of positing a basic need or potential or drive, and then seeing human troubles and maladjustment as forms of failure to achieve what our basic nature requires. Our basic need is identified in the double commandment: You shall love the Lord your God with all your heart, and your neighbor as yourself (Matt. 22:37-40). This state of proper attachment to God and neighbor is what we were made for; it is this toward which our hearts most basically incline, despite all appearances to the contrary. We are "nothing" without love, according to the apostle Paul (1 Cor. 13:2). As Saint Augustine comments, we were created with a (suppressed and often hidden) drive to praise and honor God, and our hearts are "restless" until we "rest" in God. According to Søren Kierkegaard, a human being is a "synthesis . . . of the temporal and the eternal" and does not truly become himself until he "rests transparently in the power that established [him]."[2] It is in this love and in a social setting that supports it (the kingdom of God) that we will find

---

2. Kierkegaard, *The Sickness unto Death: A Christian Psychological Exposition for Upbuilding and Awakening*, trans. Howard and Edna Hong (Princeton: Princeton University Press, 1980), pp. 13-14.

well-being — the end of anxiety, disorientation, disintegration, perverse behavior, and despair. According to ancient Hebrew theology, human beings are created in the image and likeness of God (Gen. 1:26-27; 5:1-3), and in the New Testament we find a way of elaborating this in terms of God's fatherhood of all who accept Jesus Christ (Rom. 8:15-17; Gal. 4:6). This idea — that God has fitted us by our nature to love him and find our truest identity in a filial relationship with him — also helps to explain why we yearn for what is eternal and incorruptible. Because no such condition of incorruptibility and perfect fellowship is to be found on earth, a requirement for our present psychological well-being is to have a hope of eternal life (Rom. 15:1-13).

Any Christian psychology that is developed with the help of concepts from the secular psychologies will have to remain faithful to this premise: we are made to love God and will find complete "mental health" only when we do so. It will be the task of those who work out such a psychology in detail to show how particular psychopathologies are grounded in a failure to love God and to develop therapeutic interventions that will address the pathologies by fostering the kind of filial relationship with God that was intended in creation. Since it is not obvious to many people, including many Christians, that we must love God if we are to flourish, a Christian psychology will not only need to explain in some detail how this is so and present evidence that it is so; it will also need to explain why our need to love God is so obscure to us so much of the time. Part of the answer, no doubt, is that the plethora of authority-claiming voices confuses us about what it *is* to flourish as a person. Another part of the answer would have to be in terms of our "defenses" against acknowledging God's existence and our own status as his creatures.

The "Godlessness" diagnosis of human dysfunction will not, of course, exclude other diagnoses. In whatever way a failure to love God properly is behind anorexia or clinical depression or alcoholism or juvenile delinquency or marital discord, it should still be possible to give (adjusted) diagnoses of the kinds offered in the secular therapies we surveyed — for example, inadequate early relationships, irrational self-talk, poor training, imbalances in the family ledger, and so on. It will be the business of Christian psychologists to work out the connections between the two kinds or "levels" of explanation and thereby make the needed adjustments in the secular diagnostic schemata.

The second half of the double commandment suggests that our mental well-being depends not only on loving God but also on loving our neighbor. This is not to deny the thesis of much secular psychology that our close and early relationships are crucially formative and determinative for us, but it is to say that the context on which mental health depends is broader than one's immediate family and more a matter of choice and conscious effort than can be ascribed, say, to one's early relationships with one's mother. Thus in the chapters in this second part of the book I have emphasized relationships with friends and even strangers (especially in the chapter on hospitality) and, in the manner of the cognitive therapies, have stressed our responsibility for our own healthy functioning in these and other areas. The premise underlying this concern for our relationships with virtually *everyone* is the Christian claim that since proper selfhood depends on a right relationship with a God who is our common Father, every person is essentially a close relative.

Selfhood

On the apostle Paul's view of personality, it is possible to speak of more than one self, and one person or personality can "dwell in" another for good or for ill. For example, the "old self" of the Christian is put to death with Christ (Rom. 6:6), whereafter "it is no longer I who live, but Christ who lives in me" (Gal. 2:20). The Spirit of God can dwell in a person (Rom. 8:9, 11); the Spirit of Christ is sent into the hearts of believers (Gal. 4:6). Sin, too, functions as a sort of quasi-self or personality that dwells in a person: "Now if I do what I do not want, I agree that the law is good. So then it is no longer I that do it, but sin which dwells within me" (Rom. 7:16-17). In the Gospel of John, Jesus says that the Father is "in" him and he is "in" the Father, and that he is "in" his disciples and his disciples are "in" him (John 17:20-26). One person's being indwelt by another is presumably compatible with the integrity and individual identity of both persons (when Christ lives in Paul, there is no question of Paul's confusing himself with Christ or of Christ's being reduced to Paul's "better self"). On the other hand, if sin is the indweller, the integrity of the personality *is* compromised, or at least at risk. In Romans 7, Paul seems to express confusion and dismay at the presence of sin — this alien power — in him.

How are we to understand this way of talking? Is it literally true that God's spirit is "in" a person? If so, what does this "in" mean? If it is not literally true, then how are we to understand the metaphor? So here is another task for Christian psychology. Paul's notion of the indwelling of God is obviously related to the Christian view that we are created for a relationship with God, to love him and honor him, and in those attitudes to find our health and well-being. Being in the Holy Spirit or having the Spirit of Christ in oneself is a way (the way?) of being in personal fellowship with God. Having the Spirit of God is related to prayer and to "walking by [behaving in conformity with] the Spirit" and being "led by the Spirit" and having "the desires of the Spirit" (Gal. 5:16-18). It is also obviously related to what one "sets one's mind on" (Rom. 8:9-11; Phil. 4:8-9; Col. 3:2), to issues of attention, meditation, and basic "orientation." All these connections suggest possible therapeutic interventions, and creative suggestions from practitioners of Christian psychotherapy are to be welcomed. Some light might be shed on the idea of indwelling by reflecting on Heinz Kohut's notion of a self object.

Sin and Forgiveness

Sin is without any doubt the chief diagnostic category of biblical psychology. Sin is a form of dysfunction, of failure to function as the human being was designed to function, and so it is analogous to the forms of dysfunction that are identified and addressed in the psychotherapies. In the New Testament, sin is not just a set of mis*deeds* but a perverse state of the *person* and thus a psychological state, a state of the soul. It is a "nature" that one has put on, an orientation, a matter of perverse motives (Eph. 4:22; Gal. 5:16-21; 1 John 2:16). Insofar as Christianity is a word about the overcoming of sin, a word that is at the same time instrumental in the overcoming of it, it is in the most literal sense of the word a psychotherapy — a cure for sick souls. But as a concept of psychic dysfunction, sin has three features that non-Christian concepts of dysfunction lack or tend to lack: offense against God, responsibility, and incurability by human effort. In the second section of this chapter I noted that Christian psychology holds that persons were created to love and receive love from God, and that sin, as the basic category of human dysfunction, is most basically a failure of self-realization in this relationship. For our present purpose I will let the discussion of that feature suffice and take a look at the other two distinctive features of sin.

Responsibility

The idea that the individual is responsible for his sin seems to be basic to the concept of sin, though there is inherited "sin," for which the individual is not responsible. Let me explain this paradox. Take, as an example, a man who abuses his children. To the extent that his actions and the character that lies behind his actions are due to his having been abused in his own childhood, he is not individually responsible for his sin, and so his dysfunction is only "sin." The cause of his "sin" lies outside himself. This is called inherited sin, and we all inherit some sin. But sin is always *somebody's* responsibility — Adam's if nobody else's — and whether a person can be held accountable for his sin depends on his being himself responsible for his dysfunction. The apostle Paul trades on this logic when he says, "Sin indeed was in the world before the law was given, but sin is not counted where there is no law" (Rom. 5:13). That is, without the law one does not know that the actions one is doing or the character one is promoting in oneself are evil, and so one is not, in the relevant sense, responsible for these things. Paul also trades on this notion when he says, about non-Jewish sinners, that "they show that what the law requires is written on their hearts" (Rom. 2:15). We call the actions and character faults that result from sin "sin" in the inherited sense; but real, ground-level, first-rate authentic sin is dysfunction for which the dysfunctional individual or community is *itself* responsible. Since a Christian psychology tends to diagnose human dysfunction as sin (and not just as "sin"), the supposition must be that individuals and communities (say, families) are at least partially responsible for their dysfunction. The Christian psychologist, while recognizing the power of inheritance in human dysfunction, will not be inclined to see this as the whole story, but will also ascribe some responsibility to the client. In the case of our child abuser, the psychologist will usually assume that the client was not psychologically *compelled* to abuse his children — that he knew what he was doing to be wrong and had enough resources of control to be able to abstain. Thus, a significant part of the therapy will be to bring this client to repent of his actions and to accept forgiveness from God and his family.

So in Christian terms, if a person is depressed, or anxious, or abuses drugs or alcohol, or fights with her husband, part of the diagnosis is likely to be that the individual is a sinner, and this implies not that she is totally responsible for the state she's in, but that she is at least partially responsible. One of the therapies we surveyed in Part One (RET) ascribes some responsibility to the client for his pathology, but the dominant tone of many therapies is that the client is a victim of his society, his unjust upbringing, his early self objects, poor training, or ignorance. Some therapies give the impression that the very idea that a person is responsible for his dysfunction is anti-therapeutic. ("Don't make the client feel guilty.") However, one of the chief therapeutic strategies of Christianity is forgiveness — God's forgiveness of sinners offered in Jesus Christ, and each sinner's forgiveness of the other. And forgiveness, as we saw in Chapter Ten, implies guilt; it applies only to someone who is dysfunctional *by his own responsibility*. Nor can he properly receive forgiveness unless he feels his guilt and repents of his sin. Thus the biblical psychology stresses the therapeutic importance of contrition, that emotion in which the individual regrets his state and dissociates himself from it while taking responsibility for it (Luke 3:7-9; 7:36-50; 18:9-14; 2 Cor. 7:8-10).

A worry that seems to lie behind therapists' shyness about ascribing responsibility to the client is that being "judgmental" will merely raise the client's defenses and preempt the development of therapeutic trust. Christian psychology is as much opposed as any other psychology to judgmentalism (Matt. 7:1-5), if we think of the judgmental attitude as a kind of contempt by one person, who sees himself as "righteous," of another whom he regards as inferior to himself because of the other's sinful condition. This is an alienating and untherapeutic attitude, to be sure, but the remedy need not exclude ascribing responsibility. What is pernicious about judgmentalism is not the judgment that is being made, but the contempt that alienates one human being from another. The Christian doctrine of sin is that "there is no distinction" between therapist and client in this regard, "since all have sinned and fall short of the glory of God" (Rom. 3:22-23). It is a requirement of proper Christian maturity that each one of us recognize emotionally his own sinfulness and dependency on God's grace. A pervasive attitude of contrition is a mark of Christian holiness, and surely will be a mark of the Christian therapist. Rogers and Kohut stress therapist empathy, and require it not to be an artificial attitude or mere "technique," but to make itself felt to the client out of the depths of the therapist's personality. Christian psychology agrees with this, but adds that contrition is an equally important virtue for the therapist to possess. Contrition is the attitude that will prevent judgmentalism as the therapist discusses the client's sins with her.

Incurability by Merely Human Effort

Besides being a misrelationship with God, and a kind of dysfunction for which the sufferer is to some extent responsible, sin is a condition for which there is no cure by merely human efforts. As the New Testament declares, the sinner is *"dead* [in his] trespasses and sins" (Eph. 2:1) and needs to be "born again" (John 3:1-15). Sin is by definition a condition from which one must be rescued by God. The central story of Christianity is about that rescue operation, in which God joins us humans here on earth, even to the extent of becoming one of us, and suffers as one who had responsibly offended God by his way of life — though *he* had not done so, except by virtue of his identification with us. In this act God pronounces sinners forgiven, the barrier of justice overcome, and reconciliation accomplished, and God continues to work through the Word about this rescue operation to overcome the sin in the lives of individuals and communities. So we have two tightly related psychotherapeutic acts of God: the incarnation, ministry, death, and resurrection of God's son, two thousand years ago in Palestine, and the healing work of the Holy Spirit in individuals and congregations throughout the ages and down to the present day. This means that distinctively Christian psychotherapy, no matter how extensively it uses strategies adapted from the secular therapies, will always enlist the help of God — reconciliation of the client with God through the work of the Holy Spirit — and this will mean at some time (the time may need to be very judiciously chosen) acknowledging explicitly God's saving act in Palestine two millennia ago, and prayerfully invoking present help from his Holy Spirit. It will also involve integrating the client into a faithful congregation where he may find fellowship and opportunity to partake of holy communion.

Self-Denial

Under the influence of secular therapies, Christians have grown uncomfortable with the idea of self-denial, but it is important both as a strategy against sin and as a positive part of Christian life and growth. We have been led to feel that the self is sacrosanct: just as in an earlier time it was thought never fitting to deny God, so now it seems never right to deny oneself. The analogy is helpful, because just as it was OK, in a God-fearing age, to deny idols but not to deny the *true* God, so in our age we must convince people that while it is wrong to deny one's true self, it is OK to deny false or lower selves. The schema that I developed in Chapter Two, with suggestions from Carl Rogers, can help us see this. A premise of this book is that "self" is not the name of something in the way that "kidney" is the name of an anatomical part. A self is a function of a self-interpretation, a "word" that gives the self shape and substance.

According to the Christian Word, the core of the selfhood of all of us — what we most truly are as selves, whether or not we have actualized and acknowledged this — is that we are bearers of God's image, made and intended to be his children, to love him and our neighbor and to serve in his kingdom. This is the self that Christian nurture promotes and that Christian psychotherapy restores. This self *is* sacrosanct in Christianity; it would always be wrong to deny one's nature as a child of God. Thus when the apostle Paul says, "I could wish that I myself were accursed and cut off from Christ for the sake of my brethren, my kinsmen by race" (Rom. 9:3), he speaks paradoxically: insofar as his "self-denying" wish is genuine, it expresses a love for Christ and his brethren that is not a denial but an affirmation of his true self. But all "selves" that are in opposition to this one, or even of lesser status, are candidates for denial, and this denial may be very therapeutic.

What is self-denial, and why is it so therapeutic, according to a Christian psychology? What can a therapist do to promote it? We can answer these questions by picking up some of the themes that we have identified as distinctive of Christian psychology: (a) the sociality of the Christian psychology — we are made to "transcend ourselves" toward God and others (love is the ideal); (b) the responsibility of the person according to Christianity — that we are individuals before God and one another, agents and not just patients; and (c) the reality of sin as a psychological factor.

Throughout this book I have argued that according to Christianity the human self is social: it is defined as potential "child" (of God) and "brother" or "sister" (of fellow human beings). Thus to the extent that someone is closed in upon himself, not "open" to or in fellowship with God and his human siblings, he is not self-realized, is not fully *himself,* even though he may be tremendously "selfish." We can see, then, that when a person denies himself so as to become more open to God or his fellow, he is denying not his true self but a false or pseudo or inadequate self — at minimum, a lesser self. This is not at all to deny that self-denial is painful and felt (in a way) as a denial of one's true self. For example, I may wish to do something that is easy and comfortable and satisfying (talk with my friends, read a book, write another chapter of my book), but my son wants to play a game with me or talk with me about something very interesting to him but rather boring to me. If I stop what I am doing and talk or play with him, then I am denying myself for his sake. And if my self-denial so succeeds that I enter wholeheartedly into this fatherly activity and am not just gritting my teeth and doing my fatherly *duty,* then I transcend my selfish, inadequate, or lesser self and find a truer self whose identity is "father of this boy" and "steward of God." Or let us say I find myself being rather comfortable doing what I do for God, teaching Sunday School, praying a few times a day, and so on. But a self thus "closed" to God is not the real me, so I undertake a program of self-denial — a discipline of longer, more aggressive prayers, more careful Sunday School teaching, or some such thing. If all goes best, and the light of God's countenance blesses my effort, this will not be a matter of dour duty, but I'll "find myself" in these activities, because they are works of love.

A Christian psychology sees the human self as a strong agent — not just a pawn pushed about by environmental and genetic inheritance but one who, though acting within limits set by inheritance, is decidedly an agent — an individual who himself is responsible for what he does and what he becomes. Self-denial expresses this status of responsible agency, for it is by definition something that the individual *undertakes*, not something that just happens to him. To the extent that a change is wrought by a therapist's trick and is not consciously undertaken by the client, it will lack this "agentic" character that he would give himself through self-denial. In self-denial the individual doesn't "go with the flow," thus letting the flow be responsible for his character; he takes his life and selfhood into his own hands. The fact that self-denial goes "against the grain" makes it even more agency-producing than other consciously undertaken acts. Self-denial is a way in which one's life becomes a dialogue with others, with God, and with one's upbringing and genetic endowment, a dialogue in which one takes an active part and is not just carried along.

Lastly, self-denial is required because of sin. So far I have spoken of denying the actual self not because it is bad but because it is not the essential, truest self. It is not bad to want to be alone, to desire food for oneself, to want to write a book or make some other personal success, but these desires do not express what is deepest in us, according to a Christian psychology. So we deny the lower self in the interest of the higher.

But according to biblical psychology, we not only have a lower nature that needs taming and subordinating; we also have a sinful nature that needs to die. So if I find myself in the position of the Vogelgehirns of Chapter Nine, embroiled in patterns of envy and pride, I need to die to self, to be crucified with Christ (Gal. 2:20) — not just to subordinate my invidious self to my kingdom self, but to get rid of it altogether. Christian psychotherapy will devise methods, often no doubt partially indebted to the strategies of the secular therapies, for helping individuals bring about this death (psychotherapy as assisted suicide).

Christian Psychology and the Secular Therapies

In the six therapies that we examined in Part One, we can see themes to which Christian psychology has been committed since the time of its origin. Rogerian therapy stresses the curative power of acceptance and empathy — something formally akin to the attitude that God shows to humanity in Jesus Christ, who shares our sufferings and forgives us and welcomes us into his kingdom. Ellis stresses the importance, for healthy living, of accurate and humanly proper "cognitions" — beliefs and orienting self-talk; Christianity as a healing message has always, at least in its orthodox forms, stressed the connection between proper psycho-spiritual formation and correct beliefs. Behavior therapy stresses the healing of relationships and psyche that can come from correcting behavior, reminding us of the many times that John the Baptist, Jesus, and Paul exhort their hearers to behavioral change in the interest of spiritual ends, and of James's remark that faith is perfected by works (Jas. 2:22). Nagy's contextual therapy, which centers on the healing potential of justice and reconciliation among persons who are ontologically related to one another, is reminiscent of the Pauline theme that God heals us by "justifying" us and in that way reconciling us to himself (Rom. 5:9-10). There is an obvious formal similarity between biblical psychology and Jung's emphasis on the human need to be connected with an eternal dimension. Kohut's idea that selves are formed as they find their value mirrored in the loving gaze and approval of a parent, and as they attach themselves to a parent who represents ideals to live by, is strongly reminiscent of the Christian idea that we find our spiritual selves in the love that God has lavished on us in Jesus Christ and by enlisting in the army of his kingdom.

These resemblances should not make us less hawkish in our search for differences between Christian psychology and these modern psychologies. As I argued in Part One, not only does each psychotherapy bear some resemblance to Christian psychology; each of them also, in one respect or another, contradicts Christianity. Our integration of insights and techniques from these other psychologies must therefore be done cautiously and with some precision. Still, because the therapies have developed their insights in a fairly rigorous way and have focused energetically on refining their own special techniques of person formation, it stands to reason that we can learn a lot through dialogue with them. Christian psychotherapy will be "eclectic" in bearing a number of resemblances to the secular therapies; some of these will be the result of its integrating features of those other therapies. But first and foremost Christian psychology will be true to the complexity of human nature and dysfunction and repair that has always been ingredient in the Christian psychology which this book has attempted, in some very small measure, to make explicit.

SELECTED READINGS RELATING
TO CHRISTIAN PSYCHOLOGY

Aquinas, St. Thomas. *Summa Theologica*. Translated by the fathers of the English Dominican Province. Westminster, Maryland: Christian Classics, 1981. See especially the second part.

Augustine. *Confessions*. Translated by Albert J. Outler. Philadelphia: Westminster Press, n.d.

Becker, Ernest. *The Denial of Death*. New York: The Free Press, 1973.

Bellah, Robert, Richard Madsen, William M. Sullivan, Ann Swidler, and Steven Tipton. *Habits of the Heart: Individualism and Commitment in American Life*. San Francisco: Harper & Row, 1985. See especially Chapter 5.

Collins, Gary. *The Rebuilding of Psychology*. Wheaton, Ill.: Tyndale House Publishers, 1985.

Evans, C. Stephen. *Søren Kierkegaard's Christian Psychology: Insight for Counseling and Pastoral Care*. Grand Rapids: Zondervan Publishing House, 1990.

Evans, C. Stephen, *Wisdom and Humanness in Psychology: Prospects for a Christian Approach*. Grand Rapids: Baker Book House, 1989.

Groeschel, Benedict J. *Spiritual Passages: The Psychology of*

Spiritual Development "for Those Who Seek." New York: Crossroad, 1983.

Hurding, Roger F. *The Tree of Healing.* Grand Rapids: Zondervan Publishing House, 1985.

Jones, Stanton L., and Richard E. Butman. *Modern Psychotherapies: A Comprehensive Christian Appraisal.* Downers Grove, Ill.: InterVarsity Press, 1991.

Kierkegaard, Søren. *The Concept of Anxiety: A Simple Psychologically Orienting Deliberation on the Dogmatic Issue of Hereditary Sin.* Edited and translated by Reidar Thomte in collaboration with Albert B. Anderson. Princeton: Princeton University Press, 1980.

————. *The Sickness unto Death: A Christian Psychological Exposition for Upbuilding and Awakening.* Translated by Howard and Edna Hong. Princeton: Princeton University Press, 1980.

Rieff, Philip. *The Triumph of the Therapeutic: Uses of Faith after Freud.* New York: Harper & Row, 1966.

Van Leeuwen, Mary S. *The Person in Psychology: A Contemporary Christian Appraisal.* Grand Rapids: William B. Eerdmans, 1985.

INDEX

Printed in the United States
33194LVS00007B/76-93